OXFORD
SLAVONIC PAPERS

Edited by

ROBERT AUTY   J. L. I. FENNELL

and

I. P. FOOTE

General Editor

NEW SERIES

VOLUME X

OXFORD

AT THE CLARENDON PRESS

1977

Oxford University Press, Walton Street, Oxford, OX2 6DP

OXFORD LONDON GLASGOW
NEW YORK TORONTO MELBOURNE WELLINGTON
IBADAN NAIROBI DAR ES SALAAM LUSAKA CAPE TOWN
KUALA LUMPUR SINGAPORE JAKARTA HONG KONG TOKYO
DELHI BOMBAY CALCUTTA MADRAS KARACHI

ISBN 0 19 815651 0

© *Oxford University Press 1977*

*Printed in Great Britain
at the University Press, Oxford
by Vivian Ridler
Printer to the University*

THE editorial policy of the New Series of *Oxford Slavonic Papers* in general follows that of the original series, thirteen volumes of which appeared between the years 1950 and 1967 under the editorship of Professor S. Konovalov (volumes 11–13 edited jointly with Mr. J. S. G. Simmons, who also acted as General Editor of the New Series, volumes 1 to 4). It is devoted to the publication of original contributions and documents relating to the languages, literatures, culture, and history of Russia and the other Slavonic countries, and appears annually towards the end of the year. Reviews of individual books are not normally included, but bibliographical and review articles are published from time to time.

The British System of Cyrillic transliteration (British Standard 2979: 1958) has been adopted, omitting diacritics and using -y to express -й, -ий, -iй, and -ый at the end of proper names, e.g. Sergey, Dostoevsky, Bely, Grozny. For philological work the International System (ISO R/9) is used.

ROBERT AUTY
J. L. I. FENNELL
I. P. FOOTE

The Queen's College, Oxford

CONTENTS

Le *Testament d'Abraham* en slave et en roumain

ÉMILE TURDEANU

A la mémoire d'André Vaillant

I. LES DEUX VERSIONS GRECQUES

L E *Testament d'Abraham* est le pendant naturel de l'*Apocalypse d'Abraham*. L'un raconte l'enfance du Patriarche, l'autre sa mort. L'un se situe avant le récit biblique (*Gen.* xii–xxv), l'autre après. Les deux embellissent la biographie du Patriarche, elle-même fabuleuse, avec un *excursus* eschatologique qui fait connaître à leur héros les mystères du ciel, de la mort et du jugement des âmes. Sont-ils jumeaux ou du moins apparentés?

L'*Apocalypse d'Abraham* est, selon les hypothèses les plus plausibles, d'origine juive, essénienne ou gnostique, œuvre d'un auteur palestinien du iie siècle après J.-C.; son 'composant' chrétien (chap. xxix) est une interpolation tardive.[1] Le *Testament d'Abraham* est, lui aussi, dans sa meilleure rédaction, la version courte, d'origine palestinienne, et peut-être essénienne, bien que son 'essénisme populaire',[2] vague, diffus, ne soit pas plus convaincant que celui de l'*Apocalypse*. Il daterait de la 'première moitié du premier siècle',[3] si l'on accepte son appartenance essénienne; du second siècle, si l'on veut l'associer, comme nous sommes tenté de le faire,[4] à la grande période d'efflorescence des apocalypses, et si l'on admet ne voir dans son titre de 'testament', d'ailleurs impropre, qu'une réminiscence des récits parénétiques antérieurs, comme *Les Testaments des Douze Patriarches*.

Quelles que soient la patrie et la date de composition que l'on veuille assigner au *Testament d'Abraham*, un fait est aujourd'hui acquis, et il est d'une importance capitale pour notre recherche: c'est que, en aucun

---

[1] Voir pour les différentes opinions concernant son origine, Albert-Marie Denis, *Introduction aux pseudépigraphes grecs de l'Ancien Testament* (Leyde, 1970), 37–8.

[2] Francis Schmidt, '*Le Testament d'Abraham*. Introduction, édition de la recension courte, traduction et notes' (Thèse dactylographiée, Strasbourg, 1971), i, 120. Nous remercions ici très cordialement M. Schmidt de nous avoir communiqué un exemplaire de sa thèse inédite.

[3] Ibid. 121. Voir aussi la revue bibliographique donnée par A.-M. Denis, op. cit. (n. 1), 31–7.

[4] Dans un livre récent, dont nous avons pris connaissance lorsque la rédaction du présent article était déjà achevée, le professeur Mathieu Delcor de Toulouse opte pour l'origine égyptienne du *Testament d'Abraham*: 'il ne peut guère avoir vu le jour que dans ce milieu fermé des Thérapeutes apparentés à l'essénisme' (p. 73); il serait plutôt du iie siècle que du i[er] (p. 76); 'Pour nous, les deux recensions ont vu le jour en Égypte' (p. 78). Voir M. Delcor, *'Le Testament d'Abraham': Introduction, traduction du texte grec et commentaire de la recension longue* (Leyde, 1973).

cas, la version développée, considérée pendant longtemps comme la meilleure base d'étude de l'apocryphe, ne saurait fournir une garantie suffisante d'ancienneté et de fidélité à l'original perdu. Seule la version courte peut prétendre à cet avantage. Cette opinion, que P. Riessler avait émise le premier en 1925, que N. Turner a démontrée en 1953[5] dans une thèse inédite, que, indépendamment de ces critiques, nous avons nous-même suggérée dans une brève étude publiée en 1957,[6] a été récemment reprise et confirmée, dans une thèse présentée à l'Université des Sciences humaines de Strasbourg, en 1971, par Francis Schmidt.

Selon Francis Schmidt, la version courte est plus proche de l'original perdu parce qu'elle possède, comme M. Rhodes James[7] et N. Turner l'avaient déjà remarqué, un vocabulaire et une syntaxe plus anciens et parce qu'elle recèle des influences iraniennes propres au milieu palestinien. Par contre, la version longue contient plus de cinquante mots grecs postérieurs à l'ère chrétienne et porte la marque évidente des influences égyptiennes; elle a donc été composée après la version courte et provient d'un milieu différent, qui ne peut être que l'Égypte, et probablement la ville d'Alexandrie. Elle est 'le remaniement fait en milieu juif d'Égypte d'un document issu d'un cercle juif ouvert aux influences iraniennes'.[8]

Ainsi se trouve établie l'antériorité de la version courte. La confrontation des différentes traductions du texte confirme pleinement cette conclusion. 'Les versions copte, arabe et éthiopienne du *Testament d'Abraham* dérivent de la seule recension courte et sont étroitement apparentées: l'arabe traduit le copte; l'éthiopien traduit l'arabe.'[9] Quant à la traduction slave, nous avons démontré dès 1957 qu'elle se rattache à la version courte, dont le manuscrit de la Bibliothèque Nationale de Paris, fonds grec 1613, du xve siècle, nous semblait alors être le meilleur représentant. Une heureuse fortune a fait connaître à Francis Schmidt, quelques années après la parution de cette étude, une rédaction grecque encore plus proche de la traduction slave que le manuscrit indiqué par nous. Il s'agit d'une copie du xie–xiie siècles, conservée à la Bibliothèque Ambrosienne de Milan, fonds grec n° 405

[5] Voir F. Schmidt, op. cit. (n. 2), 116–17, qui cite P. Riessler, 'Das Testament Abrahams, ein jüdisches Apokryphon' dans *Theologische Quartalschrift*, cvi (1925), 3–22, et *Altjüdisches Schrifttum ausserhalb der Bibel* (Heidelberg, 1928), 1332–3; N. Turner, 'The Testament of Abraham: a study of the original language, place of origin, authorship and relevance' (Thèse dactylographiée, Londres, 1953), résumée par l'auteur dans 'The "Testament of Abraham": Problems in Biblical Greek', *New Testament Studies*, i (1954–5), 219–23.

[6] Émile Turdeanu, 'Notes sur la tradition littéraire du *Testament d'Abraham*', *Silloge bizantina in onore di Silvio Giuseppe Mercati* (Studî bizantini e neoellenici, xi) (Rome, 1957), 405–10.

[7] M. R. James, *The Testament of Abraham: the Greek Text now first edited with an introduction and notes* (Cambridge, 1892), 50–1.

[8] F. Schmidt, op. cit. (n. 2), 118.   [9] Ibid. 15.

(G 63 sup.). Cette découverte a permis à Schmidt de situer l'origine du texte slave sur une base plus solide et de répondre positivement à la question que nous avions soulevée: 'la version courte n'est-elle pas, somme toute, un représentant plus fidèle de l'apocryphe ancien que la version longue?'[10]

Mais, si le point de départ de la traduction slave est défini aujourd'hui avec une précision satisfaisante, la carrière que le *Testament d'Abraham* s'est donnée chez les Bulgares, Macédoniens, Serbes, Croates, Ukrainiens et Russes, d'une part, et chez les Roumains, d'autre part, est loin d'être connue dans toute sa complexité. C'est à la nécessité de classer ces nombreuses rédactions, de suivre leur diffusion et de montrer le rôle culturel qu'elles ont pu jouer à travers les siècles, que répond le présent mémoire.

Pour une approche plus directe du problème, nous précisons dès ici que la plupart des matériaux que nous aurons à examiner se classent en trois groupes importants: Sl[1] et Sl[2] appuient la version B (courte) du texte grec, dont le meilleur représentant est actuellement — nous l'avons dit — le ms. E publié par Francis Schmidt; Sl[3] et Roum.[1] forment un groupe sud et nord danubien libre, dérivé du groupe précédent; Sl[4] et Roum.[2] représentent la rédaction la plus 'populaire', voire la plus aberrante, mais aussi la plus pittoresque, à laquelle a abouti le *Testament d'Abraham*. A ces groupes, le roumain ajoute un texte traduit directement d'après la version grecque longue: Roum.[3]

II. LA VERSION COURTE

Contenu des textes slaves et roumains

Les manuscrits appartenant aux groupes Sl[1] et Sl[2] sont décrits aux pp. 10–11; ceux des groupes Sl[3] et Roum.[1] aux pp. 21–2; ceux des groupes Sl[4] et Roum.[2] aux pp. 29 et 32–3. Dans le résumé ci-bas, nous faisons imprimer en italiques les passages propres aux groupes Sl[3] Roum.[1] et Sl[4] Roum.[2]

Grec B, Sl[1] et Sl[2]	*Sl[3] et Roum.[1]*	*Sl[4] et Roum.[2]*
1. La vie d'Abr. ayant touché à sa fin, Dieu envoie l'arch. Michel pour avertir son serviteur de sa mort prochaine.	(Titre:) Lorsque le Seigneur envoya l'arch. Michel pour prendre l'âme de l'hospitalier Abr.	Abr. vivait dans sa maison *et désirait voir ce qui se faisait sur la Terre.* Dieu envoie l'arch. Michel enlever son âme. Abr. n'avait plus mangé 'du pain' depuis trois jours, le diable ayant empêché tous les voyageurs de parvenir jusqu'à lui.

[10] É. Turdeanu, op. cit. (n. 6), 410.

Grec B, Sl¹ et Sl²	*Sl³ et Roum.¹*	*Sl⁴ et Roum.²*
2. L'arch. Michel, travesti en voyageur, trouve Abr. aux champs, auprès de ses laboureurs (de ses bœufs Gr B). Le patriarche l'invite à la maison, car il est soir et les bêtes fauves pourraient mettre ses jours en danger. Répondant à la question du voyageur, Abr. dit son nom et lui raconte comment Dieu lui avait ordonné de quitter sa maison et ses parents, et d'aller s'installer dans le pays qui allait lui être désigné. A cette occasion, Dieu changea son nom d'Abram en celui d'Abraham. Le voyageur reconnaît en Abr. l'homme qui avait donné hospitalité à Dieu lui-même. Se mettant en route avec son compagnon, Abr. fait venir un valet ('deux esclaves nés dans la maison, fils d'Éliézer' Sl¹), et leur ordonne d'aller chercher une monture pour le voyageur; celui-ci décline l'offre...	*L'arch. descend à l'orée de la forêt*, travesti en voyageur. *Abr. avait pour règle de ne jamais manger sans avoir un invité à sa table.* Apercevant l'arch., il va à sa rencontre *et l'interroge:* '*D'où es-tu?*' *Celui-ci répond:* '*Je suis du pays d'en haut.*' Abr. l'invite à la maison, l'arch. essaie de se dérober: il a une affaire importante, *il est fatigué.* Abr. veut envoyer chercher un cheval, mais le voyageur s'y oppose: 'Allons-y doucement!'...	L'arch., travesti en voyageur, s'approche de la maison où Abr. se tient en prières. Celui-ci le voit de loin et s'apprête à l'accueillir avec joie, en se disant qu'il va enfin pouvoir manger 'du pain'. Il sort à la rencontre du voyageur et l'invite à la maison... Abr. fait dire à la maison qu'on leur prépare le repas et veut demander une monture, mais le voyageur propose de faire route à pied...
3. (Près d'un ruisseau Sl¹), Abr. et son compagnon passent devant un chêne à 300 branches (320 Sl¹) et entendent une voix s'échapper de son tronc: 'Tu es saint, car tu as respecté le but pour lequel tu as été envoyé.' Abr. se demande en lui-même que peut être ce mystère, mais n'en parle pas à son compagnon.	Passant devant le chêne de Mambré, celui-ci se penche devant eux disant: 'Saint! Saint! Saint!' Abr. s'imagine que c'est lui l'objet de cet hommage.	Quand ils passent devant le chêne de Mambré, le feuillage dit: 'Saint! Saint! au très juste.' Ne sachant pas qui est son compagnon, Abr. pense que c'est à lui que l'hommage est adressé.
Arrivés à la maison, Abr. ordonne qu'on aille au troupeau chercher trois moutons, ensuite il demande à Isaac de rem-	Arrivés à la maison, Abr. envoie chercher *un mouton* et demande à Sarah d'apporter une bassine et de laver les pieds du voya-	Quand ils arrivent à la maison, Sarah vient, selon la coutume, laver les pieds du voyageur. Mais aussitôt elle s'écrie: 'O, mer-

Grec B, Sl¹ et Sl²	Sl³ et Roum.¹	Sl⁴ et Roum.²

plir la bassine avec de l'eau, pour laver les pieds du voyageur: 'Car je pense — dit-il — que c'est pour la dernière fois qu'il m'est donné de laver les pieds d'un invité.' Entendant ces mots, Isaac fond en larmes, son père s'attendrit et pleure lui aussi, l'arch. pleure à son tour. Tombant dans la bassine, les larmes de l'arch. se transforment en pierres précieuses.

geur, *car il est fatigué.* *S*'apercevant *que* les pieds du voyageur *n'ont pas de chair,* Sarah s'écrie: 'Ces pieds sont semblables à ceux des hommes qui ont détruit Sodome et Gomorrhe!' Abr. s'emporte: 'Comment le feu ne te brûle-t-il pas, toi qui confonds cet étranger avec un être céleste?' (Cf. Gr B, Sl¹ et Sl², § 6). Ensuite Isaac apporte le mouton et s'en va préparer le dîner.

veille! Les pieds de cet homme sont pareils à ceux des trois voyageurs qui ont détruit Sodome et Gomorrhe!' Abr. lui reproche de comparer un pécheur à un saint.

4. Attirée par les sanglots, Sarah entre dans la chambre. Abr. la rassure et la renvoie à ses besognes. Au coucher du soleil, l'arch. sort furtivement de la maison et monte au ciel adorer Dieu avec les puissances célestes. Il fait part au Seigneur de son hésitation d'enlever l'âme de son ami Abr., et lui demande de mettre dans l'esprit du patriarche l'idée de la mort. Dieu lui ordonne de redescendre dans la maison d'Abr., de vivre comme lui, et lui promet de semer la conscience de la mort dans l'esprit d'Isaac.

A l'heure du coucher du soleil, *quand les anges se réunissent,* l'arch. remonte au ciel et interroge Dieu *s'il l'autorise à manger de la viande de mouton.* Dieu lui ordonne de manger ce que les autres mangent.

A l'heure du dîner, l'arch. monte au ciel et avertit le Seigneur qu'Abr. prépare un repas de viande. Dieu lui ordonne de manger ce que les autres mangeront.

5. Il est soir, Abr. et son invité, après avoir mangé et s'être réjouis, s'en vont se coucher. Isaac veut se joindre à eux, mais son père le renvoie dans sa chambre.

Après le dîner, Abr. prépare le lit et ils se couchent.

Après le dîner, Abr. et le voyageur vont se reposer dans la même pièce, Sarah couche dans une autre maison, de même qu'Isaac et *Rébecca.*

6. Vers la 7ᵉ heure de la nuit, Isaac vient frapper à la porte de son père et se pend à son cou, en pleurs.

A minuit, Isaac se lève de son lit et vient frapper à la porte de la maison où repose son père et

A minuit, Isaac vient à la la maison où repose son père et demande de le voir pour la dernière fois.

Grec B, Sl¹ et Sl²	*Sl³ et Roum.¹*	*Sl⁴ et Roum.²*
Ses larmes font pleurer Abr. et la contagion des pleurs gagne aussitôt l'arch. Sarah accourt à nouveau au bruit des sanglots et s'enquiert de la vie de Loth, le neveu d'Abr. Le voyageur la rassure (d'une voix plus douce que celle de tous les mortels Sl¹).	demande d'embrasser *la beauté de son visage*, car il ne le verra plus. Ses pleurs réveillent Sarah. Isaac *embrasse Abr. en pleurant.*	Ses pleurs réveillent Sarah et Rébecca, ainsi qu''une foule de gens'.
Alors Sarah blâme son mari de pleurer le jour où ils ont comme hôte un envoyé du Seigneur. Abr. lui déclare que lui aussi, lavant les pieds du voyageur, y a reconnu les pieds de l'un des trois anges qu'ils avaient rencontrés sous le chêne de Mambré, et qui se dirigeaient vers Sodome pour sauver Loth.	*Voir supra,* § 3	*Voir supra,* § 3
7. A la demande d'Abr., l'arch. révèle qui il est, mais, pour lui faire comprendre sa mission, il l'invite à s'adresser à Isaac. Celui-ci raconte son rêve: Il avait sur sa tête une couronne, avec le soleil et la lune, et un homme radieux comme 'la lumière que l'on appelle le père de la lumière' descendit du ciel et lui enleva le soleil, pour la grande désolation d'Isaac, du soleil lui-même, de la lune et des étoiles. L'homme radieux les consola en leur parlant dans des termes allégoriques de la félicité de la vie céleste. Isaac ayant terminé son récit, l'arch. explique le rêve. Le soleil est Abr., qui sera enlevé au ciel, tandis que son corps restera sur la terre jusqu'à	Isaac raconte son rêve. Il avait sur la tête une couronne radieuse comme le soleil, et le voyageur la lui a enlevée. Il a donc compris que l'hôte est un archange qui veut prendre l'âme de son père. A ces paroles,	*Identique au Sl³* *Identique au Sl³*

Grec B, Sl¹ et Sl²

ce que 7000 (8000 P) ans auront passé: alors tous les corps ressusciteront. Abr. exige qu'on l'emmène avec son corps. L'arch. s'en va présenter sa requête à Dieu.

Sl³ et Roum.¹

tous fondent en larmes, l'arch. pleure lui aussi, et ses larmes deviennent des pierres précieuses. (Cf. Gr B, Sl¹ et Sl², § 3.) A la demande d'Abr., l'arch. révèle qui il est et quelle est sa mission. Abr. demande qu'il soit porté devant le Seigneur avec son corps. L'arch. s'en va au ciel et y reçoit l'ordre du Seigneur de lui amener Abr. avec son corps.

Sl⁴ et Roum.²

A la demande d'Abr., l'arch. révèle qui il est et quelle est sa mission. Épouvanté, Abr. prie le Seigneur *de ne pas l'appeler chez lui, mais de lui permettre de voir ce qui se passe sur la terre.*

8. Dieu consent et Abr. est transporté en chair et os au-dessus du 'fleuve nommé Océan'. Là, il voit deux portes, l'une petite, l'autre grande, et, assis entre les deux portes, un homme en gloire, entouré d'anges. Tantôt l'homme rit, tantôt il pleure, les pleurs dépassant sept fois le rire. Et Abr. de se laisser dire que l'homme est Adam, qui se réjouit lorsque l'âme d'un juste franchit la petite porte qui mène au paradis, et pleure en voyant la multitude des pécheurs s'engageant par la grande porte qui s'ouvre sur les peines éternelles.

Abr. est porté au ciel. *Là il adore Dieu sur le trône des chérubims. Toutes les puissances célestes s'en émerveillent.* Ensuite Dieu ordonne à l'arch. de faire voir à Abr. toute sa création et de réaliser tout ce qu'il désire. *Assis sur un trône élevé, parmi les délices du paradis,* Abr. voit un homme d'une grande beauté, qui rit un instant, ensuite pleure beaucoup. Il se fait dire que c'est Adam, qui se réjouit en voyant passer vers le paradis les âmes des justes, et pleure en voyant les pécheurs s'en aller aux peines. [Et Adam dit: 'O, mes fils, comment êtes-vous tombés dans la souillure!': Z et R.] *La suite manque dans R; Z s'arrête lui aussi quelques lignes plus loin; seul L continue jusqu'à la fin.*

Dieu consent et accorde à Abr. la puissance de voir se réaliser tout souhait qu'il exprime. L'arch. le transporte 'sur' l'atmosphère. *Au quatrième ciel* il voit un homme d'une grande beauté qui pleure beaucoup et rit peu. L'arch. lui explique que c'est Adam, qui se réjouit du salut des justes et pleure en voyant les pécheurs s'en aller aux peines.

9. Cette explication jette le trouble dans l'esprit d'Abr.: lui, qui a un corps 'large' (Gr B), ne pourra donc pas passer par la porte étroite? Mais l'arch. lui répond qu'il passera

8–11. Abr. voit deux portes, l'une large, l'autre étroite. Des anges conduisent une foule de gens vers la porte large et les précipitent vers les tortures. A la vue de la porte

8–11. Abr. voit encore un vieillard et, à ses côtés, un jeune homme: le premier tient le compte des péchés de tous les mortels. Il voit également deux portes, l'une très large,

Grec B, Sl¹ et Sl²	*Sl³ et Roum.¹*	*Sl⁴ et Roum.²*
sans difficulté. A cet instant, ils voient un ange conduisant devant la grande porte une foule de 60.000 (Gr B) pécheurs, parmi lesquels ils ne trouvent qu'une seule âme bonne, celle que l'ange tient dans ses mains: ses péchés étant égaux en nombre à ses bonnes actions, l'ange ne la conduit ni au paradis ni dans l'enfer, mais 'à un endroit qui est au milieu'. Abr. apprend que les âmes sont enlevées aux corps par la Mort, qui les conduit au lieu du jugement.	étroite, Abr. demande, inquiet, comment lui, qui a 'un corps grand', pourrait-il passer. Mais l'arch. le rassure. Il voit ensuite un ange portant [l'âme d']une femme et qui ne pouvait s'engager ni par une porte ni par l'autre. *Abr. implore le pardon de cette 'petite âme'*, mais l'arch. l'invite à assister au jugement. Là, on ouvre 'les livres': ils y trouvent toutes les bonnes actions qu'avait faites la femme, mais aussi le péché qu'elle n'avait pas avoué à son confesseur: celui d'avoir attiré à elle le mari de sa propre fille. *L'âme de la pécheresse est condamnée aux ténèbres extérieures.* Abr. veut savoir qui est celui qui a la garde des péchés. L'ange le renseigne: c'est Hénoch qui, 'en chair et os' (*s tělom*), juge les pécheurs.	l'autre très étroite, et, se tenant entre elles, [l'âme d']une femme. L'arch. lui explique que les personnages sont Hénoch et Abel, et que la femme, après avoir mené une vie juste, a pris comme amant son propre beau-fils: c'est pourquoi son âme ne peut franchir maintenant aucune des deux portes. La porte étroite mène au salut, la porte large conduit aux peines. — Mais lui, qui a un corps gros, comment pourra-t-il passer par la porte étroite? demande Abr. L'arch. le rassure en lui disant que, pour lui, la porte étroite s'élargira.

10. Dans le paradis, Abr. assiste au jugement des âmes. L'âme d'une femme implore la clémence du juge, qui lui reproche d'avoir tué sa propre fille pour lui prendre son mari. L'âme essaie de nier son crime. Le juge fait apporter par les chérubims deux livres dans lesquels sont écrits les actes des mortels. Un homme géant, coiffé de trois couronnes et tenant dans sa main un calame d'or, lit dans un livre les péchés de cette âme et la fait condamner aux peines éternelles.

11. Abr. apprend que le juge est Abel, qui fut le premier martyr; celui qui interprète les livres est Hénoch, 'le maître du ciel [et de la terre Gr B] et scribe de justice'. Hénoch ne juge pas lui-même: c'est Dieu qui juge. Hénoch inscrit les péchés dans les livres et les rapporte au jour du jugement.

12. Abr. et l'arch. s'en vont sur le firmament. Jetant son regard sur la terre, Abr. voit un homme dans les bras d'une femme mariée: il appelle le feu du ciel, qui les consume à l'instant. Ailleurs, il voit des gens calomnier d'autres gens: il les fait engloutir	Ailleurs, Abr. voit un groupe de gens assis paisiblement, que des bandits viennent attaquer et dévaliser: il appelle les fauves pour dévorer les brigands. A un autre endroit, il voit des femmes mariées s'adonnant à la luxure: il les fait engloutir	Abr. descend de nouveau sur un nuage. Il voit comment des gens paisibles sont attaqués et dévalisés: il appelle le feu sur les brigands. Ailleurs, il voit un homme et une femme s'adonnant à la luxure: il les fait engloutir par la terre. Ensuite, *il voit un*

Grec B, Sl¹ et Sl²	Sl³ et Roum.¹	Sl⁴ et Roum.²
par la terre. Dans un désert, il voit des bandits qui épient les voyageurs pour les tuer: il les fait dévorer par les fauves [lions Sl²]. Alors Dieu ordonne à l'arch. de ramener Abr. sur la terre: car, impitoyable comme il se révèle, il serait capable d'anéantir le monde tout entier.	par la terre. Ailleurs, il voit des gens qui insultent les pauvres: il les fait périr par le feu. Ailleurs, il voit un jeune homme assis: il inscrit [dans un livre] tous les péchés des mortels que lui apportent les anges, ensuite il les passe [les péchés?] à Hénoch. Abr. apprend que le jeune homme est Abel. *Ailleurs, Abr. voit des gens qui prêtent de faux serments par soif de profits: il les fait pulvériser.* Dieu ordonne à Michel de faire descendre Abr. dans sa maison, car *'celui qui n'a pas peiné pour une chose, n'a pas de pitié pour elle'.*	*homme faible maltraité par un homme fort: il fait dévorer la brute par les loups.* Voyant qu'Abr. n'a d'indulgence pour personne, Dieu ordonne à l'arch. de le déposer sur la terre, car 'n'a pas de pitié celui qui n'a pas peiné'.
13. Quand la fin des jours d'Abr. arriva, Dieu ordonna à l'arch. Michel d'envoyer chez son ami la Mort, parée d'une grande beauté. Mais ce travesti n'empêche pas Abr. d'avoir peur. Pressentant un danger, il conjure la Mort de s'en aller. Celle-ci persiste.	13-14. *Abr. vécut encore trente ans.* En lui envoyant la Mort, le Seigneur ordonne à *l'arch.* Raphaël de lui faire prendre un aspect joli et paisible. Mais Abr. prend peur de la Mort et lui demande si c'est sous cet aspect-là qu'elle se présente aux mortels. La Mort lui répond que, plutôt que de voir la face qu'elle leur montre, les pécheurs auraient mieux fait de ne pas venir au monde.	13-14. Abr. vécut encore trente ans. A l'heure de sa mort,
14. Finalement, sur les instances d'Abr., elle reprend son aspect de pourriture. Il est si terrifiant qu'à sa vue sept serviteurs d'Abr. rendent leur âme. Abr. les ressuscite par la prière. Ensuite Abr. rend lui-même son âme, comme dans un rêve. Des puissances célestes viennent la prendre et la porter à Dieu. Isaac ensevelit le corps de son père auprès des restes de Sarah.	Alors *le Seigneur,* voyant qu'Abr. a peur de mourir, *descend lui-même sur la terre en grande beauté et, venant chez Abr., lui offre trois pommes. Abr. tend les bras, prend les pommes et aussitôt rend son âme.* Gloire au Seigneur, etc.	le Seigneur descend chez lui *comme un voyageur* et lui offre *une pomme et une jolie colombe.* Abr. accepte les cadeaux et aussitôt rend son âme. 'Le 25 mars.'

III. LA VERSION COURTE INTÉGRALE

(a) Manuscrits et éditions

La version slave intégrale du *Testament* ou de la *Mort d'Abraham* comporte un grand nombre de manuscrits, qui se répartissent, selon leur caractère et leur provenance, en deux familles importantes. La famille Sl¹ comprend les copies faites en domaine orthodoxe: bulgare, serbe, roumain, ukrainien, russe. La famille Sl², catholique, contient des copies d'origine exclusivement croate.

La famille Sl¹ compte les manuscrits suivants:

1. P: Manuscrit ayant appartenu à la collection de P. I. Sevast'anov, actuellement à la Bibliothèque Publique de Moscou, n° 27. La *Mort d'Abraham* (ff. 1–6), copie moyen-bulgare du xiii° siècle, a été publiée par N. S. Tihonravov, *Apokrifičeskija skazanija*, dans le *Sbornik Otdelenija russkogo jazyka i slovesnosti Imp. Akademii nauk*, lviii (1894), 1–8 des annexes (publication posthume) et, indépendamment de Tihonravov, par G. Polívka, dans l'*Archiv für slavische Philologie*, xviii (1896), 118–25. Ce texte est malheureusement incomplet: il lui manque environ trois pages du début, qu'il faut suppléer par le texte cité plus bas.

2. A: Manuscrit n° 636 de l'Académie roumaine de Bucarest, copié en Moldavie, au monastère de Neamțu, en 1557, par le moine-diacre Ilarion, sur l'ordre de l'archevêque de Suceava Grigorié Roșca. Rédaction moyen-bulgare. Il contient un florilège de textes religieux, ainsi qu'une brève *Chronique des 'empereurs' [tsars] chrétiens*, serbes et roumains, publiée par Ioan Bogdan dans *Cronice inedite atingătoare de istoria Românilor* (Bucarest, 1895), 91–6 (description détaillée du manuscrit, pp. 83–9). La Direction de la Bibliothèque de l'Académie roumaine a eu l'obligeance de nous envoyer le microfilm de la *Mort d'Abraham* (ff. 304ʳ–315ʳ).

3. M: Manuscrit ayant appartenu à F. Miklošič, actuellement n° 149 du fonds slave de la Bibliothèque Nationale de Vienne. Le texte de la *Mort d'Abraham*, en rédaction serbo-bulgare du xvii° siècle, couvre les ff. 117ᵛ–125ᵛ. Ce texte étant encore inédit, nous sommes redevables à la Direction de la Bibliothèque de nous en avoir fourni le microfilm. Voir pour la description du manuscrit A. I. Jacimirskij, *Opisanie južnoslavjanskih i russkih zagraničnyh bibliotek*, i, dans le *Sbornik Otdelenija russkogo jazyka i slovesnosti Rossijskoj Akademii nauk*, xcviii (1921), 236–9, et, pour la bibliographie qui le concerne, Émile Turdeanu, 'L'*Apocalypse d'Abraham* en slave', dans le *Journal for the Study of Judaism*, iii (1973), 168–9.

4. C: Manuscrit n° 629 (Conev 433) de la Bibliothèque Nationale de Sofia, en rédaction moyen-bulgare du xvi° siècle. Son *incipit* (f. 105ᵛ) est identique à celui de M. Cf. B. Conev, *Opis na răkopisite i staropečatnite knigi na Narodnata Biblioteka v Sofija*, i (Sofia, 1910), 446, et notre '*Apocalypse d'Abraham* en slave', 169.

5. C¹: Manuscrit n° 509 (Conev 326) de la Bibliothèque Nationale de Sofia, copié avant 1715 en rédaction serbe mélangée avec des formes du bulgare moderne. B. Conev, op. cit., i, 315, et notre '*Apocalypse d'Abraham* en slave', 169.

6. T: Manuscrit n° 730 du monastère Sainte-Trinité-Serge de Moscou
   en rédaction russe du xvie siècle (ff. 2–10^v). Son texte a été publié par N. S. Tihonravov, *Pamjatniki otrečennoj russkoj literatury*, i
   (St-Pétersbourg, 1863), 79–90.
7. F: Manuscrit de Ujhorod (hong. Ungvár), dans la Russie subcarpatique,
   rédigé en ukrainien du xviiie siècle. Sa *Mort d'Abraham* a été publiée
   par Ivan Franko, *Apokrifi i legendi z ukraïns'kih rukopisiv*, iv (L'vov,
   1906), 104–5.

La famille Sl² comporte les copies suivantes:

8. O: MS. Canon. Lit. 414 de la Bodleian Library d'Oxford, en rédaction
   croate du xve siècle. Signalé par M. Rešetar, *Dubrovački zbornik od god.
   1520* (Srpska Kraljevska akademija. Posebna izdanja, knj. c) (Belgrade,
   1933), et décrit par Marin Tadin, 'Glagolitic Manuscripts in the Bodleian
   Library, Oxford', dans les *Oxford Slavonic Papers*, v (1954), 139–44 et
   pl. II. Ce texte glagolite, le seul complet de la famille Sl², étant lui aussi
   inédit, nous remercions très cordialement M. l'abbé Marin Tadin de
   nous en avoir fourni un déchiffrement en caractères latins, d'après un
   microfilm en sa possession.
9. J: Manuscrit ayant appartenu à l'historien Ivan Kukuljević Sakcinski,
   actuellement à la Bibliothèque de l'Académie croate de Zagreb. C'est
   un recueil de plusieurs apocryphes, copié en 1468, en caractères glagolites
   et en rédaction čakavienne. Le texte de la légende d'Abraham commence
   à peine au moment où le Patriarche arrive aux deux portes devant
   lesquelles est assis Adam: *Kada Avram vide dvoě vrata, edna mala, druga
   velika...* Il a été publié en caractères cyrilliques par V. Jagić, *Prilozi
   k historiji književnosti naroda hrvatskoga i srpskoga* (Zagreb, 1868), 25–7
   (réimpression de l'*Arkiv za povjestnicu jugoslavensku*, ix).
10. S: Manuscrit n° IV. a. 120 de la Bibliothèque de l'Académie croate de
    Zagreb. Recueil du xve siècle, en caractères glagolites et en rédaction
    ikavienne. Comme dans J, le récit commence à peine avec l'arrivée
    d'Abraham devant les portes du paradis et de l'enfer. Ce texte a été
    transcrit en caractères latins par Rudolf Strohal, *Stare hrvatske apokrifne
    priče i legende* (Bjelovar, 1917), 57–60. La Bibliothèque Nationale de
    Zagreb a bien voulu nous faire parvenir une photocopie de ce livre rare;
    qu'elle en soit remerciée.

(b) La traduction

Comme le tableau des différentes rédactions slaves l'a déjà laissé
voir, les groupes Sl¹ et Sl² appartiennent à la même traduction. Celle-ci,
à son tour, dérive de la version byzantine courte (B), connue à l'heure
actuelle dans sept manuscrits, dont le plus ancien est du xie ou xiie siècle.

La traduction, telle qu'elle se reflète dans le consensus des meilleurs
manuscrits slaves (P, A, O, et T) est, en général, correcte et se rapproche davantage du texte publié par Francis Schmidt d'après le ms.
405 (G. 63 sup.) de la Bibliothèque Ambrosienne de Milan (E). Comme
celui-ci, elle sait que, pour conduire l'archange à la maison, Abraham

fit venir $\Delta \alpha \mu \alpha \sigma \kappa \grave{o} \nu$ $'E\lambda \epsilon \acute{\epsilon} \zeta \epsilon \rho$, $\tau \grave{o} \nu$ $\upsilon \acute{i} \grave{o} \nu$ $\acute{\epsilon} \nu o \sigma \tau \hat{\omega} \nu$ $o \acute{i} \kappa o \tau \rho \acute{o} \phi \omega \nu$ $\alpha \mathring{v} \tau o \hat{v}$ (I, 12). Le seul manuscrit du groupe Sl¹ qui nous ait conservé ce texte est T (P, A et M étant lacunaires à cet endroit), et il est fautif: призва Авраамъ два дамаска, Елизорови с(ы)нове, домочѧдца своа раби-чишти 'Abraham fit venir deux Damascènes, fils d'Éliézer, nés esclaves dans sa maison'. La bonne leçon se trouve dans le manuscrit croate d'Oxford, qui dit: *I prizva Avraam Damaska, sina Elizarova domaštega rabičišta* (cf. *Gen.* xv, 2, où cependant est parlé d'Éliézer de Damas, le serviteur d'Abraham, né dans sa maison, sans aucune mention de son fils).

Les lacunes de la traduction, relativement nombreuses, ne dépassent jamais deux ou trois lignes. Le plus souvent on saute quelques mots ou de petites bribes de phrase, dont l'absence n'affecte pas la trame du récit. Les seules divergences notables par rapport à la version grecque courte apparaissent à la fin du récit. Dans sa transfiguration la plus épouvantable, la Mort se présente avec 'plusieurs têtes', lorsqu'elle n'a que deux dans le texte grec: les unes ont l'aspect des dragons (gr. $\pi \rho \acute{o} \sigma \omega \pi \alpha$ $\delta \rho \alpha \kappa \acute{o} \nu \tau \omega \nu$), d'autres ont des glaives (gr. $\acute{\rho} o \mu \phi \alpha \acute{\iota} \alpha \varsigma$), d'autres lancent du feu comme les dragons des contes populaires.

Un autre trait intéressant de la version slave (P, T) apparaît dans le passage où l'archange Michel rassure Sarah au sujet de Loth (VI, 6): 'Sarah ayant entendu, remarqua les paroles et comprit que la façon de parler de Michel est différente de tous les discours des hommes vivant *dans la tranquillité* (тихостиѭ) sur la terre, et (que) sa parole est glorieuse.' Тихость 'le calme', 'la tranquillité', c'est $\acute{\eta}$ $\acute{\eta} \sigma \upsilon \chi \acute{\iota} \alpha$. Du coup, on est tenté de penser à ce grand mouvement hésychaste lequel, partant de l'enseignement de Grégoire le Sinaïte, avait conquis l'Église bulgare dans la deuxième moitié du xIVe siècle: un disciple direct de Grégoire, Théodose, excellent orateur, l'implante à Kilifarevo, près de Tărnovo, vers 1360, et le plus grand écrivain et prédicateur de son époque, Euthyme (1371–93), l'illustre du haut de son trône patriarcal. Mais l'ancienneté du manuscrit P nous interdit de nous arrêter à cette conjecture. Si l'allusion se rapporte bien à l'hésychasme, elle ne pourra concerner que l'hésychasme sporadique, de source athonite, antérieur au grand courant du xIVe siècle. Elle remonte probablement à la traduction du xIIe siècle.

(c) La famille Sl¹: les manuscrits P, A et M

Ce qui confère au ms. P son plus grand intérêt, c'est son ancienneté. Il est écrit dans une langue où le vieux slave tardif conserve encore un certain nombre de ses traits distinctifs. Parmi ceux-ci, le plus frappant est le maintien de la désinence -те à la 3ᵉ personne du duel du présent et de l'aoriste, dans les exemples suivants: тѣжде есте nosѣ 119, 12 'ce sont les mêmes pieds', шьдша поискасте 121, 20 's'en allant, ils (l'archange Michel et Abraham) cherchèrent', et доидосте мѣста 122, 5 'ils (*idem*) parvinrent à un endroit', où l'absence de la préposition devant le complément indique, elle aussi, un trait de la langue ancienne.

Un exemple de futur imperfectif apparaît dans la proposition мнози от мира скозѣ широкаꙗ врата идѫтъ на пагоубѫ 121, 13–14 'beaucoup (de gens) de ce monde iront à leur perdition par la porte large'. Le comparatif se construit encore avec le complément au génitif: изгнилѣи мене 125, 1 'plus sordide que moi'. Mais, à part ces traits archaïques, la langue du texte est le moyen-bulgare du xiiie siècle, dont la correctitude relève d'une école littéraire.

Quelques expressions nous semblent dignes d'être notées comme étant en usage à cette époque. Tout d'abord le verbe повелѣти au sens de 'permettre': повели ми, от(ъ)че, да и азъ легѫ сь вама 118, 6 'permets-moi, père, que je couche, moi aussi, avec vous deux'. Pour 'je consens' on dit волꙗ ти даꙗ 123, 14 (valant . . . ти даѭ), littéralement 'je t'accorde la permission', comme aujourd'hui encore en bulgare дам ти воля et en roumain *îţi dau voie* 'je te permets'. Enfin, слъга чисто 124, 26 rend une expression populaire analogue au français 'tu as menti proprement'.

Une traduction probablement de la fin du xiie siècle, conservée dans une copie moyen-bulgare correcte et sans couleur dialectale, du xiiie siècle: voilà les seules indications que le ms. P nous fournit sur l'origine du *Testament d'Abraham* en slave.

Nous avons dit que le ms. P est incomplet: il lui manquent les quatre premiers chapitres du récit. Fort heureusement, le ms. 636 du fonds slave de l'Académie roumaine nous permet de compléter cette lacune et de contrôler en même temps le texte publié par Polívka. Ce manuscrit, copié en 1557 pour le monastère de Neamţu, en Moldavie, s'encadre dans la remarquable activité littéraire patronnée par un métropolite éclairé comme Grigorié Roşca.[11]

Son texte est légèrement raccourci par rapport à P, O et T. Il ne dit pas qu'Abraham était assis auprès de ses bœufs, car il était vieux (II, 1), ni qu'il voulut envoyer chercher 'une bête de somme' pour conduire le voyageur à la maison et lui éviter ainsi les dangers de la nuit (II, 5–6). Il néglige la référence de Michel à sa visite antérieure, lorsqu'Abraham fit tuer un veau pour recevoir à sa table la Trinité, et ne précise pas que les deux serviteurs du Patriarche étaient deux 'Damascènes, fils d'Éliézer'. Il omet la demande d'Isaac de coucher dans la même chambre que son père et l'archange (V, 4–5), ainsi que la

---

[11] Emil Turdeanu, 'Centres of Literary Activity in Moldavia', *Slavonic and East European Review*, xxxiv (1955), 115–18. Version française, complétée, dans la *Revue des études roumaines*, ix/x (Paris, 1965), 114–18.

remarque de Sarah que la voix de l'invité était plus douce que celle 'des gens vivant sur la terre dans la tranquillité' (cf. P et T). Il se tait également sur l'âge des enfants qui peuvent passer par la porte étroite (IX, 3). Sa lacune la plus importante est celle de P 121, 23–5: l'âme de la femme n'est conduite ni à la perdition ni à la vie, mais entre les deux portes. (IX, 9: καὶ οὐκ — μεσότητος). Il s'agit probablement de l'intervention du copiste moldave, qui ne pouvait comprendre l'existence d'une troisième mesure entre le péché et l'innocence.

Pour se racheter de ces lacunes, le ms. A contient, outre les chapitres I–IV, deux passages qui manquent dans P. Il conserve un tronçon de phrase que P et T omettent par homoeoteleuton: les deux portes du jugement conduisent à la *vie* 'et à la mort — continue A —; les portes étroites conduisent à la *vie*', et la demande d'Abraham d'être porté au lieu du jugement (qui, cependant, existe dans T). Ces particularités nous permettent d'affirmer que A ne descend pas de P, mais d'un intermédiaire très proche de lui.

Le prototype de P et de A contenait, à son tour, quelques erreurs ou particularités de lecture qui le distinguaient de l'original grec et des autres rédactions slaves. Nous en donnerons la liste plus loin, lorsque nous parlerons des caractéristiques du ms. T. Retenons pour le moment que la tradition de P et A, bien que plus fidèle dans son ensemble à la traduction, n'est pas exempte de certaines failles qu'il faut compléter par les autres témoins du texte.

La langue du ms. A confirme, elle aussi, l'intérêt particulier qu'on doit accorder à ce texte. Bien que, dans son ensemble, elle soit plus jeune que celle de P, elle conserve encore quelques-uns des traits archaïques que nous avons relevés dans le ms. P: les duels de la 3ᵉ personne de l'aoriste поискасте et обрѣтосте 310ʳ, 20, le futur imperfectif идѫтъ 310ʳ, 9, le comparatif изгнилѣи мене 314ʳ, 9, ainsi que deux des expressions que nous avons citées plus haut, p. 13. Certaines formes nous font situer son intermédiaire dans la Bulgarie occidentale: la vocalisation presque constante de ь en position forte en е: пришелъ 307ᵛ, 5, тѧжекъ 310ʳ, 1 (mais тѧжькъ 312ʳ, 8), шедше 310ʳ, 19, съчетеиы 310ᵛ, 3, праведенъ 314ᵛ, 2, etc.; le préverbe оу- dans оубоа сѧ 313ᵛ, 2 'il prit peur' pour възбоа сѧ de P; le verbe грѧдоушта 309ʳ, 13 'allant'; l'emploi exclusif de лѣпота, 'beauté', au dépens de красота, etc.

Connaissant la fidélité des scribes moldaves au moyen-bulgare, ces particularités nous font situer le modèle de la copie A dans la Bulgarie occidentale.

Parmi les témoins secondaires, la copie du ms. 149 de la Bibliothèque Nationale de Vienne, elle aussi inédite, occupe une place à part. Elle présente avec le ms. T toutes les leçons susceptibles d'émender le texte de P et de A; mais elle abrège le récit et lui donne une allure nettement plus populaire. Son accord avec T prouve qu'il a existé, dans le domaine méridional, une branche de filiation différente de celle de P et A; sa langue, formée d'un mélange de serbe et de bulgare, nous dirige, elle aussi, vers cette Bulgarie occidentale où nous avons localisé le modèle du manuscrit moldave A, et qui est, fort probablement, la patrie même de la traduction.

Voici quelques exemples du mélange des formes serbes et bulgares: сѫдїа сѫдѫтъ 123ᵛ, 14 'les juges jugent'; en regard de на рѫкѫ 122, 8 'à la main' on a trois fois въ рѫцѣ 'dans les mains'; отльченіе 119, 8 'séparation' voisine avec отлѫченна 120, 19 'séparée'; таина 'secret' fait à l'accusatif таинѫ сїю 118, 4 et таиннѹ (*sic* -nn-) 120ᵛ, 19; гредѫт въ мѫкѫ 123, 14 'ils s'en vont dans la torture' n'a rien pour surprendre.

Le moyen-bulgare a laissé plusieurs vestiges dans le texte. On rencontre par exemple: паметь смртнѫѫ (acc.) 119ᵛ, 3 'la conscience de la mort', подобѫт се пьтем твоим 123, 5 'ils imiteront ton chemin', снѫх (< снахъ) 121, 17 'j'ai enlevé', поведашѫ 120ᵛ, 19 'ils expliquèrent', несошѫ 124, 16 'ils portèrent', от Саррѫ 125ᵛ, 18 'de Sarah', etc.

Appartenant à un milieu populaire si peu rigoureux dans la rédaction de ses textes, le copiste de M ne se contente pas de simplifier la langue et de renouveler son vocabulaire, préférant цѣлева 120, 6 'il embrassa' à любызаѩ (P, A, T), вѣсть 120, 4 (et A) 'nouvelle' à наречениѥ (P, T), что еси въ сьнѣ видѣль 121, 6 (et A) 'qu'as-tu vu en rêve?' à что ти видѣниѥ съньноѥ (P, T), тѣсность 121, 19 (et T) 'étroitesse' à сънъ (P, A), etc., mais il traite également le récit à sa guise. Arrivé au moment où Abraham commence à infliger aux pécheurs ses peines impitoyables, il fait exclamer au Seigneur: 'Que de créatures a-t-il envoyées au diable!' (прѣдасть дїаволѹ), et trouve opportun d'y enchaîner un bref passage de la *Vision de saint Paul*: 'Souvent le soleil s'écria vers moi...', etc., 125ᵛ, 9–15. Le passage, qui peut n'être qu'une citation mentale, se rapporte à la version longue de l'apocalypse de Paul.

La rédaction serbo-bulgare de Vienne s'arrête avec le retour d'Abraham sur la terre.

(d) La famille Sl¹: les manuscrits T et F

Le manuscrit T, en slavon russe, descend de l'archétype slave par une branche de filiation différente de celle de P et de A. Il contient, en effet, un certain nombre de leçons qui corroborent la version B du texte grec là où, précisément, P et A sont défaillants. En échange, il est légèrement prolixe et s'accorde la liberté d'ajouter deux digressions étrangères au récit.

Voici les leçons qui sont à son avantage:

III, 6: боровы 'animaux', *tri bravi* O, три брави M (exemple cité également par Miklošič dans son *Lexicon*, s.v. брава), θρέμματα E, θρέμματα τρία A, mais крави 'vaches' A (*mq.* P).

VI, 7: како смѣи плакати са T: πῶς ἐτόλμησας κλαῦσαι; E, mais како плачеши P et A 'comment pleures-tu?' et *kako da plakati?* 'comment pleurer?' O.

VII, 7: лоуча T, τὰς ἀκτῖνας E, mais лоунѫ (acc.) P et A 'la lune' (*mq.* O).

VII, 8: молю та, господи T, παρακαλῶ σε, Κύριε E, *om.* P, A et O.

VII, 10: и отиде оубо от троуда на покои T, ἀνελήφθη γὰρ ἀπὸ κομάτου εἰς ἀνάπαυσιν E, *om.* P, A et O.

VII, 15: видѣхъ слъньце соушта (подобенъ) отца моего T, εἶδον τὸν ἥλιον γενόμενον (ὅμοιον) τοῦ πατρός μου E, mais видѣхъ слъньце отца моего въсходѧшта на nебо P et A, *vidih sln'ce otica moego vshodešta na nebesa* O 'je vis le soleil de mon père monter au ciel' ('aux cieux' O).

VII, 17: 'sept mille ans' T, ἑξακισχίλια ἔτη E, mais 'huit mille ans' P et A ('jusqu'à ce que ressuscitera le Seigneur' O).

IX, 2: горе мнѣ, что сътворю T, οὐαί μοι, τί ποιήσω ἐγώ; E, *om.* P, A et O.

X, 1: хоштоу да ма доведеши до соуднаго мѣста да бих видѣл како соудит T et A; *Hotil bim da bi me dovel do sudnega mesta da viju kako sudacǐ sudit* O, θέλω ἵνα ἀπάξῃς με εἰς τὸν τόπον τοῦ κριτερίου, ὅπως κἀγὼ θεάσωμαι πῶς κρίνει E, mais хоштѫ да сѫди сѫдит P 'je désire que le juge juge'.

X, 12: отвѣштавъ моужь T et O, ἀποκριθεὶς ὁ ἀνὴρ E, mais отвѣштавъ Авраамъ P et A.

XII, 14: на землю T, ἐπὶ τὴν γῆν E, *om.* P, A et O.

XIII, 1: рече господь Михаилоу T et O, εἶπεν δὲ Κύριος πρὸς Μιχαήλ E, *om.* P et A.

XIII, 10: La leçon de P, A, O 'et parmi les hommes' n'existe pas dans T et E.

Il ressort de ces exemples que le manuscrit T peut émender utilement les copies méridionales P, A et O, qui présentent certaines lacunes (VII, 8; VII, 10; IX, 2; XII, 14; XIII, 1) et particularités de lecture (VII, 15; XIII, 10) communes. La physionomie du prototype slave perdu est à chercher dans le consensus de ces quatre rédactions.

Quant au témoignage du manuscrit ukrainien F, tardif, raccourci et fortement remanié, il n'a qu'un intérêt local. Sa liberté et son incompréhension du texte vont parfois jusqu'à l'humour. Abraham demande à son fils d'amener 'un veau' pour conduire son invité à la maison. Il lui enjoint ensuite de laver 'les mains et les pieds' de l'invité. Les larmes de l'archange se transforment en 'flamme de feu': confusion évidente entre каменъ 'pierre' et пламенъ 'flamme'. Quand Sarah apprend que son mari quittera bientôt la terre ('dimanche matin de bonne heure', précise-t-on plus bas), elle s'en prend à l'invité: 'Comment as-tu osé nous saluer et venir comme hôte dans notre maison?' Isaac dénonce sans ambages l'archange de lui avoir dérobé, dans son rêve, le soleil qu'il avait sur sa tête — etc.

Ce texte désinvolte, populaire et moderne, montre une fois de plus comment les vieux apocryphes s'adaptent aux milieux qui les accueillent pour en faire tantôt une lecture amusante et familière, comme dans le cas présent, tantôt une lecture d'édification, comme dans les exemples qui vont suivre.

(e) La famille Sl²: le manuscrit J

Au xvᵉ siècle, la Dalmatie et la Croatie puisent leurs textes tant dans la littérature occidentale, vers laquelle les attire leur foi catholique, que dans le riche courant de traductions orthodoxes, que leur impose la tradition. Traversant les pays serbes, la *Mort d'Abraham* atteint le littoral adriatique dans la première moitié du xvᵉ siècle. Elle y revêt le dialecte čakavien et l'alphabet glagolite et, munie de ces titres, elle gagne ce droit de cité dont témoignent trois copies de l'époque.

De ces trois copies, c'est le fragment publié par Jagić qui se rapproche davantage de l'original serbe par l'aspect de sa langue, c'est la rédaction d'Oxford qui en conserve le meilleur texte et c'est le fragment de Strohal qui s'en détache le plus.

La base serbe, ékavienne (ex. *vera*) est plus évidente dans J, où le nombre des ikavismes (ex. *vira*) est plus réduit que dans les deux autres copies. Cette proportion est caractéristique du čakavien septentrional et rapproche le texte de J du *Lectionnaire* de Zadar, lui aussi du xvᵉ siècle, étudié par Milan Rešetar.[12]

Nous donnons plus bas quelques traits caractéristiques de la langue de J, afin de mieux faire ressortir son appartenance dialectale. Lorsqu'une forme se trouve également dans O, nous la faisons suivre de ce sigle entre parenthèses; lorsqu'elle diffère, nous la signalons; l'absence de toute mention signifie l'absence de la forme correspondante dans O.

La préposition *va* ou *v'* est la seule employée en regard du štokavien *u*: le trait caractérise le čakavien septentrional (Rešetar, *Rad*, cxxxiv, 104) et vaut également pour les préverbes: *vavodě* 25, 25 'il conduit', *vapijušti* 25, 39 (O) 'se lamentant', etc. La préposition *ka* à côté de *k'* apparaît seulement trois fois, toujours devant le nom d'Abraham: *ka Avramu* 25, 24; 26, 33 (mais *ka inomu člověku* O); 27, 3. Cet emploi limité aux noms propres s'accorde avec les exemples relevés dans le *Lectionnaire* de Zadar (Rešetar, ibid. 103).

La chute de la voyelle finale apparaît dans *nerĭ* 25, 32 (*razvi* O) 'seulement', *nigdorĭ* 27, 4 (O) 'personne', *nikomurĭ* 26, 18 (O) 'à personne', ce dernier accompagné de *nikomurě* 27, 12 (O). Quant à *are* 25, 31 'parce que', elle atteste une forme rare, inconnue du vieux

---

[12] Milan Rešetar, 'Primorski lekcionari XV vijeka', *Rad Jugoslavenske akademije znanosti i umjetnosti*, cxxxiv (1898), 80–160, et cxxxvi (1898), 97–199. On trouvera une vue plus large et plus complète du čakavien, dans ses rapports avec la langue de Raguse, dans les deux volumes qu'André Vaillant a consacrés à *La Langue de Dominko Zlatarić* (Travaux publiés par l'Institut d'Études slaves, vi) (Paris, 1928–31).

serbo-croate et disparue assez tôt du ragusain (cf. Vaillant, *Zlatarić*, i, 306).

La conservation du groupe *št*, dans la mesure où elle n'est pas imposée par un original štokavien, est encore un trait du čakavien de Zadar (Rešetar, *Rad*, cxxxvi, 102). Nous la trouvons constamment dans J et O: *vešti* 25, 23 (O) 'plus grand', *govorešti* 25, 39 (O) 'disant', *išteze* 27, 22 (O) 'il disparut', etc. Devant une consonne, *k* passe à *h*: *hštere* 26, 1 (*kštere* O) et *hšterĭ* 26, 8 (accusatifs; *kšter* O) 'fille'. Un serbisme caractéristique est le passage de *s* à *š* dans *biše š nim* 26, 4 (*bi š nimi* O) 'il y avait avec lui' ou 'il était avec lui'.

Dans la morphologie, on remarque tout d'abord l'emploi exclusif, pour le pluriel masculin des thèmes en *-u*, de la forme courte: on a toujours *grehe* (nom.-acc.), forme ikavienne *grehi* 26, 10 (O); 26, 19 (O); gén. pluriel *grehĭ* 26, 30, mais *grihov* O. De même, au neutre, le génitif pluriel est *del'* 26, 3 (cf. aussi Vaillant, *Zlatarić*, ii, 24); le locatif pluriel est *dĕleh'* 26, 21. Le démonstratif masculin singulier *sa* est encore vivant: *sa est' nebĕski učitel'* 26, 14 (*si* O) 'celui-ci est le maître du ciel'; mais il est concurrencé par *ov* 25, 26 (*sa* O), qui est la forme du čakavien moderne (Vaillant, ibid. ii, 151). L'interrogatif *gdo*, caractéristique du čakavien septentrional, est également attesté: *gdo esi ti?* 26, 38 (O) 'qui es-tu?'; c'est la forme courante du *Lectionnaire* de Zadar (ibid. ii, 155). Le pronom 'quoi' a, de rigueur, la forme *ča*; d'où *za-č'* 26, 1, etc. 'pourquoi?'. Le relatif masculin est, au nominatif singulier comme au nominatif pluriel, *ki*; accusatif singulier *ku* 27, 2 et 3 (O).

En ce qui concerne la conjugaison, il faut retenir le très caractéristique *viju* 'je vois', ainsi que plusieurs cas de gérondif présent en *-e* (ou *-ě*): *sidĕ* 25, 26 'étant assis', *nose* 26, 4 'portant', *imĕe* 26, 4 (*imie* O) 'ayant', etc. Ces formes sont d'autant plus intéressantes qu'elles voisinent dans J avec les formes longues du gérondif, plus anciennes: *renušta* 25, 34 (acc.) 'poussant avec force' (*reniše* O), *gredušte* 25, 29 (*gredušt'* O) et *gredušti* 25, 30 'marchant', *činešta* 26, 23 (acc.) 'faisant', *razlučajušti* 27, ii (O) 'séparant'. Les formes longues sont les seules attestées dans le *Lectionnaire* de Zadar (ibid. ii, 246).

Parmi les verbes d'un emploi plus rare, *zabivati*, imperfectif, est bien représenté: *zabivaju* 26, 11 (O) 'ils oublient', *zabivah* 26, 10 (*zabih* O) 'j'ai oublié'; il se maintient encore en čakavien (ibid. ii, 271). Le présent du verbe *vĕdĕti* apparaît sous son aspect ikavien: *vim* 27, 6 'je sais' (mais *viju* 'je vois' O). Du verbe *jęti*, avec préverbe, on a l'aoriste singulier 3ᵉ personne *ot'ě* (valant *ote*; *otĕt* O) 27, 14 'il enleva'.

Quelques mots rares complètent le tableau de ces particularités: *telesnit* 25, 31 'corpulent', *sumŭporŭ* 27, 17 'soufre', *z nutařiudu* 27, 18 (donné comme un *hapax* par le *Rječnik* de l'Académie de Zagreb, s.v.) 'de l'intérieur', *čemerĭ* 27, 19 'poison végétal' (s.-cr. *čemèrika* 'ellébore', cf. Vaillant, *Zlatarić*, i, 235).

(f) La famille Sl² : les manuscrits S et O

Si le manuscrit J présente l'intérêt d'un texte ékavien transcrit librement en čakavien septentrional avec force ikavismes, la copie publiée par Strohal nous offre une rédaction strictement ikavienne. Elle se situe donc plus au sud que J, dans la Dalmatie proprement dite. Plus encore que J, elle accuse le caractère populaire du récit, utilise la langue parlée, un style lâche avec force périphrases et mots de remplissage, avec répétitions et un vocabulaire modernisé. Mais, bien qu'elle débute exactement comme J, c'est-à-dire à peine au chapitre VIII de la version courte, et qu'elle suit le même développement, S n'est pas la réplique de J, pas plus que J ne relève pas de S. Les deux remontent à un prototype commun, dont S a gardé certains éléments que J a perdus, et inversement.

Ainsi, on note à l'avantage de S : l'âme de la pécheresse est conduite au lieu du jugement par la Mort elle-même (comme dans E IX, 10–11) ; le juge est Abel, 'le premier martyr' (le juge est le Seigneur J) et celui 'qui répond' aux questions du Seigneur est Hénoch, 'ton père' (E XI, 2–3) ; enterrement de Sarah (E XII, 15–16 ; mq. J) ; description de la Mort pourrie plus fidèle que celle de J, qui charge son tableau de touches nouvelles. Enfin, S relate comment les anges ont porté l'âme d'Abraham au ciel et comment Isaac a enseveli son corps 'dans le champ de Mambré' près de Sarah. Ces derniers détails existent en grec et dans le groupe Sl¹, sauf toutefois l'indication toponymique, qui est commune à S et O, mais qui a disparu de J avec tout le passage final.

Mais J conserve, lui aussi, certains avantages sur S. Pour nous limiter à un seul exemple, disons qu'il reproduit les paroles par lesquelles la Mort se présente à Abraham plus exactement que S : *Ja esm gorkoe ime, ja sam plač i žalost', ja sam pogiběl', ja sam smrt* : ἐγώ εἰμι ὁ πικρότερον ὄνομα, ἐγώ εἰμι ὁ κλαυθμός, ἐγώ εἰμι ἡ πτῶσις πάντων (XII, 15), mais 'Je suis la perte (*pogibel'*) de tous, je suis la mort terrible' S.

Ainsi, bien que provenant tous deux d'un seul et même prototype, incomplet, J et S ont suivi deux carrières parallèles. Le seul texte croate intégral est O, et c'est à partir de ses indications qu'il faut retracer l'histoire du *Testament d'Abraham* dans le domaine dalmato-croate. Le MS. Canon. Lit. 414 de la Bibliothèque Bodléienne d'Oxford contient un florilège caractéristique de textes byzantins et de textes occidentaux. Il a été écrit 'probablement au début du xvᵉ siècle, dans la région couverte aujourd'hui par le diocèse de Senj-Modruš',[13] et porte les notices de deux possesseurs qui se sont délectés à sa lecture, entre 1448 et 1480.

---

[13] Marin Tadin, 'Glagolitic Manuscripts in the Bodleian Library', *Oxford Slavonic Papers*, v (1954), 140.

La petite ville de Senj se situe à mi-chemin entre Zadar et Rijeka, en plein domaine čakavien, où ékavismes et ikavismes se mélangent dans une proportion variable selon le copiste et l'âge des textes. Le copiste de O est certainement plus habitué aux ikavismes que celui de J ou le rédacteur du *Lectionnaire* de Zadar.

C'est donc à partir d'un texte semblable à O comme contenu et proche de J comme langue, que s'est formée la version partielle que nous rapportent J et S. Elle est du milieu du xve siècle et du nord de la Dalmatie, peut-être même de Zadar, comme le laisserait supposer l'identité de langue entre J et le *Lectionnaire* de cette ville. Elle est courte, ne retenant que la partie finale de l'apocryphe, à partir du chapitre VIII: le jugement des âmes et la mort d'Abraham. Son but est d'illustrer l'existence d'un jugement céleste qui décide du sort de l'âme immédiatement après la mort, et de fournir ainsi aux bons et aux mauvais croyants un exemple de ce que peut les attendre, les uns et les autres, dans la vie éternelle.

Rien ne nous permet de savoir si, telle qu'elle a été détachée de l'ensemble de l'apocryphe, cette section a servi ou non comme lecture d'édification. Mais si nous pensons à la fortune qu'ont connue plusieurs autres apocryphes, cet usage nous semble des plus naturels. Nous savons, par exemple, que les chapitres VII–XVI de la *Vision de saint Paul* ont été publiés par Božidar Vuković comme une pièce autonome, dans son *Zbornik za putnike* paru à Venise, en 1520, et qu'ils ont été repris ensuite dans les *Prologues* russes;[14] qu'un ecclésiastique russe du xve siècle a tiré de la même *Vision de saint Paul* une section à lire 'le jeudi de la 5e semaine du Carême', sur la nécessité de la prière 'de jour et de nuit';[15] que l'*Apocalypse de Baruch* a fourni à un moraliste russe du xve siècle le thème d'un apologue sur les méfaits de l'abus du vin;[16] et nous n'avons pas hésité à ajouter à ces exemples le petit fragment, le seul retrouvé en serbe, des *Testaments des Douze Patriarches*, qui dénonce les tentations que les femmes font subir aux hommes pieux.[17]

Dans ce processus de récupération des apocryphes par l'Église et peut-être également par certaines gens de bonne volonté, pour en tirer un enseignement direct, facile et pittoresque à la fois, la rédaction fragmentaire du *Testament d'Abraham* a pu jouer auprès des masses populaires un rôle plus actif que la rédaction longue, plus livresque et plus 'anecdotique' dans sa partie consacrée à la biographie terrestre du Patriarche.

---

[14] É. Turdeanu, 'La *Vision de saint Paul* dans la tradition littéraire des Slaves orthodoxes', *Die Welt der Slaven*, i (1956), 423–7.

[15] Ibid. 427–9.

[16] É. Turdeanu, 'L'*Apocalypse de Baruch* en slave', *Revue des études slaves*, xlviii (1969), 44–8.

[17] Idem, 'Les *Testaments des Douze Patriarches* en slave', *Journal for the Study of Judaism*, i (1971), 181–4.

IV. LES VERSIONS DE LA *PALAEA*

A. Les caractères communs

Dans deux études antérieures, l'une consacrée à la *Palaea* byzantine,[18] l'autre à l'*Apocalypse d'Abraham*,[19] nous avons constaté l'apparition, en Macédoine slave, à la fin du XIVe siècle et au début du XVe siècle, de deux versions abrégées du cycle de six légendes ayant pour protagoniste le Patriarche Abraham. La première de ces six légendes est l'*Apocalypse d'Abraham*, la dernière la *Mort d'Abraham*. Les deux résultent de la contamination des vieux apocryphes respectifs avec la *Palaea* byzantine, dont la rédaction intégrale a été traduite en Macédoine dès le XIIe siècle.

C'est dans le cadre que nous avons tracé pour l'*Apocalypse d'Abraham* qu'il convient de situer l'étude des versions abrégées de la *Mort d'Abraham*. Elles contiennent un seul et même récit écourté, contaminé et enrichi d'un thème d'origine populaire. Cependant, elles traitent ce récit d'une manière assez différente pour se donner, chacune, une individualité propre. Aussi les désignons-nous sous deux sigles différents, Sl³ et Sl⁴. A leur tour, elles s'associent deux versions roumaines correspondantes, que nous indiquons par Roum.¹ et Roum.²

Compte tenu des éléments nouveaux qu'ils possèdent en commun, mais aussi des différences importantes qui les séparent, la filiation de Sl³ et Sl⁴ peut être envisagée de deux manières: (a) Les deux procèdent, par deux voies de filiation indépendantes, d'un seul et même prototype; (b) Sl⁴ est tributaire de Sl³. La première hypothèse soulève une objection majeure: aucun manuscrit n'a conservé un récit qui corresponde au Sl³ et Sl⁴ tout en ignorant les particularités de chacun de ces groupes. D'autre part, la seconde hypothèse trouve une confirmation dans l'histoire de l'*Apocalypse d'Abraham*, où nous avons pu suivre sans difficulté le passage de la première version abrégée à la deuxième, plus libre et plus inventive. Aussi prenons-nous le parti de considérer la première version abrégée de la *Mort d'Abraham* comme la source directe de la deuxième.

B. La première version abrégée

(a) *Contenu et analyse*

Tout comme la version intégrale, cette nouvelle version compte deux familles de manuscrits: l'une appartient au domaine slave, l'autre au domaine roumain.

La famille Sl³ est formée de quatre manuscrits que nous avons déjà rencontrés et décrits au sujet de l'*Apocalypse d'Abraham*: L, en slavon

---

[18] 'La *Palaea* byzantine chez les Slaves du sud et chez les Roumains', *Revue des études slaves*, xl (1964) (*Mélanges André Vaillant*), 195–206.
[19] 'L'*Apocalypse d'Abraham* en slave', *Journal for the Study of Judaism*, iii (1973), 153–80.

serbe du XVe siècle, publié par P. A. Lavrov, *Apokrifičeskie teksty* (Saint-Pétersbourg, 1899), 78–81 (réimpression du *Sbornik Otdelenija russkogo jazyka i slovesnosti Imp. Akademii nauk*, lxvii); *belgr.*, en slavon serbe du XIVe siècle, inédit et détruit dans l'incendie de la Bibliothèque Nationale de Belgrade, en avril 1940; B[1], serbe du XVIIIe siècle, inédit et détruit dans le même incendie; Z, copié à Raguse, en 1520, et publié pour la première fois par V. Jagić, dans *Prilozi k historiji književnosti naroda hrvatskoga i srbskoga* (Zagreb, 1868), 22–4, ensuite par Milan Rešetar, *Libro od mnozijeh razloga. Dubrovački ćirilski zbornik od god. 1520* (Zbornik za istoriju, jezik i književnost srpskog naroda, xv) (Sr. Karlovci, 1926), 57–9. Voir également la nouvelle description de Vladimir Mošin, *Ćirilski rukopisi Jugoslavenske akademije*, i (Zagreb, 1955), 71–3.

La famille roumaine compte à l'heure actuelle une seule copie: R: texte copié en Transylvanie, vers la fin du XVIe siècle, par le pope Grigorié du village de Măhaciu, près de Turda, dans son fameux *Codex Sturdzanus*. Edité par B. Petriceicu-Hasdeu, *Cărțile poporane ale Românilor în secolul XVI* (Bucarest, 1879), 189–94. Un fac-similé dans N. Cartojan, *Istoria literaturii române vechi*, i (Bucarest, 1940), 68.

Cette nouvelle version n'est pas un simple résumé de la version courte intégrale, loin de là. Si elle en garde certaines parties, en les condensant, elle en omet d'autres, et en nombre (voir plus haut, pp. 3–9). Elle change également l'ordre de certains épisodes, ramenant, par exemple, au début du récit, les révélations que, dans B, Sl[1] et Sl[2], Sarah ne fait que plus tard. Mais surtout elle ajoute des incidents et des détails nouveaux, qui accusent son originalité.

Ces éléments nouveaux peuvent être répartis en deux groupes: les uns sont communs aux deux versions Sl[3] Roum.[1] et Sl[4] Roum.[2], les autres sont propres à la seule version Sl[3] Roum.[1]

Ceux qui caractérisent les deux versions sont:

§ 2. Le diable ayant 'fermé' toutes les routes qui mènent à la maison d'Abraham, celui-ci se voit contraint de jeûner plusieurs jours avant de rencontrer un voyageur et de l'inviter à sa table. (L'obstruction du diable manque dans L.)

§ 3. Lavant les pieds du voyageur, Sarah reconnaît en lui un être céleste, semblable aux trois étrangers qui ont détruit Sodome et Gomorrhe. Sa remarque lui attire le reproche naïf d'Abraham.

§ 4. Avant le dîner, Michel remonte au ciel dans le seul but de demander au Seigneur s'il doit ou non accepter le repas de viande que lui prépare Abraham.

§ 9. Abraham voit tout d'abord Adam et ensuite les deux portes qui conduisent au paradis et à l'enfer.

§ 13. Après sa visite au ciel, Abraham vit encore trente ans. A l'heure de son trépas, le Seigneur descend lui-même sur la terre pour lui offrir 'trois pommes' (Sl[3] Roum.[1]) ou 'une pomme et une jolie colombe' (Sl[4]

Roum.[2]). Abraham tend les mains pour recevoir le présent et aussitôt rend son âme.

Les additions propres au groupe Sl[3] Roum.[1] sont:

§ 2. Michel descend à l'orée d'une forêt. Abraham demande à Isaac de l'accompagner à la recherche d'un voyageur, car il sent ses forces faiblir, tellement il a faim. (Cette invitation manque dans L, mais existe dans Z et R: nous la considérons comme remontant au prototype.)

§ 8. Conduit au ciel, Abraham adore Dieu sur son trône porté par des chérubims. Étonnement et joie des puissances célestes à sa vue.

§ 9. Abraham demande le pardon de l'âme qui a fait autant de bien que de mal.

(Le ms. Z s'arrête ici; R saute tout le reste du récit jusqu'au passage final.)

§ 11. En regard du nom d'Hénoch, on lit la citation: 'L'Église d'Hénoch ne répond pas sur la terre et personne n'appelle son nom' (L).

§ 12. Parmi les crimes qu'Abraham voit du haut du firmament et les châtiments qu'il inflige aux mortels, L introduit le châtiment des parjures.

§ 13. L'heure de la fin d'Abraham étant venue, c'est à l'archange Raphaël que Dieu ordonne de parer la Mort et de l'envoyer chez le Patriarche sous un aspect agréable (cf. B, Sl[1] et Sl[2]: l'archange Michel).

§ 14. Le Seigneur descend lui-même dans la maison de son ami et lui offre trois jolies pommes, dont la vue entraîne sa mort.

Nous parlerons plus loin des différences secondaires qui séparent le manuscrit L des textes ragusain (Z) et roumain (R).

Parmi les particularités relevées plus haut, les deux premières confirment d'une manière inattendue la relation que nous venons d'établir entre la nouvelle version de la *Mort d'Abraham* et le cycle des légendes consacrées au Patriarche dans la *Palaea*. L'épisode du diable qui bloque les chemins conduisant à la demeure d'Abraham, afin d'obliger le Patriarche à renoncer à sa coutume de ne jamais s'asseoir à table sans un invité à ses côtés, est emprunté au récit de la *Palaea* qui porte, dans L, le titre de *L'hospitalité d'Abraham: 'Slovo' sur la Sainte Trinité*.[20] C'est à la suite du jeûne prolongé d'Abraham — trois jours, selon ce récit — que lui apparaît la Sainte Trinité sous l'aspect des trois anges. Cependant l'apocryphe ne suit pas les lignes de la *Genèse* xviii, mais raconte que les voyageurs, invités par le Patriarche à sa table, déclinent l'offre: немоштно есть намь приїти, понеже бръза работа намь есть L 74, 9–10 'il nous est impossible de venir, car nous avons une affaire urgente' — paroles qui, dans la *Mort d'Abraham*, reviennent presque littéralement dans la bouche de l'archange: великоу работоу имамь [...], не мошно

---

[20] P. A. Lavrov, *Apokrifičeskie teksty*, 73–6. Cf. également une version grecque apparentée, dans A. Vasiliev, *Anecdota graeco-byzantina* (Moscou, 1893), 214.

есть мнѣ L 79, 3, 5 'J'ai une affaire importante [...], il ne m'est pas possible.' Abraham réitère son invitation auprès des trois anges, invoquant l'amour de Dieu: прїидѣте кь мнѣ аште любите бога вашего 74, 10–11; 'venez chez moi si vous aimez votre Dieu', exactement comme il le fait, dans la *Mort d'Abraham*, auprès de l'archange: прїиди вь домь мои аште любиши бога твоего 79, 4: 'viens dans ma maison si tu aimes ton Dieu.' Finalement, les trois anges cèdent aux supplications du Patriarche et s'en vont avec lui à la maison. Abraham ordonne qu'on aille amener un veau (посла принести юнца 74, 15) et demande à Sarah de laver les pieds des voyageurs. Sarah s'étonne de voir que les pieds des étrangers n'ont pas de consistance corporelle: беспльтни сьт 74, 19. Toutes situations que l'on retrouve également dans la *Mort d'Abraham* où, arrivé à la maison avec son invité, le Patriarche envoie qu'on lui apporte un mouton (посла принести овче 79, 10) et Sarah s'exclame, en voulant laver les pieds de l'archange: беспльтни соуть 79, 13. Ce n'est qu'à partir de la scène du dîner que les deux apocryphes se séparent nettement, l'*Hospitalité d'Abraham* se rapprochant davantage de la *Genèse* xviii, 9 et suiv.

Enfin, l'appât à l'aide duquel le Seigneur lui-même fait rendre à Abraham son dernier soupir, en lui offrant trois pommes, est un thème de folklore. N. Načov, l'éditeur du manuscrit de Tikveč, l'avait déjà signalé en Bulgarie, dans plusieurs poésies populaires,[21] dont une publiée dans le célèbre recueil d'Auguste Dozon (nº 15).[22] Pour s'emparer de l'âme de Janka, jeune fille malade et innocente, les anges envoyés par Dieu offrent à ses parents deux pommes d'or, ensuite ils présentent à Janka une troisième pomme d'or. La jeune fille sourit, ses parents pensent qu'elle a guéri et s'éloignent de son lit, alors les anges prennent son âme. La pomme d'or est une promesse du paradis et n'est offerte qu'aux âmes pures. Le peuple roumain se représente lui aussi le paradis comme un jardin aux fruits d'or.[23] Dans un poème du poète persan Djāmī (1414–92), poème résumé par l'abbé Migne dans son *Dictionnaire des apocryphes*, ii, col. 425–6, on apprend que Joseph, le fils de Jacob, 'averti par l'ange Gabriel que son heure était venue [...] respira l'odeur d'un fruit venant des jardins du paradis que l'ange lui présenta, et à l'instant son âme cessa d'animer son corps'.

En conclusion, la nouvelle version nous apparaît comme un récit entièrement récrit à l'aide de trois sources plus importantes: (a) au début, l'*Hospitalité d'Abraham*; (b) ensuite, la *Mort d'Abraham*, dans la forme de B, Sl¹ et Sl²; (c) à la fin, un thème de folklore. L'ensemble

---

[21] *Sbornik za narodni umotvorenija, nauka i knižnina*, x (1894), 154–5.

[22] *Chansons populaires bulgares inédites*, publiées et traduites par Auguste Dozon (Paris, 1875), 21–2 et 175–8.

[23] Voir Paul-Henri Stahl, 'L'organisation magique du territoire villageois roumain', *L'Homme*, xiii, 161; idem, *La dendrolatrie dans le folklore et l'art rustique du XIXᵉ siècle en Roumanie* (Archivio Internazionale di Etnografia e Preistoria, xi) (Turin, 1959), 67–8.

est écourté, bien serré et unitaire. Le récit s'adapte avec justesse au cycle de la *Palaea* dont il forme le dernier chaînon.

(b) *Les manuscrits L et* Z

Que nous apprennent les manuscrits L et Z sur la carrière de l'apocryphe?

Le ms. L, en slavon serbe du xvᵉ siècle, aux traits dialectaux orientaux, n'est pas sans laisser percer ça et là des formes qui trahissent son original bulgare. Ainsi, la confusion de ѫ et de ѧ, caractéristique du moyen-bulgare, est apparente dans le participe présent глаголю 'parlant', rendant глаголѭ (< глаголѧ) 78, 25, 79, 8, 79, 25, etc., et dans плачешти се 79, 24, 79, 31 'se lamentant' pour плачѧшти сѧ (< плачѫшти сѧ). La confusion de oy (< ѫ) et de o relève d'une prononciation orientale et macédonienne, fréquente dans le *Sbornik* de Tikveč (N). On a, par exemple, потника 78, 30 en regard de поутем 79, 7, et l'expression възлюбленомо ми Авраамоу 81, 16 'à mon bien aimé Abraham'. Les jers, confondus et notés invariablement ь, sont conservés, tant en position forte qu'en position faible: вѣньць слъньцны 79, 29 'la couronne du soleil', où ц note, comme souvent en moyen-bulgare, ч: слъньчни; voir encore троудьнь 79, 12 'fatigué', беспльтни 79, 13 'sans corps', црькьвь 80, 29, et, pour ц au lieu de ч: ц͠ка, ц͠кы, etc. (courant, pour чловѣка, acc., чловѣкы, etc.). La diphtongue ѣ est d'emploi général, mais non pas absolu: ꙗдѣше 78, 29 'il mangeait', сѣдешта 78, 30 'étant assis' (acc.), снѣдь 79, 17 'nourriture', мѣстѣ 81, 1 'dans l'endroit' (loc.), mais aussi нозе 79, 12 'les pieds'. Une fois on a a au lieu de ѣ: всах 81, 4 'tous' (acc.). Le préverbe въ- (orthographié вь-) se maintient à côté de sa forme serbe оу-: вьзети 79, 30 'enlever' et оузе 79, 29 'il enleva'. Le texte bulgare qu'a utilisé le remanieur serbe était récent. Il employait народь 80, 15 'foule' à côté de люде 80, 31 'les gens' et сньмиште (chez Miklošič συναγωγή, *conventus*) au sens, inconnu par ailleurs, de 'lit': вьзлегь на сньмишти, Исак же вь полоу ношть вьста от сньмишта своего 79, 23–4: 's'étant couché dans le lit, Isaac se leva à minuit de son lit.' La seule forme de duel présent en -те que nous rencontrons dans le texte n'est que la transcription de la désinence -тѣ, usuelle avec un sujet féminin: и прострѣть роуцѣ свои да примете ихь 81, 24-5 'et il tendit ses mains pour qu'elles (les mains) les reçoivent'.

Ce texte bulgare, qui n'était vraisemblablement pas plus ancien que la fin du xivᵉ siècle, a été repris par un copiste serbe qui, sans se donner la peine d'éliminer tous les traits du slavon bulgare, a néanmoins soigneusement évité les voyelles nasales et y a introduit un petit nombre de formes propres à la langue populaire. Parmi ces particularités, notons: le passage de *s* à *š* dans ш нимь 79, 21 'avec lui', ou dans приношахоу 81, 3 'ils apportaient', et le développement d'une spirante devant la gutturale, dans льхко (< льгько) 79, 7 'lentement', dû probablement à l'analogie avec тихко 'doucement', 'calmement'. La quantité est notée parfois avec une double voyelle: грѣхь тьь 80, 25 'ce péché'. Un autre trait populaire est le diminutif доуштица (pour доушица?) 80, 20 'petite âme'.[24]

La version dont L nous offre aujourd'hui la rédaction la plus con- servatrice a eu une large diffusion: un de ses descendants apparaît à Raguse, vers 1520, un autre en Transylvanie, au xvie siècle, où il donne naissance à la traduction roumaine.

Tout en s'apparentant de près à L, la rédaction ragusaine (Z) s'identifie au texte roumain dans plus d'un trait caractéristique. En voici un premier. Lorsque Sarah révèle à son mari et à Isaac que le voyageur qu'ils viennent d'accueillir dans leur maison est un être céleste, semblable aux trois anges qui détruisirent Sodome et Gomorrhe, le ms. L, du groupe Sl³, et les mss. H et N, du groupe Sl⁴, ajoutent que, ayant entendu sa femme, Abraham l'a sévèrement réprimandée pour sa légèreté de confondre une créature mortelle avec un être céleste: Z et R attribuent cette apostrophe à Isaac. Plus loin, Z et R sont les seuls à mettre dans la bouche d'Adam, affligé par la vue des foules condam- nées aux peines éternelles, ces paroles: 'O, mes fils, pourquoi vous êtes-vous souillés ainsi?' (Z 24, 28–9; R p. 194.)

Les autres différences que l'on constate entre le texte de L et celui de Z et R ne sont pas expressives, les omissions de L pouvant être im- putées à son propre copiste, Z étant fortement dilué, R jouant entre les deux un rôle d'équilibre.

La différence essentielle entre L et Z réside dans leur langue. Tandis que L conserve sa structure slavonne, avec même une dose assez forte de bulgarismes, Z est écrit dans la langue vivante à Raguse au début du xvie siècle. C'est le štokavien courant, jékavien (ex. *vjera*), sans čakavismes. Les quelques formes qui ont incité M. Rešetar à chercher l'origine du texte dans la littérature čakavienne en glagolite,[25] ne nous paraissent pas résister à la critique. Une de ces formes, о божијех рꙑјечех, où le mot *riječ* aurait, comme en domaine čakavien, le sens de 'chose', n'existe ni dans l'édition de Jagić ni dans celle de Rešetar lui-même.[26] La deuxième forme, веде 24, 4 (Reš. 7, 14) 'vraiment', remplace, comme adverbe, la forme vieux-bulgare, encore utilisée au xive siècle, вѣдѣ 'je sais',[27] et correspond à вѣмь de L 79, 30 (et même

---

[24] La lecture de Lavrov оу (б)рати своихь 'auprès de ses frères' doit être corrigée en оу ратаи своихь 'auprès de ses laboureurs'.

[25] M. Rešetar, *Libro od mnozijeh razloga. Dubrovački ćirilski zbornik od god. 1520* (Zbornik za istoriju, jezik i književnost srpskog naroda, xv) (Sr. Karlovci, 1926), 51.

[26] M. Rešetar renvoie au chapitre 7, alinéa 8, de son édition (n. 25). Nous n'avons pas réussi à repérer dans son texte les mots cités.

[27] Cf. Henri Boissin, *Le Manassès moyen-bulgare. Étude linguistique* (Paris, 1946), 89.

à *văd* 'je vois' de R, où cette forme est due à la confusion courante entre
вѣдѣти et видѣти). Enfin, тисna 24, 30 (Reš. 7, 22) 'étroite', doublet de
тиескna 24, 29 (Reš. 7, 21 et 22) peut facilement s'expliquer par
l'influence orale du čakavien qui, dans la seconde moitié du xvᵉ
siècle, effleure le parler de Raguse.[28] Cet ikavisme n'est d'ailleurs pas
isolé dans le texte: on lui ajoutera заповидие 23, 35 (Reš, 7, 11) 'il
ordonna'.

Sa parenté étroite avec le texte roumain montre que Z, loin de sortir
de la littérature glagolite du xvᵉ siècle, tire son origine d'un prototype
de l'est, de la Serbie sinon de la Bulgarie occidentale. Les rédactions
glagolites de la *Mort d'Abraham*, on l'a déjà vu, n'ont rien de commun
avec la forme écourtée de notre apocryphe.

Malgré sa dépendance d'un modèle slavon, le copiste de Z n'est
nullement soucieux de respecter son original. Il rejette constamment
les formes slavonnes au profit de la langue parlée. Tout en le moder-
nisant pour le rendre plus accessible, il repense son texte, le farcit de
paraphrases inutiles et, qui plus est, il en change même, de temps à
autre, le sens. Comme exemple de sa désinvolture, il suffit de citer, en
traduction, quelques lignes du début, où les matériaux de remplissage
sont imprimés en italiques:

Abraham avait l'habitude de ne jamais rien goûter à sa maison sans un
invité; et *les Juifs* savaient cela et bloquèrent toutes les routes *qui traversaient
ces montagnes* [et] *conduisaient à la maison d'Abraham*, afin que personne ne pût
venir à Abraham, *de nulle part.* S e p t jours passèrent depuis qu'Abraham
n'avait rien goûté, *parce qu'il n'y avait aucun hôte dans sa maison, comme ils en
venaient auparavant...*, etc.

Ce texte refondu, bourré d'incidentes et de répétitions, n'est pas
sans engager de graves responsabilités quant à l'exactitude du récit.
Il veut que les routes aient été bloquées par 'les Juifs' et non pas par le
diable, et qu'Abraham ait jeûné pendant 'sept' jours au lieu de trois.
Il transcrit mal son original en affirmant que le Patriarche exigea
qu'on le porte au ciel afin de voir 'le corps (*tijelo* 24, 10) de mon Seigneur', lorsqu'en réalité il demanda d'être porté *s tijelom* (cf. L 80, 1)
'en chair et os' afin de voir le Seigneur.

Pour fâcheux qu'ils soient, ces détails ne sauraient effacer le mérite
de Z, qui est de nous fournir un des premiers textes štokaviens, de
caractère populaire, rédigé en écriture cyrillique. Aussi sa contribution
à l'étude du croate parlé au xviᵉ siècle, et de son vocabulaire en
particulier, a été appréciée à sa juste valeur. Milan Rešetar a con-
sacré à la langue du *Zbornik* de 1520 une étude exhaustive, et le Dictionnaire de l'Académie de Zagreb a largement puisé dans son trésor.

[28] Voir André Vaillant, 'Les origines de la langue littéraire ragusaine', *Revue des études
slaves*, iv (1924), 222–51.

(c) *Le texte roumain*

Publiant sur deux colonnes parallèles le fragment roumain de la *Mort d'Abraham*, tiré du *Codex Sturdzanus* (R), et le texte d'une rédaction en moyen-bulgare découvert à Bucarest (H), Bogdan Petriceicu-Hasdeu croyait pouvoir identifier, dans le deuxième, le modèle du premier. Il allait même jusqu'à attribuer au pope Grigorié, le copiste, d'une partie du *Codex Sturdzanus*, le rôle d'avoir traduit l'apocryphe, vers 1600, 'en abrégeant et en complétant' en même temps son original.[29] L'assertion de Hasdeu, acceptée par Moses Gaster,[30] a été contestée par A. N. Veselovskij,[31] sans que celui-ci ait pris la peine de chercher la source du texte roumain. Ce fut N. Cartojan qui, le premier, a indiqué la ressemblance du texte roumain avec 'la rédaction serbe' (Z),[32] mais, ignorant la copie L, il n'a pas poussé plus loin ses observations.

En réalité, l'apocryphe roumain est le fidèle reflet d'une forme slave, serbe ou moyen-bulgare, qui, tout en étant très proche de Z, lui était incomparablement supérieure. Elle ne mettait pas au compte des Juifs les méfaits du diable et ignorait les autres inadvertances de Z. La trame de son récit était, elle aussi, plus solide. Aussi R nous offre-t-il aujourd'hui un texte qui se place avec bonheur entre L et Z, en confirmant les leçons de l'un ou de l'autre, en complétant leurs lacunes et en dénonçant les interpolations de Z. Son seul défaut est d'être incomplet.

Voici, à titre d'exemple, un passage où R appuie Z. Les mots en italiques manquent dans L:

Arhaggelŭ dzise: Slabu sămtŭ, *pičoarele mă doru*. Şi dzise Avram *lui Isacu fiiului său*: Do-te *acasă* şi adu calulu să ducemu cestu ospe co noi. Arhagg(e)lŭ dzise: *No usteni fečorul*, ce blămu cătiliru...

Voici également deux passages parmi d'autres, où R concorde avec L. Les mots en italiques manquent dans Z:

Îr acela čas arhaggelŭ se dose în geroe [*sic*: cerŭure î]r'apusul soarelui, *cândo se adora îngerii*, şi se închiră Domnolui, grăi: Domne! Avram *va să dea mie carne de* berbece de să mărâncu... (p. 191) ('Abraham a préparé un mouton pour me l'offrir à manger' Z).

Iarăşi deştiînse îngerul şi află masa gata şi mâîncă *Avram cu îngerul*; şi gătă patu de ospeţi şi se colcară. Şi în miadză-noapte scolă-se Isacu diîn patul său şi *stătu îraintea uşiei caseei*, grăi cu glas mare... (p. 192).

[29] B. Petriceicu-Hasdeu, *Cărţile poporane ale Românilor în secolul XVI* (Bucarest, 1879), 188.

[30] M. Gaster, *Literatura populară română* (Bucarest, 1883), 312.

[31] A. N. Veselovskij, 'Razyskanija po oblasti russkogo duhovnogo stiha, VI: Duhovnye sjužety v literature i narodnoj poezii rumyn', *Sbornik Otdelenija russkogo jazyka i slovesnosti Imp. Akademii nauk*, xxxii (1883), 18.

[32] N. Cartojan, *Cărţile populare în literatura românească*, i (Bucarest, 1929), 85–6, note; 2ᵉ éd. (Bucarest, 1974), 109–10, note.

On peut donc conclure, sans même avoir recours à d'autres preuves, que le texte roumain ignore les nombreuses interpolations et paraphrases de Z et complète les menues lacunes de L.

On sait, par ailleurs, que ce texte du xvie siècle occupe une place notable dans la formation de la langue littéraire roumaine. Il appartient aux premiers écrits non canoniques, sinon laïques, traduits dans cette langue. Il présente deux particularités frappantes: l'une phonétique, le rhotacisme, soit le passage de -n- intervocalique à -r- dans les éléments d'origine latine (*adora, închiră, mărâncu*, etc. pour *aduna, închină, mănâncu*), qui le situe dans la Transylvanie du nord; l'autre strictement graphique, la notation de *u* par *o* (*do-te, no, se dose, cândo, se adora, se colcară, scolă-se*, etc., pour *du-te, nu, se duse, cându, se aduna, se culcară, sculă-se*, etc.) à laquelle il ne faut attribuer aucune valeur phonétique.[33]

Traduite d'après un modèle venu probablement de Serbie, d'où un autre manuscrit du même type est allé, quelques dizaines d'années plus tôt, porter ce même texte en Dalmatie, pour y être récrit dans la langue parlée à Raguse, la rédaction du *Codex Sturdzanus* témoigne de l'existence, à l'ouest comme au nord de la Péninsule balkanique — et d'ailleurs comme dans toute l'Europe du xvie siècle — d'un puissant courant national et populaire, qui a imposé le passage des ouvrages écrits dans les langues surannées du Moyen Age, aux langues vivantes, parlées par toutes les couches sociales.

Pour modeste qu'il soit, l'apocryphe du *Codex Sturdzanus* se range parmi les signes avant-coureurs de la renaissance littéraire roumaine.

C. La deuxième version abrégée

(a) *Les textes slaves*

La deuxième version abrégée de la *Mort d'Abraham* se trouve, elle aussi, tout comme la version correspondante de l'*Apocalypse d'Abraham*, dans deux manuscrits slaves qui forment le groupe Sl[4]: N (serbo-macédonien du xve siècle) et H (moyen-bulgare de Moldavie, de la fin du xvie siècle). Le texte de N a été publié par N. A. Načov, dans le *Sbornik za narodni umotvorenija, nauka i knižnina*, viii (1892), 411–13, et reproduit par B. Angelov et M. Genov, *Stara bălgarska literatura (IX–XVIII v.) v priměri, prěvodi i bibliografija*, 194–6; celui de H a paru dans B. Petriceicu-Hasdeu, *Cărțile poporane ale Românilor în secolul XVI* (Bucarest, 1879), 189–94. Voir également notre 'Apocalypse d'Abraham en slave' (n. 19), 176. Deux manuscrits roumains de la même version forment le groupe Roum.[2], dont nous parlerons plus loin.

Les manuscrits de cette version présentent, en général, le même texte que Sl[3] et Roum.[1], mais ils ignorent, bien entendu, les particularités

---

[33] C'est, du moins, l'opinion d'Al. Rosetti, voir sa *Istoria limbii romăne dela origini pînă în secolul al XVII-lea* (Bucarest, 1968), 499.

qui sont propres à ces familles (voir *supra*, p. 22, traits communs, et 23, différences) et ajoutent, à leur tour, quelques détails originaux.

Voici le tableau de leurs additions et remaniements:

(i) Le début est nouveau, avec un détail invraisemblable: 'Abraham vivait dans sa maison *et désirait voir tout ce qui se faisait sur la terre*; et il se tenait en prière devant Dieu...'

(ii) Les quatre manuscrits nous indiquent, avec un soin particulier, comment les hôtes et leur invité se sont répartis pour dormir: 'Quand fut le moment de se coucher, Abraham [alla se coucher] avec l'invité, comme il avait coutume, et Sarah dans une autre maison, [et] Isaac *avec Rébecca.*' La mention de Rébecca est pour le moins surprenante, selon la *Genèse* xxiv, Isaac ne s'étant marié qu'après la mort de sa mère. Mais le rédacteur de Sl⁴ ne prend pas la peine de contrôler ses souvenirs bibliques; il se contente de suivre la *Palaea historica*,[34] qui, effectivement, situe le mariage d'Isaac avec Rébecca du vivant même de Sarah. Aussi fait-il intervenir Rébecca une seconde fois, 'avec une multitude de gens', lorsque, apeuré par son rêve, Isaac court à la porte de son père.

(iii) Abraham rencontre Adam 'au quatrième ciel', où se trouvent également les deux portes de la vie éternelle. Ceci est contraire à B, Sl¹ et Sl² (le détail manque dans Sl³, ce qui explique peut-être la liberté de Sl⁴), qui affirment que l'archange Michel porta le Patriarche sur un nuage au-dessus du fleuve Océan, et que c'est là qu'il vit Adam et les deux portes fatidiques.

(iv) Descendant sur la terre pour prendre l'âme d'Abraham avec ses propres mains, le Seigneur offre à son ami, comme appât, 'une pomme et une jolie colombe' (trois jolies pommes, Sl³).

A ces différences près, Sl⁴ reproduit le même récit écourté, adapté à la *Palaea*, que nous avons déjà rencontré dans Sl³ et Roum.¹ Son remanieur se révèle un esprit original, qui se soucie peu de précision ou de chronologie, et qui prête au récit ses connaissances bibliques douteuses, redevables à la *Palaea historica*, ainsi que son goût capricieux du pittoresque.

A défaut d'autres informations, peut-on identifier la personnalité de ce remanieur selon les touches qu'il a données à sa version? A notre avis, il n'est autre que le scribe qui, pour la première fois, a réuni les matériaux que nous présentent aujourd'hui, dans deux copies tardives, le *Sbornik* de Tikveč et celui de Bucarest. Ce lettré aimait les légendes naïves de la *Palaea* et trouvait un charme particulier aux petits récits pseudo-historiques qui dénonçaient les méfaits de certaines femmes célèbres comme la perfide Dalila (*Le Dit de Samson et de sa femme*), l'épouse rusée du prophète Élie ou la vicieuse Théophano (*Le Dit de l'empereur Nicéphore II Phocas*). Il n'a pas hésité non plus à marquer de sa curieuse personnalité l'*Apocalypse d'Abraham* et la *Mort d'Abraham*.

---

[34] Voir l'édition d'A. Vasiliev (n. 20), 223.

Les particularités de Sl⁴ revêtent ce caractère fantaisiste qui donne une marque originale, et malgré tout sympathique, à l'ensemble des récits contenus dans le *Sbornik* de Tikveč et dans celui de Bucarest.

Mais, si leur contenu est identique, les deux manuscrits divergent radicalement du point de vue de leur rédaction: celui de Tikveč est serbo-macédonien, celui de Bucarest est moyen-bulgare. Le premier est vulgarisant et novateur, faisant de larges concessions à la langue parlée; le deuxième est conservateur et puriste, fidèle à la tradition du meilleur slavon bulgare. Malheureusement, H omet toute une section du texte, qui dans N occupe plus de vingt lignes imprimées: 413, 4–28, après les mots и въпроси Авраамъ емоу. Il s'agit vraisemblablement d'un feuillet perdu.[35] B. Petriceicu-Hasdeu n'a pas remarqué cette lacune qui rend son texte inintelligible à l'endroit respectif (p. 194, l. 14). Les deux rédactions dérivent d'un prototype serbo-macédonien, probablement du début du xvᵉ siècle, que N reproduit avec force touches populaires, que H transcrit en un moyen-bulgare de bon aloi, conforme à la tradition littéraire de la Moldavie. Nous avons largement illustré cette tendance puriste des scribes moldaves, indiquée tout d'abord par André Mazon,[36] dans notre étude sur *Le Dit de l'empereur Nicéphore II Phocas et de son épouse Théophano*,[37] ainsi que dans d'autres articles.[38] La *Mort d'Abraham* nous en fournit, elle aussi, quelques exemples expressifs.

L'écart qui existe entre N et H est celui qui sépare une expression comme Аврамь ротѣше Сарроу N, où le verbe ротити, inconnu du bulgare, a le sens propre au serbe parlé de 'gronder' et même d''injurier', de Авраамъ въспрѣштааше Саррѣ H 190, 24 'Abraham réprimanda Sarah', où la construction du verbe въспрѣштати avec le datif est respectée. Une phrase comme егда быст на ложи, възлеже Аврамь сь гостѣмь ꙗкоже имаше наоукоу N 'quand il fut à la maison, Abraham se coucha avec l'invité, comme il en avait l'habitude', se dit dans H 191, 11–13: егда быст възлешти Авраамоу съ гостем ꙗко бѣ емоу обычаи, avec le datif du sujet exigé par la proposition infinitive; наоукъ est serbe, обычаи bulgare, mais en roumain *năuc* signifie 'étourdi' et seul *obicei* a gardé son sens de 'coutume'. Le copiste de H, un Moldave et peut-être un Roumain, préfère normalement обычаи, *obicei*. Enfin, au populaire да се тебѣ нагледамь de N 'afin que je te regarde' correspond dans H 191, 20 le savant да сѧ тебе наблюдж 'afin que je t'observe', et цѣловаше de N 'il embrassa' est en regard de

[35] Le manuscrit 740 des Archives d'État de Bucarest a seize lignes sur une page, avec seulement quatre ou cinq mots dans une ligne: voir les trois pages reproduites en fac-similés par George Ivaşcu, *Istoria literaturii române*, i (Bucarest, 1969), en regard de la p. 35, et les six planches qui accompagnent notre étude sur *Le Dit de l'empereur Nicéphore II Phocas* (n. 37).
[36] André Mazon, 'Le Dit d'Alexandre le Vieil', *Revue des études slaves*, xx (1942), 13–40.
[37] Thessalonique, 1976: édition de l'Association hellénique d'Études slaves.
[38] Cités dans l'ouvrage indiqué plus haut (n. 37), 48–9.

облобызажшти 'embrassant' de H 192, 4, qui, au xvie siècle, est un archaïsme d'école.

Ces différences sont caractéristiques des milieux auxquels les manuscrits N et H ont été destinés. L'un appartient à la littérature mi-savante mi-populaire de la Macédoine serbe; l'autre à la littérature 'de classe', puisque réservée aux cercles ecclésiastiques et à un nombre infime de gens connaissant le slavon, de Moldavie. Considérés l'un par rapport à l'autre, ils se situent aux extrémités opposées des usages littéraires de l'époque.

Pour trouver le correspondant naturel de manuscrit N, écrit dans une langue vivante et pittoresque, à l'intention d'une large masse de lecteurs, c'est la traduction roumaine qu'il faut évoquer.

(b) *Les textes roumains*

La traduction roumaine de la deuxième version courte nous est connue dans deux manuscrits, appartenant tous deux à la Bibliothèque de l'Académie roumaine de Bucarest.[39]

Le manuscrit 2158, signalé par N. Cartojan comme le représentant d'une nouvelle version 'traduite du grec',[40] est tout simplement la copie d'une traduction de la version slave représentée dans les pays roumains par le manuscrit H. Elle est de Valachie, du xviiie siècle, et a été faite d'après un original moldave ou transylvain: au lieu de *şi au venit şi Sara* (VI, 4), elle transcrit *şi au venit şi seara* 'le soir est venu', ce qui laisse supposer à son départ une rédaction intermédiaire *şi au venit şi sara* — *sara* étant une forme phonétique de la Transylvanie du nord et de la Moldavie. Le manuscrit 5299, copié en Transylvanie au début du xixe siècle, par un certain pope Ioan Felea, qui n'indique pas la localité où il vivait, présente lui aussi au même endroit *au venit seara*, mais cette forme coexistait en Transylvanie du sud avec *sara*. D'ailleurs, le caractère transylvain du manuscrit 5299 saute aux yeux: il emploie *oaspeţ* (singulier) pour *oaspe*, *să mânc*, *să mânce* pour *să mănânc*, *să mănânce* 'que je mange', 'qu'il mange', *pâne* pour *pâine* 'pain', *să merjem* pour *să mergem* 'que nous marchions', *jinere* pour *ginere* 'gendre', etc. La forme *pedestru* 'à pied' est commune aux deux copies. Nous pensons que cette nouvelle traduction a été faite quelque part en Transylvanie centrale, mais que la copie 5299 est de la Transylvanie du sud-est (Făgăraş–Sibiu–Braşov), où *seara* est une forme courante. Quant à la copie 2158, elle est indubitablement valaque. Cette nouvelle traduction de la *Mort d'Abraham* est donc la deuxième faite en Transylvanie, après celle du *Codex Sturdzanus*.

La nouvelle traduction suit de près la version slave NH. Mais elle

---

[39] Nous remercions ici la Direction de la Bibliothèque et M. Dan Zamfirescu pour nous avoir procuré le microfilm de ces textes inédits.

[40] N. Cartojan, op. cit. (n. 32), i, 88; 2e éd., 113. Dans les deux éditions il faut lire 'Codex Sturdzanus' au lieu de 'Codex Neagoeanus'.

contient aussi des leçons qui manquent dans H et qui existent dans N, ainsi que toute la partie omise accidentellement dans H. Par ailleurs, le ms. 5299, bien que plus jeune, est plus complet que 2158, puisqu'il conserve, entre autres, le récit du rêve d'Isaac, que son aîné de Valachie a trouvé bon de sauter.

Malgré sa fidélité à la deuxième version slave courte, le texte roumain présente, dans ses deux copies, plusieurs omissions, dont deux sont à retenir: il supprime le rôle du diable qui ferme les chemins conduisant à la maison d'Abraham et la réprimande que celui-ci adresse à son épouse. Nous ne croyons pas nous tromper en pensant qu'il faut voir dans ces omissions l'intervention délibérée d'un remanieur qui n'accepte pas l'idée que le diable ait pu nuire au grand Patriarche et que celui-ci ait pu gronder sa femme comme un quelconque mortel. Il y avait là, à ses yeux, de mauvais exemples pour les lecteurs.

D'où vient le prototype des nouveaux textes roumains? Pour répondre à cette question, nous devons considérer le contenu des manuscrits 2158 et 5299 dans son ensemble. Ils contiennent, notamment, après d'autres textes sans intérêt pour notre sujet, la *Légende d'Adam et d'Ève*, les trois *Légendes des croix du Golgotha*, les six légendes du *Cycle d'Abraham* et un florilège de fables tiré du *Physiologue*. Tous ces textes, à l'exception des chapitres du *Physiologue*, se retrouvent également dans H. Tous, à l'exception de la *Légende d'Adam et d'Ève* et des *Légendes des trois croix du Golgotha*, existent également dans N. Tous, sauf la *Mort d'Abraham* et les chapitres du *Physiologue*, font partie d'un manuscrit serbe tardif, B[2] (voir notre '*Apocalypse d'Abraham* en slave', p. 176). Et tous, moins les *Légendes des trois croix du Golgotha*, se lisent également dans le manuscrit n° 629 de la Bibliothèque Nationale de Sofia, en rédaction bulgare du XVIᵉ siècle.[41]

Cet ensemble nous conduit à un fonds de littérature semi-populaire qui, constitué en Macédoine serbe, au XIVᵉ siècle, à partir de divers apocryphes anciens et de bon aloi, s'est largement diffusé les siècles suivants dans des manuscrits serbes et bulgares et, par leur intermédiaire, dans les pays roumains. Nous avons étudié ailleurs, avec une documentation sensiblement plus riche, la genèse et le rayonnement de cette littérature.[42] Nous nous contentons d'ajouter ici que le manuscrit valaque 2158 et le manuscrit transylvain 5299 représentent, dans leur ensemble, un fleuron de cette tradition sud-slave.

V. LA TRADUCTION ROUMAINE DE LA VERSION GRECQUE LONGUE (Roum.³)

Cette nouvelle traduction roumaine a été faite dans la première moitié du XVIIIᵉ siècle d'après un original grec de la version longue.

---

[41] Voir la comparaison détaillée de ces manuscrits et les conclusions qui en résultent dans notre étude sur *Le Dit de l'empereur Nicéphore II Phocas*, (n. 37), 36–40.

[42] Ouvrage cité (n. 37) et '*La Palaea* byzantine' (n. 18).

Moses Gaster l'a publiée dans les *Transactions of the Society of Biblical Archaeology* de Londres, ix, pt. 1 (1887), 195–9 (introduction) et 200–26 (texte et traduction anglaise), d'après trois manuscrits qui se trouvaient alors en sa possession: l'un de 1777, l'autre de la fin du xviiie siècle, le troisième de 1813. Ils sont conservés actuellement à la Bibliothèque de l'Académie roumaine de Bucarest, qui a racheté la collection de manuscrits de l'éminent savant, et portent respectivement les cotes 1151, 1157 et 1158.[43] Le texte de Gaster a permis à Montague Rhodes James d'établir qu'il est 'dans son ensemble, une forme abrégée et pas très fidèle de la recension longue', et que, 'somme toute, cette version montre une grande ressemblance avec le texte des manuscrits C, D. Elle ne contient aucun détail qui n'apparaisse dans ceux-ci'.[44] Précisons que C est un manuscrit du xvie siècle appartenant à la Bibliothèque Bodléïenne d'Oxford (MS. Canon. Gr. 19), D un manuscrit du xve siècle de la Bibliothèque Nationale de Paris (Fonds grec 1556). Dans l'apparat qui accompagne l'édition de James, la version roumaine (sigle R) se situe toujours en compagnie de ces deux manuscrits, mais aussi aux côtés du ms. E, qui est 'du xiiie siècle (?)'[45] et appartient à la Bibliothèque Nationale de Vienne (Cod. Theol. Gr. 237). Comme ces trois manuscrits, R omet, par exemple, toute la section des chapitres V et VI qui décrit l'intervention de Sarah lorsque Isaac vient raconter son rêve à son père. Un examen attentif de l'apparat de James nous permet d'affirmer que toutes les omissions qui y sont indiquées sous les sigles C, D, E, caractérisent également la version roumaine. Elles devraient figurer, avec les autres variantes communes à ce groupe, dans une nouvelle édition de la version longue.

Parlant des résultats acquis par Gaster et par James, N. Cartojan précise que la version roumaine longue, dont il donne un résumé détaillé, 'nous est connue jusqu'à présent dans au moins huit manuscrits'. Cet inventaire comporte: les trois rédactions utilisées par Gaster et cinq manuscrits inédits du fonds roumain de l'Académie roumaine, à savoir: n° 44 (Valachie, xviiie siècle);[46] 2339 (Bucarest, 1826); 2629 (Banat, début du xixe siècle); 3013 (xixe siècle); 4278 (1760).[47]

A l'inventaire établi par N. Cartojan on doit ajouter:

9. Ms. n° 1491 appartenant à la Métropole orthodoxe de Sibiu.[48] Après une rédaction du roman de *Barlaam et Josaphat*, que nous avons eu l'occasion

[43] On trouvera leur description détaillée dans G. Strempel, Florica Moisil et L. Stoianovici, *Catalogul manuscriselor românești* (Académie roumaine), iv (1062–1380) (Bucarest, 1967), 201–7 (copie faite à Bucarest par un Moldave, Andonachi Berhecianu); 223–6 (copie de Moldavie, sans début ni fin); 227–8 (copie valaque datée de 1813).

[44] *The Testament of Abraham* (n. 7), 6.   [45] Ibid. 2.

[46] Décrit par Ioan Bianu, *Catalogul manuscriptelor românești* (Académie roumaine), i (Bucarest, 1907), 104–7.

[47] N. Cartojan, op. cit. (n. 32), i, 90; 2e éd., 114–15.

[48] Décrit par le Général P. V. Năsturel, *Vieața Sfinților Varlaam și Ioasaf* [...] (Bucarest, 1904), p. xxxviii–xxxix.

d'étudier jadis sur place,[49] il contient une 'Apocalypse (*sic*) d'Abraham' qui commence par les mots: 'Abraham a vécu sa vie en tout 175 ans.' Cent soixante-quinze ans, c'est la durée de la vie d'Abraham donnée par les rédactions grecques D et E, ainsi que par *toutes* les rédactions roumaines du 'type Gaster'. Le dernier feuillet conservé se termine avec les mots: 'Şi veni şi Sara, muĭarea lui, iarăşi într'acelaşi chip văitându-se cu amar...': or, ces mots font défaut dans l'édition de Gaster, ce qui prouve que les lacunes de R ne remontent pas toutes au prototype.

10. Manuscrit du Maramureş (nord-ouest de la Roumanie), du XVIIIe siècle, propriété d'une famille du village de Dragomireşti, signalé et résumé par Florea Florescu, 'Un apocalips maramureşean. Cuvânt de arătare pentru viaţa Patriarhului Avram', dans *Sociologie românească* i, (Bucarest, 1936), 40–1. Comme dans toutes les copies de la version roumaine longue, ce texte assigne à Abraham 175 ans de vie et situe sa rencontre avec l'archange à *Driĭa cea neagră*. Or, comme Gaster l'avait déjà montré, il s'agit tout simplement de δρῦς τῆς Μαμβρῆ 'le chêne de Mambré', mais le traducteur a pris δρῦς pour un nom propre, *Driĭa*, et le nom propre Μαμβρῆ pour l'adjectif μαύρη 'noire', *neagră*.

11. Ms. n° 3110 de la Bibliothèque de l'Académie roumaine (BAR) de Bucarest, provenant de Transylvanie. La *Mort d'Abraham* (ff. 67[v]–79) est signée au f. 79: 'S'au scris prin mine Iacov Popa din Lud[işor], 1781, zi 13 ianuarie': 'Copié par moi Iacov Popa de Ludişor, le 13 janvier 1781.' La commune de Ludişor se trouve près de la ville de Făgăraş, dans la Transylvanie méridionale.[50]

12. Ms. n° 3162 de la BAR, copié en Valachie. La *Mort d'Abraham* (ff. 40–3) est insérée entre un texte daté de novembre 1780 et un autre se rapportant à un événement de 1798.[51] Ce texte ne contient que le début du récit, jusqu'au paragraphe 15 de l'édition de Gaster.

13. Ms. n° 1972 de la BAR, du début du XIXe siècle, en provenance du monastère de Cernica, près de Bucarest. C'est un recueil de textes hagiographiques qui contient, entre autres, la vie de saint Démètre-le-Nouveau dit Basarabov et la vie de saint Jean-le-Nouveau de Suceava.

14. Ms. n° 5210 de la BAR, du début du XIXe siècle. Porte une date '1813' et la signature de Ioan Popovici de Bran, en Transylvanie (près de Braşov). Mais celui-ci peut n'avoir été que le propriétaire du manuscrit.

15. Ms. n° 4252 de la BAR, en provenance du Banat (sud-ouest de la Roumanie). La *Mort d'Abraham* (ff. 19–29[v]) est signée par Petru Popovici, qui a fini de la copier le 6 mars 1832.[52]

Les 13 copies identifiées jusqu'à présent dans la Bibliothèque de l'Académie roumaine de Bucarest sont loin d'épuiser les ressources de ce fonds, qui compte à l'heure actuelle plus de 6000 manuscrits. En

[49] E. Turdeanu, '*Varlaam şi Ioasaf*. Versiunile traducerii lui Udrişte Năsturel', *Biserica Ortodoxă Română*, lii (1934), 477–82, avec un fac-similé.
[50] G. Strempel, *Copişti de manuscrise româneşti până la 1800*, i (Bucarest, 1959), 180, note.
[51] Cf. aussi Dan Simonescu, *Cronici şi povestiri româneşti versificate (sec. XVII–XVIII)* (Bucarest, 1967), 305–6.
[52] Utilisé également par C. Ciuchindel, *Povestea lui Archirie Filosoful* (Bucarest, 1976), qui le date de 1839 (p. 83).

attendant que d'autres recherches faites sur place[53] viennent compléter notre documentation, nous croyons utile de fixer les caractéristiques les plus saillantes des cinq rédactions signalées ici pour la première fois et dont la Direction de la Bibliothèque a bien voulu nous procurer le microfilm.

Mais tout d'abord il nous faut dire que la collation même rapide des copies roumaines montre que l'édition de Gaster ne peut nullement servir de référence. Son texte est largement corrompu et parfois, comme dans le paragraphe 23, tout à fait inintelligible. Nos copies donnent en général raison à la rédaction *b* de cette édition sans que, pourtant, elles aient la netteté souhaitable. Elles gardent certaines formes anciennes de la traduction, comme *toapsec* 'poison' < lat. *toxicum* (*toapsecul morţii*); *blem* 'marchons' < lat. *ambulemus* (n° 1972 a également *blemaţi* 141ᵛ, 12 'allez'); *pedestri* 'à pied' < lat. *pedester* devenu *pedestrus*, pl. *pedestri*; le vocatif *oame* < lat. *homo*. Elles se plaisent à donner une forte teinte chrétienne au récit : Abel est semblable 'à l'image du Christ', le deuxième jugement sera celui des douze apôtres (XIII, 6 : des douze tribus d'Israël), le troisième jugement sera celui 'de notre Seigneur et Sauveur Jésus-Christ'.

A ces traits communs, chaque manuscrit ajoute ses particularités propres. Ms. n° 3110 enrichit la liste des mots anciens avec des formes comme *despuitorĭul* 76, 3 'le seigneur', 'le maître', du verbe *a despune* < lat. *disponere*; *să mă răpaus* 77, 3 'que je me repose', *m'aş răposa* 78ᵛ, 8 'je me reposerais' < lat. *repausare*: le mot signifie aujourd'hui 'mourir'. Il affirme que les anges du jugement tiennent dans leurs mains 'un Évangile' 74, 11, et commet une grossière confusion entre Abraham et Moïse lorsqu'il fait dire à Dieu s'adressant à l'archange : 'Va chez mon ami Abraham et dis-lui ceci : Je suis le Seigneur Dieu qui l'ai fait sortir *de la terre d'Égypte et de la maison du servage...*' (72, 8–10). Ce texte s'achève avec une mention qui montre bien son emploi comme lecture d'édification : 'Après ceci dis les prières de pardon (*iertăciuni*) et le Notre Père.'

Le manuscrit valaque 1972 et le manuscrit transylvain 5210 transfèrent la résidence d'Abraham de *Driĭa cea Neagră* près d'un endroit plus connu, *Marea* (*cea*) *Neagră* 'la mer Noire'. Plus fantaisiste encore, le ms. 1972 se permet une allégation que l'on pourrait qualifier de 'scandaleuse' si elle n'était pas due à une mauvaise lecture. Quand Abraham constata que les larmes de l'archange se transformaient en pierres précieuses, 'il s'empara aussitôt [et] furtivement des pierres — dit le texte — et les cacha seul [et] secrètement dans sa chambre' (*în cămara lui*, au lieu de : 'il cacha le secret dans son cœur', *în inima lui*).

---

[53] Le catalogue imprimé de ce fonds compte quatre volumes (cf. *supra*, n. 43) et ne couvre que 1,380 manuscrits. Pour le reste, nous sommes tributaires des notes que nous avons prises à la BAR il y a de très nombreuses années et qui sont, forcément, incomplètes.

Comme pour lui donner le change, le ms. 5210 prétend que Dieu bénit Abraham d'avoir 'des biens nombreux (*avere multă*) comme les étoiles du ciel et le sable de la mer'. Ces bévues — et elles ne sont pas les seules — prouvent qu'il n'y a aucune relation directe entre les deux manuscrits, si ce n'est qu'ils possèdent dans leur proche ascendance un intermédiaire valaque, qui situe la demeure d'Abraham 'près de la mer Noire'. Copié dans la même région que le ms. 3110 — la Transylvanie du sud — le ms. 5210 contient lui aussi les exemples déjà cités où le verbe *a se răpausa* a conservé son sens ancien de 'se reposer'. Parmi ses formes dialectales on retiendra encore *pretin* 54^v, 14 'ami', *mânile* 56^v, 12 'les mains', *striinii* 46, 11 'les étrangers', *precep* 50, 17 'je comprends', *să morĭu* 51, 15 'que je meure', *să înghiţă* 51, 15 'qu'il engloutisse', *răşchirate* 49^v, 15 'écartées', etc.

Enfin, le ms. 4252, de 1832, nous offre une rédaction partiellement écourtée: les paragraphes 12–16 et 55–6 de l'édition de Gaster sont réduits à quelques lignes et les omissions de deux ou trois lignes y sont nombreuses. Du point de vue dialectal, deux particularités sont plus frappantes: la réduction de la diphtongue *oa*, qui n'est jamais notée, à *o* (ouvert) et un subjonctif comme *să puni* 20, 11 'que tu mets', qui ne s'entend que dans le Banat.

Il est évident qu'un classement plus rigoureux des 15 manuscrits signalés ici ne pourrait être entrepris que lorsqu'on aura réuni tous les témoins que les bibliothèques roumaines, et en premier lieu celle de l'Académie roumaine, sont susceptibles de contenir. Les matériaux dont nous disposons à l'heure actuelle ne sont pas moins révélateurs pour la large diffusion du texte sur tous les territoires roumains: la Moldavie, qui comprenait avant 1812 également la Bessarabie (ms. BAR 1157), la Valachie (ms. BAR 44, 1151, 1158, 1972, 2339, 3013, 3162, 4278), le Maramureş (*supra* n° 10), la Transylvanie proprement-dite (ms. de Sibiu, BAR 3110, 5210), le Banat (ms. BAR 2629, 4252).

Tous ces manuscrits témoignent de l'unité culturelle étroite et permanente dans laquelle ont vécu les Roumains aux siècles passés, en dépit du destin historique qui les a séparés en trois, et parfois même en quatre ou cinq entités politiques différentes.

VI. LA COUPE DE LA MORT

La grande diffusion du *Testament d'Abraham* dans les pays roumains ne pouvait ne pas laisser de traces dans leur folklore, particulièrement vivant et réceptif.

N. Cartojan a déjà reconnu cette influence dans la façon dont le peuple se représente la Mort cherchant sa victime une coupe à la main, pour la lui faire boire. Elle lui laisse entendre que la coupe contient du vin, lorsqu'en réalité elle est remplie du poison fatal. Le thème a été noté dans plusieurs *bocete*, ou complaintes, que les pleureuses ou la mère ou la sœur du défunt récitent près du cercueil.[54]

Aux exemples déjà relevés nous ajoutons ici un texte recueilli plus récemment (1933). Il provient du village de Drăguş, dans cette Transyl-vanie méridionale où nous avons vu circuler au moins deux manuscrits du *Testament d'Abraham* (BAR 3110 et 5210):

> *Vine Moartea pin grădină*
> *C-un pahar de vin în mînă;*
> *Şi ea mă roagă că-i vin*
> *Da el e amar venin.*[55]

> La Mort s'amène par le jardin
> Un verre de vin à la main;
> Elle me l'offre comme du vin
> Mais c'est de l'amer vénin.

La voici donc cette coupe amère, τὸ πικρὸν ποτήριον, qui accompagne la Mort dans certaines représentations iconographiques juives[56] et que le *Testament d'Abraham* a passée au folklore roumain. Les copies de la légende appellent le poison fatal *toapsecul morţii*, et la persévérance même avec laquelle elles gardent le mot *toapsec*, un survivant en voie de disparition du lat. *toxicum*, montre qu'il s'agit en l'occurrence d'une expression populaire, qui a dû être courante jusqu'au XIXe siècle.

[54] N. Cartojan, op. cit. (n. 32), i, 89; 2e éd., 114
[55] Ernest Bernea, *Poezii populare în lumina etnografiei* (Bucarest, 1976), 100.
[56] F. Schmidt, op. cit. (n. 2), i, 100, note 42.

ADDENDUM

Cette étude était déjà présentée aux *Oxford Slavonic Papers* lorsqu'a paru le recueil édité par W. E. Nickelsburg Jr., *Studies on the Testament of Abraham* (Missoula, Montana, 1976). Aux pp. 310–26 de ce recueil on trouve la traduction anglaise des manuscrits slaves P et T, avec variantes de sept manuscrits grecs. La traduction est due à Donald S. Cooper, qui assume également les notes critiques de l'apparat, et à Harry B. Weber.

A Further Note on Sir Jerome Bowes

By ROBERT CROSKEY

God made men; & men made mony.
God made bees; & bees made hony.
God made owles, & apes & asses:
God made Sir Jerome Bowes, & Sr Jerome Bowes made Glasses.

THE reputation of Sir Jerome Bowes, Queen Elizabeth's ambassador to Ivan IV in 1583–4, long survived the man himself. Evidence of this was recently discovered by J. Luria in the form of the above verse— found in the margin of a copy of *Purchas, his Pilgrimage* which formerly belonged to the East India Company. Luria concludes that this marginal note was made towards the middle of the seventeenth century.[1]

A remarkable circumstance, the fact that in 1621 this same verse was the instance for a quarrel between two members of Parliament, allows us to learn somewhat more about the verse, and even to discover its author. Since the quarrel led to blows, and, eventually, to drawn swords, the matter was considered serious enough for a formal parliamentary investigation. According to testimony given by Sir Charles Morrison, one of the principals in the quarrel, this is what happened:

He [Sir Charles Morrison] asked Mr. Glanvyle what pattent that was, which Mr. Glanvile said was the pattent of glasses. Then he replied it made him remember the song of Sir Joshug Percy, God made man and man made mony. Mr. Cooke [Clement Coke] asked him which side he was of. He replied, indifferent. Nay, said Mr. Cooke, you are for the asses. He replied, yes, if they had longe eares. They satt together a good while, he nothing misdoubting either by Mr. Cooks countenance or words any offence taken by him. Soone after he went out; and upon the stayres whispered why or wherfore he knowes not what and so answered. Soone after Mr. Cook gave him a push on the neck and at his risinge gave him a slapp with his glove and by his thrust he fell upon the backe of Sir Edward Mountague. He [Sir Charles] went into the hall for to get a sword.[2]

---

[1] J. Luria, 'An Unpublished Epigram on an English Ambassador in Russia', *Oxford Slavonic Papers*, N.S. vii (1974), 13–17. Possibly Purchas would not have been consulted much later. According to Pepys, his reputation was in decline by the 1660s: 'Purchas his work was sold for 4 or 5s. before the Fire of London, being valued but as so much waste paper.' See 'Samuel Pepys's Naval Minutes', ed. J. R. Tanner, *Publications of the Naval Records Society*, lx (1926), 123.

[2] *Commons Debates, 1621*, comp. and ed. Wallace Notestein, *et al.* (New Haven, 1935), vi, 144–5, testimony of 8 May. The quarrel took place on 30 April (ibid. iv, 315). Clement Coke was judged to be the guilty party, and he was ordered to make a public apology to Morrison in Parliament. This was done on 15 May and Coke resumed his seat (ibid. iv, 346).

Other testimony by Mr. Glanvile refers specifically to Sir Jerome Bowes in connection with the verse.[3]

The parliamentary testimony gives some interesting information about the verse. In 1621, as may be expected, the verse was already considered an 'old rhime'. Bowes had been granted the glass monopoly in 1592, and the verse undoubtedly dates to the period between 1592 and Bowes's death in 1616. The verse in one instance is referred to as a song, so it may have been sung or chanted.[4] The author, according to Sir Charles Morrison, was 'Sir Joshug Percy'. This must be Sir Jocelyn Percy (1579?–1631), the seventh son of the eighth Earl of Northumberland. Little is known of Jocelyn Percy, except that he participated in Essex's attempted coup of 1601, and later served in Ireland.[5] He also at one time planned to enter the service of the King of Spain.[6]

Percy found Bowes a likely target for witticism on at least one other occasion: Ben Jonson noted that Percy rapped on Bowes's breast and asked if he was within.[7] If there was any personal animus behind Percy's sallies at Bowes, the reason for it has not survived.

As for the verse itself, the note found by Luria records the oldest known variant of a still current nursery rhyme.[8] It is tempting to speculate that the Percy verse is the prototype for the later versions, and some of the parliamentary testimony could be interpreted to support this argument. However, the evidence is ambiguous, and the surest conclusion would seem to be simply that the Percy variant was rather widely known in the early seventeenth century.[9]

---

[3] *Commons Debates*, iii, 215, testimony of 9 May: 'Mr. Glanveile saith That Sir Charls Morison went on with the old rhime of God made man, man made mony, etc., and stayed at that part, God made Sir Jerome Bowes, etc., King made Judges, and theay, etc. and he could not goe through with the rhime and intreated me to helpe him; but what past more twixt Mr. Cooke and him I knowe not but by report.'

[4] It is of some interest to note that versions of the verse collected from American blacks in the mid nineteenth and early twentieth centuries were also sung. See Newman I. White, *American Negro Folk-songs* (Hatboro, Pennsylvania, 1965 reprint of 1928 ed.), 255, 382.

[5] See the entry on the eighth earl in *D.N.B.*, xv (1909), 856, and *Calendar of State Papers, Ireland, 1 Nov. 1600–31 July 1601* (1905), 386.

[6] G. Brenan, *A History of the House of Percy*, ii (1902), 147.

[7] Drummond reports that Jonson recalled this remark in 1619. See *Ben Jonson, the Man and his Work*, ed. C. H. Herford and P. Simpson, i (Oxford, 1925), 148.

[8] The most recent version is noted by Iona and Peter Opie, *The Lore and Language of Schoolchildren* (Oxford, 1959), 361. Iona Opie kindly supplied the information that Percy's is the oldest recorded variant, and she also gave me the references in nn. 4 and 9 to other versions of the verse.

[9] Iona Opie believes the basic version of the verse to be as follows:

> God made man, and man made money;
> God made bees and bees make honey;
> God made Satain, Satain made sin;
> God made hell, and put Satain in.

This verse was recorded in a Bible dated 1676, carried to Ireland by settlers from Scotland. See *Notes and Queries*, 11th series, xii, no. 300 (25 Sept. 1915), 250. This is the second earliest report of the verse.

This verse is not the only mention of Bowes in the seventeenth century to survive. Pepys, in his diary entry for 5 September 1662, recorded two anecdotes concerning Bowes which he heard while at dinner with the officers of the customs, men chosen from among the most important merchants.[10] According to the first anecdote, Bowes supposedly was offended because some Russian noblemen preceded him up the stairs to his reception by Ivan IV. Bowes

would not go up till the Emperor had ordered those two men to be dragged down-stairs, with their heads knocking upon every stair till they were killed. And when he was come up, they demanded his sword of him before he entered the room. He told them, if they would have his sword, they should have his boots too. And so caused his boots to be pulled off, and his night-gown and night-cap and slippers to be sent for; and made the Emperor stay till he could go in his night-dress, since he might not go as a soldier.

In a second incident, Ivan, to show his power over his subjects, ordered one to jump out the window in Bowes's presence. The man died from the fall, and Bowes remarked that

his mistress did set more by, and did make better use of the necks of her subjects: but said that, to show what her subjects would do for her, he would, and did, fling down his gantlett before the Emperor; and challenged all the nobility there to take it up, in defence of the Emperor against his Queen: for which, at this very day, the name of Sir Jerom Bowes is famous and honoured there.

Probably Bowes became the subject of Pepys's dinner conversation in connection with the impending arrival of a Russian ambassador, and the prospects this held for improved trade after the breach in relations which had occurred at the time of the Civil War.[11]

During the same period, the 1660s, Dr. Samuel Collins, physician to Tsar Aleksey Mikhailovich, also recorded anecdotes concerning Bowes.[12] According to Collins, Ivan IV supposedly had the French ambassador's

[10] *The Diary of Samuel Pepys, M.A., F.R.S.*, ed. H. B. Wheatly, ii (1903), 308. Both this anecdote and the Collins anecdote following are noted in the entry on Bowes in *D.N.B.*, ii (1908), 965–6.

[11] On Anglo-Russian relations at this time, see S. Konovalov, 'England and Russia: Three Embassies, 1662–5', *Oxford Slavonic Papers*, x (1962), 60–104. The tsar's agent, John Hebdon, was in England before the dispatch of the Russian embassy, and departed on 16 September 1662 to meet the ambassadorial party at Gravesend; see I. Lubimenko, *Les Relations commerciales et politiques de l'Angleterre avec la Russie avant Pierre le Grand* (Paris, 1933), 237, n. 3, and A. Lodyzhensky 'Russkoe posol'stvo v Angliyu v 1662 g.', *Istoricheskii vestnik* (1880), 446. It is tempting to speculate that Hebdon related the Bowes anecdotes at Pepys's dinner. He was in London at the time and was later acquainted with Pepys; see the *Diary* (n. 10), iii, 150–1. Unfortunately, there is no evidence that he was present at the dinner.

[12] *The Present State of Russia* (London, 1671), 49–51. Collins's work is discussed in L. Loewenson, 'The Works of Robert Boyle and "The Present State of Russia" by Samuel Collins (1671)', *Slavonic and East European Review*, xxxiii (1955), 470–85. Also note the entry in *D.N.B.*, iv (1908), 831–2. Collins arrived in London in 1662 with the Russian embassy. He was apparently recruited into the tsar's service by John Hebdon in 1661.

hat nailed to his head, after which incident Bowes appeared before the Tsar wearing his hat.[13] When Ivan inquired how Bowes dared do such a thing, Bowes replied that the French ambassador

represented a cowardly King of *France*, but I am the Embassador of the invincible Queen of *England*, who does not vail her Bonnet, nor bare her Head, to any Prince living; and if any of her Ministers shall receive any affront abroad, she is able to revenge her own quarrel. Look you there (quoth *Juan Vasilowidg* to his *Boyars*), there is a brave Fellow indeed, that dares to do and say thus much for his Mistris; which Whoreson of you all dare do so much for me, your Master?

Though more fantastic, the Collins anecdotes are in some ways more explicable than Pepys's stories. Collins's book is apparently based on letters sent to Robert Boyle in the period 1663–5, roughly the time of the Carlisle embassy's visit to Muscovy.[14] The Carlisle embassy of 1664 seems to have increased interest in Bowes's mission—the two embassies were remarkably similar: both ambassadors attempted unsuccessfully to restore English trading privileges, both were plagued by problems of protocol and hostile Russian bureaucrats, both concluded with the return of the Russian gifts by the English ambassador.[15] It is clear that the issues of Bowes's embassy were remembered by both the English and the Russians, though Bowes's name did not find its way into the printed English account of the embassy.[16]

Incredible though the stories of Pepys and Collins are, a comparison with Bowes's own accounts of his embassy reveals that they reflect actual events to a certain degree.[17] The question of whether Bowes or the Tsar's representative should remove his hat did arise on one occasion,[18] and the matter of whether or not Bowes should wear his sword in the Tsar's presence also related to fact. Even mention of Bowes's nightgown reflects historical reality, though in a humorously distorted

---

[13] The account of this incident derives from the story of Vlad the Impaler (Dracula), which reached Muscovy late in the fifteenth century. In this earlier version the ambassadors had been sent to Vlad by the Sultan; their refusal to remove their caps was similarly punished. See *Povest' o Drakule*, ed. Ya. S. Lur'e (L., 1964), 66, n. 20. Despite the derivative nature of this anecdote, it may have been inspired by the problems of hat etiquette during Bowes's mission.

[14] Collins was in London with the Russian embassy which left England on 5 July 1663. Apparently, he met Boyle during this visit to England. Boyle's book containing excerpts from the letters sent by Collins appeared in 1665. See Loewenson, op. cit. (n. 12), 473, 478, 483.

[15] Compare Carlisle's account of his embassy in G. Miege, *A Relation of Three Embassies* (London, 1669), 435–60, with Bowes's account of his mission found in Hakluyt's *The Principal Navigations, Voyages, Traffiques and Discoveries of the English Nation*, iii (Glasgow, 1903), 463–85.

[16] The English remembered the hostility of Russian bureaucrats, Ivan's private conversations with the English ambassador, and the halcyon days of the English trade. The Russians remembered Ivan's proposed English marriage. See Miege, op. cit. (n. 15), 249, 450.

[17] Bowes wrote two fairly lengthy accounts of his embassy. One is cited above, n. 15, the other may be found in G. Tolstoy (ed.), *The First Forty Years of Intercourse between England and Russia, 1553–1593* (Spb., 1875), 231–5.

[18] Ibid. 231.

fashion: Bowes, when required to remove his sword before entering the Tsar's presence, sent for a 'longar garment meetar to be worne without a sword', but he was not allowed to change clothes before his reception.[19]

As noted in the anecdotes of both Collins and Pepys, Bowes did stoutly defend the honour of the queen:

After I had bene dyvers tymes before the emperor and had often had conference with his cowncell and that he fownd I had not comyssion to yeld to every demande that he thowght reasonable, he one day emongst other used theis speaches. 'I doo not esteme (quoted he) the Queene your mystris for my fellowe: ther bee that are her bettars, yea hir worstars' wheruntto answeringe as I thought ffytt (wheche no way was unreasonable) he towld me in furye, he would throwe me owt of the doores, and bad me gett me home.[20]

These anecdotes are remarkable for their favourable portrayal of Bowes. By the 1660s the failure of Bowes's mission and the disagreements after his return between him and the Muscovy Company seem to have been forgotten,[21] and Bowes was admired for his stout spirit and defence of Elizabeth's and England's honour.

It is not clear to what extent the fluctuations in Bowes's reputation and fortunes represent the varying strengths of parties at the English court. Luria contends that Burghley was a patron of Bowes and that Bowes's disagreements with Sir Jerome Horsey, a prominent figure in Russo-English relations in the 1580s, reflected differences between Burghley and Walsingham, a known supporter of Horsey.[22] This explanation is not entirely satisfactory. There is evidence to tie Bowes to Burghley very late in the century, after Walsingham's death,[23] but in 1583, at the time of the embassy, Bowes appealed to Walsingham, not Burghley, for assistance in a personal matter.[24] Bowes's translation of Innocent Gentillet's *An Apology or Defense for the Christians of France which are of the Evangelicall or reformed religion, for the satisfiing of such as wil*

---

[19] Ibid. 233–4. In the account published by Hakluyt (n. 15), 471, the sword incident is described as having taken place during an audience with Ivan IV. This incident is also mentioned quite laconically in the Russian account of the embassy, 'Pamyatniki diplomaticheskikh snoshenii Moskovskogo gosudarstva s Anglieyu', ii (1581–1604), ed. K. N. Bestuzhev-Ryumin, in *Sbornik Imperatorskogo Russkogo istoricheskogo obshchestva*, xxxviii (1883), 103. Here the audience is with Ivan. [20] Tolstoy, op. cit. (n. 17), 232.

[21] For details of the failure of the mission see: T. S. Willan, *The Early History of the Russia Company, 1553–1603* (Manchester, 1956), 166, and Ya. S. Lur'e, 'Angliiskaya politika na Rusi v kontse XVI veka', *Uchenye zapiski Leningradskogo pedagogicheskogo instituta im. A. I. Gertsena*, lxi (1947), 123; on Bowes's disagreements with the Muscovy Company, see *Calendar of State Papers, Foreign Series, of the reign of Elizabeth*, xix (1916), 132–3.

[22] Luria has developed this argument in a number of articles, the most important of which is his 'Angliiskaya politika' (n. 21), 129–31, 135–8. See also his 'Unpublished Epigram' (n. 1), 15–17, and the related articles, 'Russko-angliiskie otnosheniya i mezhdunarodnaya politika vtoroi poloviny XVI v.' in A. A. Zimin (ed.), *Mezhdunarodnye svyazi Rossii do XVII v.: sbornik statei* (M., 1961), 419–43, and 'Pis'ma Dzheroma Gorseya', *Uchenye zapiski Leningradskogo gosudarstvennogo universiteta*, lxxiii, *Seriya istoricheskikh nauk*, viii (1941), 189–201.

[23] Conyers Read, *Lord Burghley and Queen Elizabeth* (New York, 1960), 529.

[24] *Calendar of State Papers* (n. 21), xviii (1914), 44.

not live in peace and concord with them (London, 1579) indicates that Bowes and Walsingham were similar in their religious views. In 1586 Burghley did in fact support Horsey when his dispute involving Bowes was tried in council;[25] it should also be noted that the disagreements between Walsingham and Burghley were resolved by early 1587.[26] The possible political nature of Bowes's quarrel with Horsey remains obscure.

The Percy verse seems to indicate that it was primarily Bowes's management of the drinking glass monopoly after his return to England which attracted disapproval and ridicule. What exactly Bowes did in his handling of the monopoly to cause such an attitude has so far remained unexplained. There are, however, two incidents connected with Bowes and the monopoly which may have inspired the humorous verse. The first dates from 1598, when the English ambassador in France felt compelled to write to Robert Cecil and complain of Bowes's activities:

> Monsr Zamett the great Banquier here, who is so much esteemed by the king, and all this Cort, as I doubt not yor honor knoweth hath of late sundrie tymes complayned to me that having loden at Venice certein Cases of glasses for his own provision and to present to his frends here the w[ch] were Conveyed in a shipp of London, and appoynted to be sent from thence to Roan, S[r] Jerom Bowes doth seeke to confiscatt the said glasses by vertue of his lycence, He hath hereof Complayned to the k[ing]: and procured him to wryte unto her ma[tie] or yo[r] honor, and I beseech yo[r] honor be pleased to take order that such extremities maie not be exercised w[ch] are of ill favor.[27]

Six years later, in 1604, another incident involving Bowes arose when a Francis Verseline (probably a connection of the previous holder of the monopoly, Giacopo Verselini) attempted to acquire the drinking glass monopoly.[28] This attempt was supported by King James, who proposed that Bowes be granted the rent of the monopoly, £300 a year, for Bowes's lifetime, although Bowes's monopoly was valid for only three more years. Bowes refused to relinquish the monopoly under these conditions. Further investigation revealed that Bowes had not paid the rent of 100 marks a year for the preceding nine years he had held the monopoly.

[25] Luria's assertion to the contrary ('Angliiskaya politika' (n. 21), 135) seems to be based on a misunderstanding. Horsey's mention in his 'Travels' of 'my lord Treasurer' as his supporter (see *Russia at the Close of the Sixteenth Century*, ed. E. A. Bond (1856), 216) refers to Burghley, who was in fact Lord Treasurer, rather than to Christopher Hatton, as might be concluded from the ambiguous syntax of the passage.

[26] See Conyers Read, 'Walsingham and Burghley in Queen Elizabeth's Privy Council', *English Historical Review*, xxviii (1913), 58.

[27] *The Edmondes Papers: a Selection from the Correspondence of Sir Thomas Edmondes, Envoy from Queen Elizabeth at the French Court*, ed. G. G. Butler (1913), 369, letter of 28 August 1598.

[28] *Calendar of the Manuscripts of the Most Honorable the Marquess of Salisbury, preserved at Hatfield House, Hertfordshire*, Pt. 23, Addenda, 1562–1605 (1973), 179, document dated after August 1604; on Giacopo Verselini, see W. H. Price, *The English Patents of Monopoly* (Boston, 1906), 69.

The outcome of the first incident is unknown, but Bowes prevailed in the second case, and his patent of monopoly was renewed in 1606, only to be cancelled, however, in 1614. The cancellation does not seem to have been readily accepted by Bowes's associates, but Bowes himself was granted a pension.[29]

As the verse discovered by Luria indicates, Bowes's commercial exploits were not held in high esteem, but his service as ambassador in Muscovy—actually no more successful than his handling of the drinking glass monopoly—was admired for its boldness and dash, qualities which were emphasized in the anecdotes which circulated a remarkable length of time after his death.

[29] Price, op. cit. (n. 28), 70–2. A grant of £600 a year was given to Bowes on 17 March 1616, about a week before his death, in consideration of his former rents. See *Calendar of State Papers, Domestic, 1611–1618* (1858), 355. As late as 1621, £600 of the yearly rent of £1,000 from the monopoly went to Bowes's executors. See *Commons Debates, 1621* (n. 2), iv, 354.

Azbuka znakami lits: Egyptian Hieroglyphs in the Privy Chancellery Archive*

By DANIEL CLARKE WAUGH

In 1713 the compiler of an inventory to the papers that remained from the Chancellery of Privy Affairs (*Prikaz tainykh del*) of Tsar Aleksey Mikhailovich (reigned 1645–76) noted a file that contained among other items an '*azbuka znakami lits*' (alphabet in pictorial signs).[1] Although this file has survived to our day (it is now in the Tsentral'nyi gosudarstvennyi arkhiv drevnikh aktov (TsGADA) in Moscow, *fond* 27, *delo* 312) and has been used by scholars, the '*azbuka*' has been ignored.[2] It is the purpose of this brief communication to discuss the nature and origins of this so-called 'alphabet'.

Its manuscript consists of two loose sheets, one approximately the size of a Muscovite *stolbets* (i.e. about 45 × 17 cm., and prepared by halving a full sheet of paper lengthwise) and the other of the same length but half the width. Both sheets have writing on recto and verso, the wider one containing two columns and the narrower one a single column of figures on each side (Plates I–II). A quick glance suggests that the figures are Egyptian hieroglyphs.[3] My initial impression was that the hieroglyphs could well be a conglomeration of genuine and imaginary ones, not necessarily representing a coherent text. Some of

* This research was made possible by financial support from the International Research and Exchanges Board, the American Council of Learned Societies, and the Russian and East European Program of the Institute for Comparative and Foreign Area Studies at the University of Washington.

[1] See the 'Opis' delam Prikaza tainykh del 1713 goda', in *Zapiski Otdeleniya russkoi i slavyanskoi arkheologii Imperatorskogo Russkogo arkheologicheskogo obshchestva*, ii (1861), 7. The entry reads in full: '*Izobrazhenie znaka, yavl'shchagosya na nebesi v Vengerskoi zemle 1672 g. i znaki zh chervyam v toi zhe zemle, kotorye byli s velikim snegom vo 181 godu, da azbuka s znakami lits*.' The next line in the inventory is '*listki pisany po azbuke*', presumably referring to a different item. The (on the evidence of the handwriting) seventeenth-century table of contents for the file (TsGADA, *fond* 27 (Papers of the *Prikaz tainykh del*), no. 312, f. 1), from which the inventory entry appears to have been copied, reads '*azbuka znakami lits*' for the item that concerns us here.

[2] For example, I. Ya. Gurlyand described and published the texts of the first two items in the file but did not mention the third (*Prikaz velikogo gosudarya tainykh del* (Yaroslavl', 1902), 380–2).

[3] TsGADA, *fond* 27, no. 312, ff. 8–9. Note that f. 8ᵛ is a copy of the top two-thirds of f. 8ʳ, and the left column on f. 9ᵛ is likewise a copy of the top two-thirds of the right column on f. 9ʳ.

the signs have been rendered as human figures by the copyist and do not seem to coincide with known Egyptian hieroglyphic signs. Initially, then, the prospects of discovering the source for the drawings appeared to be slim.

One significant detail provided a clue as to where one might begin a search for the source. Each set of figures is enclosed in a long rectangle, at the end of which is a triangular point. The shape suggested is that of an obelisk. A search of literature pertaining to the evolution of Egyptology revealed that Egyptian obelisks had been of particular interest in Europe during the sixteenth and seventeenth centuries.[4] A number of obelisks had been transported to Europe in late Roman times; as part of the rebuilding and decoration of the Baroque era, especially in Rome under papal sponsorship, some of the long since fallen monoliths were raised in prominent locations. The interest in obelisks was connected not only with city planning and decoration: most of the obelisks bore hieroglyphic inscriptions. During the Renaissance, there had developed an increasing interest in the interpretation of Egyptian hieroglyphs, in part because many people felt that they had particular mystical or religious significance that might be related to the prevalent cabalistic and Hermetic theories.

In the seventeenth century a German Jesuit, Athanasius Kircher, undertook a massive scholarly project—the compilation of a complete catalogue of all known Egyptian obelisks and their inscriptions, along with an explanation of their history and an attempt at interpretation. Kircher's *magnum opus*, the three-volume *Oedipus Aegyptiacus* published in 1652–4, was indeed the most complete collection of material on Egyptian obelisks in Europe in the middle of the seventeenth century and long afterwards.[5] Since my search in earlier publications discussing hieroglyphs and obelisks had failed to provide any clues to the origin of the drawings in Muscovy, it was logical to turn to Kircher. Moreover, since the archive of the Tsar's Privy Chancellery contained so many translations, including the other items in the file with the hieroglyphs, it seemed reasonable to look for the source in a printed book such as Kircher's, containing detailed engravings of the obelisks he described.

Among them was the famous 'Theodosian' or Hippodrome obelisk raised toward the end of the fourth century in the Constantinople Hippodrome by the order of Emperor Theodosius I and standing on the same location today in what is now called the Atmeydan or Horse Square. This monument, dating from the time of Tuthmosis III (1490–

---

[4] I have relied primarily on the excellent survey by Erik Iversen, *The Myth of Egypt and its Hieroglyphs in European Tradition* (Copenhagen, 1961), and the same author's authoritative *Obelisks in Exile*, 2 vols. (Copenhagen, 1968–72).

[5] Athanasii Kircheri, *Oedipus Aegyptiacus. Hoc Est Vniuersalis Hieroglyphicae Veterum Doctrinae temporum iniuria abolitae Instauratio . . .*, 3 vols. in 4 (Rome, 1652–4). I have used the copy in Harvard University's Houghton Library.

1436 B.C.), had become an object of attention for visitors to the imperial city long before the Turkish conquest and remained so subsequently. Yet Kircher had provided the first thorough description and reasonably accurate representation of the obelisk; there appear to have been no other such depictions of it widespread in Europe before the end of the seventeenth century.[6] As he explains, he had to write to the Imperial resident in Istanbul in order to obtain an accurate drawing from which to make an engraving. The resident turned to his Greek interpreter Panaioti Nicusio for assistance. It happened that some time earlier Nicusio had made drawings of the obelisk and its hieroglyphs 'per mia curiosità', and it was these which were sent to Kircher.[7]

Kircher's engraving (Plate III) reveals that the Theodosian obelisk was, indeed, the source for the drawings in the Tsar's archive. However, as becomes clear from a comparison of the engraving and the drawings with accurate modern representations of the obelisk, Kircher's edition could not have served as the source for the manuscript illustrations.[8] For despite the fact that some of the hieroglyphs in the drawings are 'anthropomorphized' versions of what is actually on the obelisk, the drawings are nonetheless closer to the original than is Kircher's engraving. One additional feature of the drawings should be noted. The artist did not depict a complete side of the obelisk in one long strip, but divided each side approximately in half, surrounding each set of figures with a frame and adding a pointed tip, thus giving each half of the inscription the appearance of belonging to a distinct side of the obelisk. Perhaps this was done because drawings of two sides of the monument were not available—what we have is the complete text of the inscriptions on the north-east and south-west faces only.

Having located the source for the drawings, our next task was to determine how they came to Moscow. Two facts derived from the manuscript provided a clue. First, the paper contains fragments of what appears to be the watermark 'three crescents'. This paper was uncommon in Muscovy but widespread in the Ottoman Empire and the

---

[6] Kircher, op. cit. (n. 5), iii, 304–16. For the complete history of the Theodosian obelisk, see Iversen, *Obelisks* (n. 4), ii, 9–33, and Gerda Bruns, *Der Obelisk und seine Basis auf dem Hippodrom zu Konstantinopel* (Istanbuler Forschungen. Herausgegeben von der Abteilung Istanbul des Archäologischen Institutes des Deutschen Reiches, Bd. 7) (Istanbul, 1935), 1–11. While Bruns's historical excursus has been superseded by Iversen's, her book is valuable for its discussion of the inscriptions on pp. 21–9, where one finds their text in German translation, and for a variety of archaeological details.

[7] Kircher, op. cit. (n. 5), iii, 305.

[8] Compare Kircher's engraving (Plate III) with the photographs in Bruns, *Der Obelisk* (for example, fig. 2 = Plate IV), which are reproduced in Iversen, *Obelisks*, ii, figs. 6–9. The clearest accurate reproductions of the inscriptions are in the magnificent portfolios of R. Lepsius, *Denkmäler aus Aegypten und Aethiopien* (Berlin, 1849–59), Abt. III, Bd. v, pl. 60. I have no evidence to suggest that Kircher's *Oedipus Aegyptiacus* was known in Muscovy; for two of his works that apparently were, see A. I. Sobolevsky, *Perevodnaya literatura Moskovskoi Rusi XIV–XVII vekov* (Spb., 1903), 94, 182.

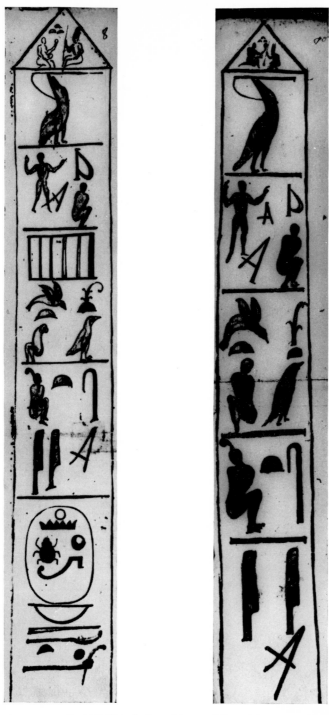

I. TsGADA, *fond* 27, *delo* 312, f. 8ʳ and 8ᵛ

II. TsGADA, *fond* 27, *delo* 312, f. 9ʳ and 9ᵛ

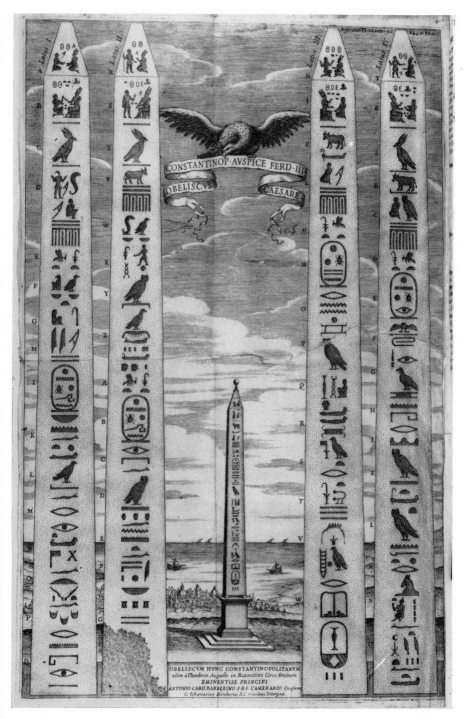

III. The Hippodrome obelisk: the engraving in Kircher's *Oedipus Aegyptiacus* (1652-4)

IV. The Hippodrome obelisk, south-west face

(Reproduced by permission of the Deutsches Archäologisches Institut, Abteilung Istanbul)

Caucasus.[9] Second, there is a small Greek inscription written upside down at the top of folio 8ʳ (. . . νφιλα).[10] It seems reasonable to conclude then that the original source of the drawings was Istanbul itself, where the Phanariot Greek interpreters for foreign visitors had ample opportunity and incentive to supply curiosities—as had been done to fulfil Kircher's request. Muscovy's channels of communication with Istanbul were many—in addition to frequent diplomatic exchanges, there was active trade (much of it in Greek hands) and a steady stream of Orthodox clerics seeking alms in Muscovy. The best we can suggest regarding a date for the transmission of the drawings is the early 1670s—certainly not later than 1676, when the Privy Chancellery was closed. The file in which the hieroglyphs are found contains two other items, both dating from the early 1670s. It may be, of course, that the presence of the three items in one file is merely the work of the archivist and is not evidence for the date when the copies were received.

The last question we would wish to answer regarding the drawings is how they were understood in Muscovy. It is of some interest that the seventeenth-century table of contents for the file and, following that, the 1713 inventory, term the hieroglyphs an 'alphabet'. Even Kircher, who was the outstanding Egyptologist of his day, failed to understand the hieroglyphic script as an alphabet, but rather adhered to the common Renaissance view that they were mystical symbols. It would, of course, be foolish to argue that in Muscovy anyone really understood the nature of hieroglyphs: there is no basis here for talking even of the beginnings of Russian Egyptology. The designation 'alphabet' possibly resulted from the interpretation of the hieroglyphs as something akin to diplomatic cipher (*azbuka*), examples of which were in the archive of the Privy Chancellery.[11]

The file in which the drawings are found has a common denominator that provides another explanation of the way in which Muscovites viewed the hieroglyphs. The first item in the file is a watercolour of fantastic insects which, according to the legend, appeared in Hungary during a snow storm and proceeded to devour each other. The second item, sent to Moscow by Varlaam Yasinsky, the Rector of the Kievan College, is a depiction and explanation of complex signs that purportedly appeared in the heavens over Hungary predicting the union

---

[9] See R. Pataridze, 'Tre lune', *Paleografiuli dziebani*, ii (Tbilisi, 1969), 59–102 (in Georgian with Russian summary), also V. Nikolaev, *Watermarks of the Medieval Ottoman Documents in Bulgarian Archives* (Sofia, 1954), *passim*. The watermark fragments visible in the manuscript are insufficient for dating purposes.

[10] Although the first two or three letters on the microfilm I received are unclear, the inscription might be read from the original. Not knowing Greek, I was unable to provide a sufficiently accurate *de visu* copy to be of much use to Professor Pierre MacKay, who kindly deciphered what he could for me.

[11] A probable example is the item mentioned in n. 1 above; see also *Dela Tainogo prikaza*, i (Russkaya istoricheskaya biblioteka, 21) (Spb., 1907), col. 19.

of Poland, Muscovy, and the Habsburg Empire to defeat the Turks.[12] In each case, the compiler of the table of contents for the file termed the items depicted '*znaki*' or signs. It is understandable how in Muscovy, where tales of portents were common, and in particular at the court of Aleksey Mikhailovich, who had a personal interest in astrology, such curiosities would be appreciated.

In this connection, I believe that we can make some suggestions regarding the significance of the hieroglyphs for the study of Muscovite court culture. By themselves they are no more than curiosities. However, they are important if seen as one of many items of evidence that could provide us with a better picture than we have had previously of Muscovite cultural development in the seventeenth century. For it seems to me that the papers formerly housed in the archive of Tsar Aleksey Mikhailovich's Privy Chancellery contain a great deal that is little known but worthy of study. That chancellery served as an instrument for the Tsar to effect his will in matters he considered to be particularly deserving of his personal attention. As one can see from the inventories drawn up after the Tsar died, the Privy Chancellery archive contained, among other things, the Tsar's personal papers and a variety of material which was intended to keep him both informed and amused.[13] There were numerous books and pamphlets, some of them translated from foreign sources, there was a long run of the translated news compilations known as *kuranty*, there were instructions to the Tsar's English agent, John Hebdon, and much more. It is only by analysing carefully the contents of this archive—not merely by looking at the inventories but also by trying to locate the sources for individual items—that we will enlarge our picture of the ruler whose inquisitiveness has been likened to that of his more famous son, Peter the Great, and at whose court were sown the seeds of the cultural transformation that was to grow in subsequent decades.[14]

[12] For description and publication of the texts, see n. 2; see also Sobolevsky, *Perevodnaya literatura* (n. 8), 247–8. The two other pictures in the file have yet to be published. For the textual history of the explanation for the signs in the heavens, see my 'Seventeenth-century Muscovite Pamphlets with Turkish Themes: toward a Study of Muscovite Literary Culture in its European Setting' (Unpublished Ph.D. dissertation, Harvard University, 1972), i, 298–305.

[13] The inventories have been published in *Dela Tainogo prikaza*, i (n. 11) and in the book cited in n. 1. One finds a variety of interesting material about the Privy Chancellery and court culture scattered through the two basic studies of the institution, Gurlyand's *Prikaz* (n. 2), and A. I. Zaozersky, *Tsarskaya votchina XVII veka: iz istorii khozyaistvennoi i prikaznoi politiki tsarya Alekseya Mikhailovicha*, 2 ed. (M., 1937).

[14] Cf. S. M. Solov'ev, *Istoriya Rossii s drevneishikh vremen*, vi (M., 1961), 29.

Scottish Cannon-founders and the Russian Navy, 1768–85*

By R. P. BARTLETT

1

By the third quarter of the eighteenth century, Peter the Great's navy had fallen into a state of considerable disorder and inefficiency. After his death, and throughout the mid-eighteenth century, little was done to maintain his creation, and despite some Russian successes at sea in the Seven Years War, the Russian government thereafter was very conscious of the navy's deficiencies. An official Commission had already been set up to deal with its reorganization when Peter III was over-thrown in June 1762;[1] and Catherine II showed herself equally con-cerned to improve Russia's armed forces, both the army and the navy. The latter presented a daunting task: not only modern equipment was needed, but a complete revision of seamanship and skills. 'We have ships, and people on them, in plenty; but we have neither a fleet, nor sailors', Catherine wrote to N. I. Panin in 1765, after a disastrous naval review.[2]

Efforts at renewal were pushed forward in all areas. The official establishment of men, ships, and equipment was revised. Russians were sent to train in foreign navies, and foreign officers recruited for Russia, particularly Britons; the most outstanding foreigner acquired in this way was Samuel Greig, and the highest ranking at the time of his appointment, Rear-Admiral Sir Charles Knowles, who spent four years (1771–4) in Catherine's service.[3] In addition, new ships were com-missioned; skilled workers were sought abroad for Russian shipyards; and similar measures were taken in the field of armaments.

Russia emerged from the Seven Years War with a large artillery park, both naval and military. But it still fell below the establishment set in 1757; much of it was outworn or outmoded, and the establish-ment levels defined by the Naval Commission in the 1760s were higher than before. The principal lack, and the principal difficulties which the government was to encounter, lay in the production of iron can-non, which formed the bulk of naval armament in Russia as they did

* An earlier version of this paper was read to the Study Group on Eighteenth-century Russia at its meeting in July 1976.

[1] L. Beskrovny, *Russkaya armiya i flot v XVIII v.* (M., 1958), 331.
[2] *Sbornik Imperatorskogo Russkogo istoricheskogo obshchestva* (hereafter *SIRIO*), x (1872), 23.
[3] See A. G. Cross, 'Samuel Greig, Catherine the Great's Scottish Admiral', *Mariner's Mirror*, lx (1974), 251–65; P. H. Clendenning, 'Admiral Sir Charles Knowles and Russia, 1771–1774', *Mariner's Mirror*, lxi (1975), 39–49.

elsewhere. Brass cannon could be made fairly readily, but they distorted and wore out more quickly in use, and were more expensive. The skills developed in Peter I's time had not been adequately maintained. Catherine II lamented to Sir Charles Knowles:

Nous possédions cy devant l'art de fondre des Canons de Fer, pour nos Vaisseaux et Fortresses. A notre honte il faut avouer que nous avons oublié cet art utile, et qu'à présent quelquefois de Cent Canons de Fer, a l'épreuve il n'en reste souvent que dix en entier. . . . En revanche nos Canons de cuivre sont parfaitement bien fondûs, mais ceux de fer nous sont également neces-saires, et ils sont à meilleur marché.[4]

The high failure rate to which Catherine referred had several causes, the most basic of which were interrelated. There was a severe lack generally of skilled labour capable of manning and carrying through the different stages of the casting process; and more specifically, master-founders were not available who could ensure the correct composition of the gun-metal and achieve a flawless cast. The presence or absence of such a competent workman was usually decisive for the success of sustained operations. At the same time the state of metal-lurgical chemistry in this period was such that achieving the right proportions and qualities in the metal was a matter of feel and flair, almost as much an art as an exact science.[5] This was a problem of European technology in the eighteenth century, and its effects were not confined to Russia, as will be seen.

In its attempts to increase and regularize naval artillery production, the government looked in particular to three of the state metallurgical groups created by Peter I in the early years of the century: the Kamen-skii foundry, one of the last Urals plants now remaining under state control; the Petrovskii complex around Lake Onega in the Olonets region north of St. Petersburg, which had supplied the Baltic fleet; and the Lipetsk foundries, near Voronezh. Some private iron-masters also took government contracts, initially usually for munitions: notably the Demidov foundry at Nizhnii Tagil in the Urals, and the Batashev works on the middle and lower reaches of the Oka.[6]

---

[4] Admiralty Library, London, Admiral Sir Charles Knowles, 'Copies of documents relative to his service in the Russian Admiralty, 1770–4' (hereafter Knowles Papers), f. 5: 'The Empress' reply to Knowles's Second Memorandum', para. 9 (n.d., probably 1771). I am grateful to the Librarian of the Admiralty Library for permission to consult these papers. In quotations from these and other documents the orthography of the original is retained.

[5] Cf. the comments on this problem in V. Rodzevich, *Istoricheskoe opisanie Peterburgskogo arsenala za 200 let ego sushchestvovaniya, 1712–1912* (Spb., 1914), 18–19. These relate to the Petrine period, but are valid for later times as well, and for both brass and iron casting.

[6] In general, besides Beskrovny (n. 1), see N. I. Pavlenko, *Istoriya metallurgii v Rossii XVIII veka* (M., 1962); Ya. A. Balagurov, *Formirovanie rabochikh kadrov Olonetskikh Petrovskikh zavodov (pervaya polovina XVIII v.)* (Petrozavodsk, 1955); idem, *Olonetskie gornye zavody v doreformennyi period* (Petrozavodsk, 1958); A. Martynov, V. Zhdanov, *Iz proshlogo Lipetskogo kraya* (Lipetsk, 1959), chap. xi 'Lipskaya manufaktura'.

These three state complexes had each developed differently in the post-Petrine period. While the Urals iron industry had grown steadily during the century, the Olonets and Lipetsk foundries, like the navy they were designed to serve, fell into decline once the urgent need for cannon in the Great Northern War had passed. In particular, by the 1760s, the skilled labour force of the Olonets complex had been dispersed.[7] In 1755 the Lipetsk works, in a run-down state, passed into the private ownership of Prince Petr Ivanovich Repnin. His bid to obtain control of the Olonets foundries as well was unsuccessful;[8] but these were now in such poor condition that, while munitions could be produced there, the College of Mines declared in 1761 that 'it considers it extremely dangerous to take upon itself and to promise the casting of cannon at the Petrovskii foundries because production there has stopped and they are generally in a ruined state'.[9]

Consequently, the efforts of the Admiralty College in the early 1760s were concentrated principally on the Kamenskii works. However, the Urals cannon repeatedly failed to come up to specification, a failure ascribed to 'the preparation of poor ores, and the inadequacies of the blast-furnaces and the craftsmen'.[10] In 1766 plans were therefore made to restore the Olonets foundries, and new contracts were also authorized with private producers: notably the Batashev foundries were to produce 'cannon and other things' needed for the army and the fleet in the south.[11] But the Admiralty rejected as exorbitant a proposal from Repnin for cannon production at Lipetsk.[12]

The difficulties of the Kamenskii foundry continued. Of 613 guns cast there between April 1763 and September 1768, only 123 were accepted as sound, and on further inspection in St. Petersburg even some of these had to be rejected.[13] In November 1768, in a final effort to put things right, the authorities sent Captain of naval artillery F. Pasynkov to take charge of the works. But results did not improve, and in December 1769, despite the continuing war with Turkey and the consequent urgent need for cannon, gun-founding at the Kamenskii works was stopped.[14]

The Turkish declaration of war in September 1768 had taken Russia by surprise. There was no doubt in the minds of observers in the 1760s that Catherine intended to make war on Turkey as soon as it suited

[7] Balagurov, *Formirovanie* (n. 6), 29.   [8] Ibid. 30–1.

[9] F. Veselago, *Materialy dlya istorii russkogo flota* (hereafter *MIRF*), 17 vols. (Spb., 1865–1904), xi, 30–1, Minutes of the meeting of the Admiralty College Board (hereafter CM), 25 June 1762 (unless otherwise indicated, all dates in Russian documents are given in the Old Style, those in western sources in New Style).

[10] *MIRF* xi, 252, CM 16 Mar. 1766.

[11] Ibid. 264–5, 463, CM 19 June 1766, 13 Feb. 1769; Beskrovny, op. cit. (n. 1), 351.

[12] *MIRF* xi, 253, CM 16 Mar. 1766.   [13] Ibid. 349, n. 1.

[14] Ibid. 422–3, Admiralty College report to H.I.H., 15 Dec. 1769; ibid. 525–6, CM 23 Dec. 1769; Beskrovny, op. cit. (n. 1), 357–8.

her;[15] but in September 1768 the time was not yet ripe. The Russian forces were unprepared, and until the last moment Nikita Panin, in charge of foreign affairs, had thought that he could bribe the Turkish officials and postpone the final crisis.[16] The outbreak of hostilities intensified the search for an assured and adequate supply of naval artillery. In November Catherine personally demanded the dispatch of special inspectors to the Kamenskii, Lipetsk, and Olonets foundries; and while Pasynkov set out for the Urals, General (*general-tseikhmeister*) Demidov was sent to Lake Onega, and Captain of naval artillery Ivan Dmitriev assigned to make trial castings at Lipetsk.[17] In addition, 'by the exact desire of H. I. H.', Panin wrote to the Russian ambassador in Stockholm for a skilled Swedish cannon-founder: a duplication of similar instructions sent at this time—according to Klyuchevsky[18]—to London, and a repetition of an identical request in 1766 which had met with no success.[19] The problem was pressing: in December the College calculated that the existing naval provision fell short of the prescribed war-time establishment (including reserves) by 4,956 guns.[20]

During the next two years the most strenuous efforts were made to establish and improve artillery production. The arrival of General Demidov at Konchezersk brought some urgency to the restoration work there; but he failed to achieve any immediate prospect of reliable cannon production, and from November 1769 growing labour unrest repeatedly halted the work of the foundry altogether.[21] The stoppages formed part of a wider disturbance among the Karelian peasantry, often referred to as the Kizhi rising, which lasted from 1769 to 1771; it had finally to be put down by military force, and it provoked an official enquiry.[22] (One particular source of grievance proved to be Demidov's rigour in driving on the reconstruction at Konchezersk.[23]) In the wake of the enquiry M. F. Soimonov, the President of the College of Mines, made an extensive inspection of the whole Olonets metallurgical complex. The upshot of these investigations was a decision

---

[15] See, for example, *Dispatches and Correspondence of John, Second Earl of Buckinghamshire, Ambassador to the Court of Catherine II of Russia, 1762–1765*, 2 vols. (1902), ii, 97–8: Buckingham to Sandwich, 4 Nov. 1763.

[16] M. S. Anderson, 'Great Britain and the Russo-Turkish War, 1768–74', *English Historical Review*, lxix (1954), 40.

[17] *MIRF* xi, 326, Confirmed Admiralty report to H.I.H., 12 Nov. 1768; ibid. 348, CM 9 Nov. 1768.

[18] V. O. Klyuchevsky, *Sochineniya*, v (M., 1958), 47.

[19] *MIRF* xi, 269, CM 1 Sept. 1766; *SIRIO*, lxxxvii (1893), 262, no. 1766, Panin to Ostermann, 20 Dec. 1768.

[20] *MIRF* xi, 454, CM 31 Jan. 1769. 5,478 iron guns were in service, 1,478 were still needed, as were 3,478 for the reserve. Figures are as given.

[21] Ibid. 600, CM 15 Jan. 1770; Beskrovny, op. cit. (n. 1), 354.

[22] V. Semevsky, *Krest'yane v tsarstvovanie imp. Ekateriny II* (Spb., 1901), ii, 457–502; S. M. Levidova, *Istoriya Onezhskogo (byvshego Aleksandrovskogo) zavoda*, i (Petrozavodsk, 1938), chap. ii.

[23] Levidova, op. cit. (n. 22), 21–2.

to construct a completely new foundry, to be called the Aleksandrovskii zavod, on the river Lososinka, above the existing Petrovskii works. This foundry became operational in 1774.[24]

The Petrovskie zavody themselves no longer formed part of the state complex, having been made over in 1765 to two Frenchmen, Barral and Chanoni, who had come to the area in 1765 to set up a zinc works.[25] In trying to renew cannon production, the authorities considered involving Barral and Chanoni: already in 1767 the Frenchmen had had negotiations to expand into gun manufacture, and had even pursued the matter so far as to obtain French government permission for the recruitment of a master-founder from France.[26] In May 1769 the College of Mines again proposed their services to the Admiralty College, but the Frenchmen's conditions proved quite unacceptable and this time, too, the negotiations brought no results.[27]

Besides the attempts to restore cannon production at the Kamenskii and Olonets foundries, a variety of other measures were undertaken. The Admiralty College tried to find skilled workers at private plants, who might be transferred.[28] It ordered the repair, by a secret process, of some of the many defective cannon available.[29] And the search for skilled personnel abroad was also resumed: the College decided in April 1769 to write yet again to the Russian ministers in Sweden, Saxony, and Britain.[30]

This renewed request, like the others, brought no immediate result. The envoy in Stockholm replied in July that, as before, he could not fulfil the commission: most skilled workers in Sweden were at private works and so indebted to their employers that they could not leave, but the main obstacle lay in the attitude of the Swedish government, which forbade the emigration of such people.[31] In October Count I. Chernyshev, Vice-President of the Admiralty Board, wrote from London of his continuing inability to find a suitable master-founder, despite 'many discussions and correspondence with different people, in other countries'. He was continuing the search and at the same time was also

---

[24] L. A. Gol'denberg, *Mikhail Fedorovich Soimonov (1730–1804)* (M., 1973), 27–41; Balagurov, *Olonetskie gornye zavody* (n. 6), 18–20.

[25] On Barral and Chanoni, see Pavlenko, *Istoriya metallurgii* (n. 6), 210–13; V.-E. Veuclin, *La Ville de Lyon et la Russie sous Pierre le Grand et Catherine II* . . . (Lyon, 1894), 8–10; idem, *L'Amitié franco-russe, ses origines: le génie français et la Russie sous Catherine II* (Lisieux, 1896), 8–10.

[26] Archives Nationales, Paris: Archives étrangères, B¹987, Corr. Cons. St-Pétersbourg, Rossignol to Praslin, Moscow, 9 Sept. 1767; same to same, Moscow, 25 Jan. 1768.

[27] *MIRF* xi, 483, 699, CM 6 May 1769, 12 Jan. 1771.

[28] Ibid. 348–9, CM 14 Nov. 1768.

[29] Ibid. 517, 521, CM 12, 19 Nov. 1769. Lt.-Col. Nartov, whose father had developed the process, for which the authorities had assigned 1,500 roubles annually from 1752, was instructed to carry out the work. By May 1770 he had repaired 52 guns (ibid. 618, CM 14 May 1770). Cf. the very scathing account of Nartov's process in Rodzevich, op. cit. (n. 5), 134–7. A recent study of Nartov senior is F. N. Zagorsky's *Andrey Nartov, 1693–1756* (L., 1969).

[30] *MIRF* xi, 480, CM 30 Apr. 1769.   [31] Ibid. 489, CM 20 July 1769.

trying to find 'yet another one, only not a simple master-founder, but an originator (*uchreditel'*) or entrepreneur (*zavoditel'*), however not at the expense of the Admiralty funds alone'.[32] Two months later Chernyshev could announce the engagement of some other needed professions— a rope-maker, block-maker, caulker, and tackle-maker—from Holland.[33] But it was only eighteen months later that the quest for a foreign founder succeeded. After a further approach by the Admiralty College, Count A. Musin-Pushkin in London finally engaged two British cannon-founders in May 1771.[34]

Still in 1769, the Admiralty College pursued the possibility of further contracts with private Russian suppliers. The Batashev foundries were already producing small-calibre artillery for the government, and in response to a new approach they undertook to try their hand at large-calibre weapons as well. During the second half of 1769 they test-cast 70 guns, of which 28 passed the Admiralty's inspection.[35] This first beginning marked the start of a long and relatively profitable involvement of the Batashev works in naval ordnance production: from 1770 to 1774 they produced nearly 1,900 naval guns of various calibres, and they remained suppliers throughout the rest of the century.[36]

The new Batashev production was complemented by some small success at the third group of foundries to which the Admiralty had sent an inspector in 1769, the Lipetsk works of Prince Repnin. Although they were not at that time producing cannon, their potential importance for the supply of the armed forces in the south was obvious, and the government bought them back from Repnin, 'especially because they are extremely suitable for the casting of cannon and shells', in 1769.[37] Following his arrival at the foundries early in that year, Dmitriev had been carrying out casting in relatively small quantities, but with some encouraging results, to judge by his report of October 1769. In January 1771 the Admiralty College stated that Lipetsk had by then produced 121 guns of various calibre.[38] This production was to continue during the 1770s. In October 1772 Dmitriev's successor Gannibal reported the casting of 33 relatively large-calibre guns of which, however, only 9 withstood proof, and in 1778 236 guns were ordered to be sent to Archangel 'from the Lipetsk foundries, out of the cannon cast there up to the present time'.[39]

But such levels of production, and the high proportion of defective guns, even taken together with the early achievements of the Batashev

---

[32] *MIRF* xi, 514–15, CM 29 Oct. 1769.   [33] Ibid. 524–5, CM 16 Dec. 1769.
[34] Ibid. 724, CM 21 June 1771.
[35] Ibid. 501–2, CM 28 Aug. 1769; Beskrovny, op. cit. (n. 1), 352.
[36] Beskrovny, op. cit. (n. 1), 351–2.
[37] Ibid. 353.   [38] *MIRF* xi, 522, CM 27 Nov. 1769; 698, CM 12 Jan. 1771.
[39] Ibid. xii, 472, CM 21 Sept. 1778; 119, CM 11 Oct. 1772. There seem to be no grounds for the assertion by Beskrovny (loc. cit. (n. 37)) that Lipetsk produced no new cannon in this period.

group, offered no solution to the problems of the Admiralty College in 1770 and early 1771, as the war and the concomitant urgent need for cannon continued. In January 1771 Catherine addressed a number of 'points' or questions to the College, of which the fifth asked: 'What is happening with the casting of iron cannon, are we engaging a master-founder abroad, and have we set up a premium (*preis*) for our founders?' In reply to the first part of the question, the College listed the modest achievements of the Batashevs and Lipetsk, mentioned its at this time continuing lack of success in Sweden, Saxony, and Britain, and the abortive negotiations with Barral and Chanoni. On the second point it added: 'As to the encouragement of our own craftsmen, the College has promised no premium.'[40] Not surprisingly, plans for a premium scheme were soon put forward;[41] but the College of Mines had reservations and, with or without a premium, the requisite supply of large-calibre guns remained out of reach. In November 1771 the Admiralty College told the College of Mines that while Batashev had sufficient reliable capacity for its small-calibre requirements, it needed as a matter of urgency over 600 30-pounder and other cannon.[42] So, with no secure large-calibre supply at home, in February 1772 the Admiralty took the final logical step of ordering guns from abroad. One thousand tons of cannon were ordered from Scotland, through the St. Petersburg house of Thompson, Peters, and Co., who were agents in the matter for Carron Company of Falkirk.[43]

The first consignment of 45 Scottish guns reached Cronstadt in June 1772.[44] And although (as will be seen) they were by no means entirely satisfactory, from this point onwards the shortage of large-calibre cannon became less chronic: already in March 1773 the College's Artillery Office was confident of meeting its urgent requirements, with ordnance from both Carron and the Batashev foundries.[45]

2

Carron Company, one of the outstanding British metallurgical enterprises of the eighteenth century, founded in 1759, had first started producing cannon in 1761; and by the end of the decade they had succeeded in interesting the British Board of Ordnance as well as other buyers in their guns. However, in their early years in this field, they experienced difficulties not unlike those of the Russian foundries in

[40] *MIRF* xi, 698–9, CM 12 Jan. 1771.   [41] Ibid. 702–4, CM 28 Feb. 1771.

[42] Ibid. 712, 750–1, 753–4, CM 18 Apr., 4, 18 Nov. 1771. At the same time 1,014 defective cannon were awaiting repair by Nartov, and the College was considering reports on new lighter guns now in use in the British navy, which had also been recommended by Knowles; see Clendenning, op. cit. (n. 3), 44. But these were not (as Clendenning states) Carronades: the latter only came into use from late 1778.

[43] *MIRF* xii, 5, 66, Imperial decree to Admiralty College, 9 Feb. 1772, CM 10 Feb. 1772.

[44] Ibid. 11, 89, Confirmed report to H.I.H., June 1772, CM 11 June 1772.

[45] Ibid. 190–1, CM 8 Mar. 1773.

producing reliable gun-metals and sound cannon. In fact, shortly after Carron secured the Russian order, the Woolwich Board of Ordnance suspended all further dealings with the Company (June 1773). It was not until 1775 that Carron solved the metallurgical problems which were troubling them; and only with the development of the revolutionary Carronade naval gun from 1778 did they establish themselves as outstanding ordnance founders on a European scale.[46] These problems were reflected in their dealings with the Russian Admiralty.

Carron's previous connections with Russia had been limited to the purchase of Russian iron, and their first negotiations on that subject with the firm of Thompson, Peters, and Co. seem to have taken place in April 1770.[47] This house then became Carron's established St. Petersburg correspondent in the years following. The contract concluded by Thompson, Peters with the Russian Admiralty in February 1772[48] stipulated delivery in the same year of 1,000 tons of iron cannon at £13 per ton, to be tested under Russian proof regulations. These were somewhat more severe than the British proof requirements. Carron, through their agents, offered only 32-pounder guns, which the Russian Admiralty accepted as being practically of equal calibre with the 30-pounder guns they wanted. In fact, Carron were stretching themselves to take on the new order, offering a large quantity at short notice and low price. The first cargo, of forty-five pieces, was shipped on board the *Stirling*, Capt. Miller, which left Borrowstowness on 5 June, and arrived in Cronstadt 16 days later.[49] With the guns went a Carron clerk, John McKenzie, who was to attend the proof, and whom Carron recommended in a fulsome letter to Sir Charles Knowles. Carron's managing director, Charles Gascoigne, wrote in confident tone. To Thompson, Peters he declared his hope 'that our ordnance will answer your most sanguine expectations as well with Respect to quality as to Neatness of finishing, as we apprehend that nothing has been seen in Russia equal to their Exterior'. To Knowles he wrote: 'We flatter ourselves that from the Excellence of our Ordnance, and our capacity of Executing large orders in a shorter time than any other Foundry in Europe, we shall obtain some degree of your attention and favour.' He added: 'Permit us, Sir, to Express our Warm Wishes that under your Auspices:

[46] R. Campbell, *Carron Company* (Edinburgh–London, 1961), 82–91. On the Carronade and its introduction, see in particular C. Ffoulkes, *The Gun-founders of England*, 2 ed. (1969), 39, 82–4, 104, pl. XIII; *Scots Magazine* (1779), 452; P. Padfield, *Guns at Sea* (1973), 105–10. I wish to acknowledge valuable assistance received from Professor Campbell in the early stages of this work, and the kind permission granted me by Carron Company and the Keeper of the Records of Scotland to use the Carron Papers in the Scottish Record Office.

[47] Scottish Record Office, Carron Papers, GD 58/1/10, f. 266, Charles Gascoigne to Thompson, Peters (London office), 25 Apr. 1770.

[48] *MIRF* xiii, 66–7, CM 10 Feb. 1772.

[49] Carron Papers, GD 58/1/12, ff. 73–4, Gascoigne to Thompson, Peters (St. Petersburg office), 6 June 1772; *MIRF* xii, 89, CM 11 June 1772.

The Glory of Her Imperial Majesty's arms may be proclaimed from the mouths of our Artillery at the Gates of Constantinople.'[50]

Such optimism was, however, somewhat premature. At the first proof, three guns exploded; in fact, General Demidov—now back in St. Petersburg after his assignment at Konchezersk and in charge at the proof—used the occasion to recommend additional safety precautions for those present against flying fragments of Scottish metal.[51] Carron had overlooked the extent to which the Russian proof was severer than that practised at Woolwich: not only was stronger gunpowder used, but two balls instead of one. 'We apprehend', wrote Gascoigne, 'that exclusive of the greater Weight and Strength of the Russian powder, the Severity of the prooff is Increased by the Addition of one Ball in a Ratio of four to one'—a quite unnecessary test, he asserted, especially if (as at Woolwich) minimum weight was an important consideration in gun manufacture.

The object of our Board of Ordnance is, to procure, as far as is consistent with perfect Security, the Lightest and most manageable Guns, and . . . the old modells of their Artillery, were reduced to the plan of our Guns. It is difficult to Assign any good Reason for the Extraordinary Prooff required at Cronstadt, unless the Russian Admiralty are Indifferent about the Weight of their Guns. On this principle we could adapt Guns to any Degree of prooff.

Carron wanted Thompson, Peters to persuade the Russians that the Woolwich proof was adequate. At the same time they requested information on a further proposed order for 2,000 tons of cannon for the following year, which the company was obviously anxious to secure.[52]

The Russian proof-masters also found fault, initially, with the calibre of the Scottish guns. They took exception as well to an increase in weight beyond the specifications of the contract. Carron explained this as a mistake in the specification: a shrunken wooden pattern had been

---

[50] Carron Papers, GD 58/1/12, ff. 70–1, Gascoigne to Knowles, 4 June 1772. This is a letter written to a stranger, and there is no direct evidence to link Knowles with the Carron contract. Clendenning's statement (op. cit. (n. 3), 44) that Knowles ordered guns from Carron evidently relates to a request from Knowles to Catherine in April 1772 that 990 guns should be cast (where unspecified) for the southern fleet. Catherine rejected this: 'il me seroit impossible de faire fondre et de vous envoyer au bout de quelques mois 990 Canons et Licornes dont vous dites avoir besoin . . ., nous n'avons gueres fondu je pense autant de Canons dans deux Guerres consecutives que nous avons eu.' (Knowles Papers, ff. 17ᵛ, 21, Knowles to Catherine, 17 Apr. 1772, Catherine to Knowles, 11 June 1772.)

[51] MIRF xii, 98–9, CM 26 June 1772.

[52] Carron Papers, GD 58/1/12, ff. 117–18, Gascoigne to Thompson, Peters (St. Petersburg office), 3 Aug. 1772; f. 122, W. Lyons to Thompson, Peters (St. Petersburg office), 7 Aug. 1772. The new lighter designs mentioned by Gascoigne might be the new British guns considered by the Russian Admiralty in 1769–71, see MIRF xi, 523, 753. In fact, the Scottish 32-pounder guns were lighter than the Russian 30-pounders, see MIRF xii, 103, CM 27 July 1772.

used in casting the cannon whose weight had formed the basis of their offer. But the company was unwilling to reduce the weight of the guns they were supplying without some concession on the severity of the proof.[53]

During the 1772 season Carron shipped out 337 cannon to Cronstadt. The last consignment of 70 pieces was delayed at Helsingör by the late season; but for the 267 guns proved by the Russian Admiralty the rejection rate, although better than that of the Russian foundries, was still high—only 190 were accepted.[54] In December, Gascoigne wrote to Thompson, Peters in St. Petersburg:

We unfortunately undertook too much within the Limited time when we engaged to deliver 1000 Tons at Petersburgh in six mo[s], and have suffered severely by precipitating matters so as to execute the order within the time. Our Honour is now engaged, and we are more than ever solicitous to be permitted to send some guns in the next summer, which we consent to risque against Cannon of any other Foundry in Europe and if they do not answer the utmost Wishes and Expectations of the Russian Admiralty, we do not desire Sixpence for them.[55]

To Thompson, Peters's London office he added:

We owe it . . . to them [the firm's St. Petersburg branch] and to ourselves to Remove the Disgrace and to this we conceive you may be instrumental. The object then of this Letter is, to request your application to His Excellency [the Russian Ambassador] to permit us to send out in the Spring, as many 32 p[rs] as will Compleat the order, & these we consent to be tried against any Guns in Russia or in any manner that the Russian Admiralty may think proper.[56]

This application gained Carron's objective: in 1773 the company sent out a further 191 guns.[57] But these cannon fared no better than the earlier ones, and in August Gascoigne again had to make his apologies:

We are truly sorry to find the last two Proofs have been so unsuccessful, and the more so as we had a better opinion of the Paisleys Cargo than we find it deserved. Your Remarks on the Metal is [sic] just it contains too much Phlogiston, and is in the Workmens language too Rich. We did not till very

[53] *MIRF* xii, 102–3, CM 13, 23, 27 July 1772. Knowles and Demidov declared that the difference in calibre was not crucial, and these guns were accepted. Carron Papers, GD 58/1/12, f. 133, W. Lyons to Thompson, Peters (St. Petersburg office), 19 Aug. 1772; f. 452, Gascoigne to Thompson, Peters (St. Petersburg office), 5 Apr. 1773.

[54] Carron Papers, GD 58/6/9, Invoice book, 1772–5(i), ff. 15, 25, 35, 43, 52: total cost £10,675. 5s. 5d. On the delay at Helsingör and proof of the guns, see Carron Papers, GD 58/1/12, f. 314, Gascoigne to N. Fenwick, Elsineur, 8 Jan. 1773, and *MIRF* xii, 109, 118, 122, CM 25 Aug., 8 Oct., 20 Nov. 1772.

[55] Carron Papers, GD 58/1/12, ff. 267–8, 7 Dec. 1772.

[56] Ibid., f. 296, 28 Dec. 1772. The weight of cannon already sent was nearly 1,000 tons. Carron evidently wished to complete 1,000 tons of acceptable guns.

[57] Ibid., GD 58/6/9, Invoice book, 1772–5(i), ff. 114, 134, 153, invoices totalling £5,611. 7s. 10d.

lately discover this, which we have Corrected to our Satisfaction, but the discovery comes too late to avail ourselves of it for the Russian guns. [58]

Although Carron Company were thus able to complete the order of 1772, their repeatedly expressed hopes of further contracts from Russia were not fulfilled. Even their request for 'Permission to send one Cargo of Thirty or Forty pieces in the Spring to regain the Character of the [Carron] Works, and these at any price',[59] fell on deaf ears. The situation in Russia was no longer as critical as it had been in 1772 and, in fact, the Russian Admiralty was having difficulty in providing gun-carriages and shot for the new artillery supplied both by Carron and by the Batashev foundries: so much so that instead of 30-pounders they decided in March 1773 to arm their 66-gun ships for the year's campaign with old 24-pounders for which carriages and shot were readily available.[60] The gradual success of the Batashev works, and the commissioning in 1774 of the new Aleksandrovsk foundry under A. S. Yartsov raised Russia's own home production capacity (even though the Aleksandrovsk works in its turn had many teething troubles, as will be seen). In 1772 or 1773 Carron Company obtained a large order from the Spanish government (although this, too, caused the company a lot of problems); and the Carronade, introduced in 1779, soon secured their reputation in the widest circles. But the Carron invoice books show no further significant dispatches of cannon to Russia until 1785.[61]

However, Carron Company's connections with Russia in the early 1770s were not limited to the supply of cannon. In 1773, at the instigation of Sir Charles Knowles, the Russian Admiralty decided to instal a steam pump at Cronstadt for the new naval dry docks there; and the order for the machine went to Carron Company. The installation took several years to complete, involving a stay of some length in Russia for numbers of Carron workmen; the pumping machinery when finally

[58] Ibid., GD 58/1/13, f. 63, Gascoigne to Thompson, Peters (St. Petersburg office), 16 Aug. 1773. Cf. f. 163, the same to the same, 13 Oct. 1773: '. . . In the first Instance we made the Guns too hard & sharp, & discovering that Error We fell into the contrary Extreme, too rich & soft, but had we been fortunate in the Execution the price was too low to Manufacture with Profit. . . .' The presence of such elements as sulphur or phosphorus in the ore critically affected the quality of metal produced. Another important factor was the carbon level: the wrong carbon content rendered gun-metal either too hard and brittle or too soft and malleable. For advice here and elsewhere on technical points I am grateful to my colleagues Dr. F. Celoria and Dr. H. Torrens.

[59] Ibid., f. 209, Gascoigne to Thompson, Peters (St. Petersburg office), 9 Nov. 1773; cf. ff. 63-4, 163-4; ibid., GD 58/1/12, f. 549 on hopes of further gun sales to Russia.

[60] *MIRF* xii, 190-1, CM 8 Mar. 1773.

[61] Carron Papers, GD 58/6/19, Invoice book, 1784-9(i), ff. 88-9, 97, 111. In 1777 and 1779 Carron sent out minor items of ordnance for Admiral Samuel Greig—also 'a Milk Cow in Calf' for Lady Greig. Ibid., GD 58/6/12, Invoice book, 1775-8(ii), ff. 229, 331; GD 58/6/14, Invoice book, 1778-81(i), f. 102; GD 58/1/18, f. 548, Gascoigne to J. Balfour, 8 Sept. 1780.

in operation worked well, and was very advanced for its time.[62] And in addition to the Cronstadt 'fire engine', Carron Company also unwittingly supplied the master cannon-founder for whom the Russian government had been looking for so long.

3

As we have seen, the search for skilled foreign workmen in this field had been protracted and quite unsuccessful; and it had become particularly urgent since the beginning of the war. Catherine wrote to Knowles, evidently in 1771: 'On se donne depuis deux ans toutes les peines possibles pour avoir un habile Fondeur de Canons de Fer, mais inutilement.'[63] Among names proposed for the job at this time was James Watt, whom John Robison recommended to Catherine 'because', he wrote to Watt, 'I was well acquainted with your knowledge in Metallurgy and Mechanics, and your intimate acquaintance with all the processes as carried on at Carron.'[64] But Watt was now too well established to be tempted. It was, however, finally in Britain that the Russian government found what it was looking for.

British law at this time forbade, of course, both foreign recruitment of British workmen, and the export of British industrial machinery. International competition in industry was intense and direct: entrepreneurs of all European countries were as eager to discover and purloin their rivals' secrets as they were to protect their own, and governments supported these attitudes. In 1770, for example, a Swiss firm wrote to Matthew Boulton, whose Soho ironworks in Birmingham were famous throughout Europe:

> We know you are not unacquainted with the establishment of our hardware factory; no less are we acquainted with the bonds you wish to place upon it. You fulfilled, Sir, the duty of a good citizen in persecuting us, and when you wished to do us the most harm, we considered you moved by patriotic zeal rather than ill will. . . . But at the same time we hope that after thus having done you justice, your own sense of what is fair will do us the grace of rendering what is just in its turn. Our reasons for building our factory were exactly those which made you oppose it, patriotic zeal. . . .[65]

Boulton added his voice to the chorus of complaint made by Britain's leading iron-masters on the subject of worker emigration in the 1760s[66]

---

[62] Clendenning, op. cit. (n. 3), 45–6 and references; Cross, 'Samuel Greig' (n. 3), 256–7; E. Robinson, 'The Transference of British Technology to Russia: a Preliminary Enquiry', *Great Britain and her World, 1750–1914: Essays in Honour of W. O. Henderson*, ed. B. Ratcliffe (Manchester, 1975), 9–10; Carron Letter Books, GD 58/1/13, 14, 15 *passim*.

[63] Knowles Papers, f. 5.　　　　　[64] Robinson, op. cit. (n. 62), 7.

[65] E. Robinson, 'The International Exchange of Men and Machines, 1750–1800', in: A. Musson and E. Robinson, *Science and Technology in the Industrial Revolution* (Manchester, 1969), 217.

[66] See, for example, *Calendar of Home Office Papers, 1760–5* (1878), 480, 571–2, 601, 605–6, 620; ibid. *1766–9* (1879), 61, 68–9.

—even though at one point he seems to have considered favourably the prospect of transferring his own enterprise to Sweden[67]—and in general the British authorities were watchful over both foreign visitors to Britain and workers leaving the country. There were legal difficulties for similar reasons over the work-force for the Carron pumping engine at Cronstadt.[68]

In these circumstances Russian diplomats seeking workers for Russia had to move with caution. The two men whom Musin-Pushkin finally engaged, Adam Ramage and Joseph Powell, were Carron Company employees. According to their own later account, they were first approached by John Burn or Burns, a Falkirk merchant, and engaged ostensibly to work for 'merchants in His Majesty's Dominions in America'. When they met the supposed merchants in London, these turned out to be the later Russian consul, Alexander Baxter, and Musin-Pushkin himself, with whom both men then signed a contract forthwith to go to Russia.[69] The terms of the contracts, dated 24 May 1771, stipulated that both men were to serve as 'Master Ironfounder or Moulder' in any Russian foundry, for six years in the first instance; though they could be dismissed at the end of one year if they should prove inexpert. Musin-Pushkin promised full travel expenses from Scotland to Russia and back again; a free house and firing; and a salary of £100, or 500 roubles, starting on their arrival in St. Petersburg. Each man promised to instruct at least one apprentice, with a bounty of 50 roubles for each apprentice so trained.[70]

Powell and Ramage left London shortly after completion of their contract, reaching St. Petersburg at the end of June. They put up at the 'English House' of Alexander Frazer; and although a private house was rented for them, they stayed on at Frazer's *traktir* in expectation of early departure to their new place of work.[71] But contrary to their assumptions, their departure from St. Petersburg was delayed. Summer turned to autumn, and the Admiralty showed no inclination

[67] Robinson, op. cit. (n. 65), 224–7.

[68] P. Zabarinsky, 'Pervye "ognevye" mashiny v Kronshtadtskom portu', *Trudy Instituta istorii nauki i tekhniki*, Seriya II, vyp. 7 (M.–L., 1936), 52.

[69] PRO S.P. 91/88, ff. 283–90, Cathcart to Suffolk, St. Petersburg, 25 Nov./6 Dec. 1771, enclosing a copy of Ramage's contract, signed by Musin-Pushkin. Further copies, signed by Powell and Ramage and witnessed by Mikhail Tatishchev, are in Tsentral'nyi gosudarstvennyi arkhiv drevnikh aktov, Moscow (TsGADA), *fond* 271 (College of Mines), *kn.* 2065, *delo* 19, 'Ob otpravlenii aglinskikh masterov Dzhozef Povelya i Radmezha [*sic*] na lipetskie zavody i o uchinenii vovsem s nimi posile kontraktov, raschetov', *listy* 718–19.

[70] Ibid. Both men made provision for their families, who remained in Scotland. Ramage proposed to allow his wife £20, and Powell his £30, annually, to be paid by quarterly instalments through Burns. Irregular payments of this money later caused Musin-Pushkin trouble with the wives (ibid., *list* 858r–v, Musin-Pushkin to Soimonov, 1/12 Mar. 1779). Burns's expenses 'incurred in the seeking out, entertaining and engaging of two master-founders and blacksmiths' were £3, and his fee for recruitment was £500 (ibid., *listy* 722, 911r–v).

[71] Ibid., *listy* 721–4, I. Chernyshev to A. A. Vyazemsky, 7 Oct. 1771, and enclosures.

to assign them to a post in a state foundry, or to honour the other articles of their contract. Finally, their credit ran out and they turned in desperation to the British Ambassador, Lord Cathcart.[72] His intervention with N. I. Panin at last produced a response: at the end of October an Imperial decree to the College of Mines directed that Powell and Ramage should be sent to the Lipetsk works, to take charge of the casting of cannon there, and the College was enjoined to observe exactly all the points of their contracts.[73] As companion and interpreter they were given a student just returned from England, Semen Matveevsky, who received with his appointment the rank of Collegiate Interpreter, and who stayed with them until the expiry of their contract.[74] Accompanied by Matveevsky and two soldiers, the two founders travelled to Lipetsk, carefully skirting Moscow, which was still in the grip of the plague of 1771.[75]

The six-year term of service at Lipetsk proved a harsh experience for Ramage and Powell. There were difficulties with the works management and health problems. Ramage in fact died before expiry of his contract, in 1775,[76] and by the end in 1777 Powell was very ill, 'his person', in the words of the British Consul-General Walter Shairp, 'being decayed and infirm'.[77] Powell had satisfied the College of Mines by his work; but in doing so he had deprived himself of his job. The College informed him that as he had satisfactorily trained two apprentices, who could now continue the work without him, he was no longer required at Lipetsk.[78]

Powell's initial reaction was to desire to return to Scotland. But his affairs at Lipetsk had become somewhat involved, and he was dissatisfied with the settlement of matters between him and the College of Mines. His claims and pretensions dragged on, and he incurred considerable debts living the while in an inn in St. Petersburg.[79] His principal claim against the College was that he had trained far more than the two apprentices for whom he had received payment: to the

---

[72] PRO, S.P. 91/88, ff. 283–6. Cathcart's dispatch deals generally with the problems of specialist personnel recruited by Musin-Pushkin, several of whom experienced difficulties. Another case, whose contract is also appended here, was the instrument-maker Francis Morgan.

[73] TsGADA, *fond* 271, *kn.* 2065, *list* 717, decree of 1 Nov. 1771. This states that Powell and Ramage had been 'engaged by Our will from London especially for those works', but there is no other evidence that the initial request to Musin-Pushkin was dictated for Lipetsk alone. Lipetsk came under the College of Mines, while the original contracts appear to have been made under the Admiralty, which met the men's expenses in St. Petersburg.

[74] Ibid., *list* 725. On Matveevsky, see A. G. Cross, 'Russian Students in Eighteenth-century Oxford (1766–76)', *Journal of European Studies*, v (1975), 91–110.

[75] TsGADA, *fond* 271, *kn.* 2065, *list* 743, Enquiry from College of Mines to Yamskaya kantselyariya on alternative routes, n.d.

[76] Ibid., *list* 746. Ramage died at Lipetsk on 16 Oct.

[77] Ibid., *list* 822[r–v], Shairp to College of Mines, 28 Oct. 1777.

[78] Ibid., *listy* 806, 825.   [79] Ibid., *listy* 800, 823.

College he claimed fifty, to Shairp, whose help he sought to enlist with mediocre success, forty-three.[80] Powell's pretensions in the matter of the apprentices were finally rejected in April 1778: payment was limited to the sums already made over for the two apprentices recognized by the College, Yakov Seleznev and Petr Chekmenev.[81]

A month before this final decision Powell sent a further petition to the College. Instead of returning home, as he had previously intended, he now wished, he said, to show the government a new and unknown method of casting cannon, which consisted in 'bringing the iron to the finest quality', before casting. In return he asked that his contract should be renewed at an increased salary of 600 roubles; and he later added as an afterthought the request that the College should 'reward him with a rank' (*nagradit' menya chinom*) as well.[82]

At about the time that Powell submitted his petition, the College had received a complaint about the casting of cannon at the Aleksandrovsk foundry at Petrozavodsk. According to the petitioner, *nakhodyashchiisya na olonetskikh petrovskikh zavodakh podmaster'e petr chekmenev*, the poor quality of the cannon being produced there was a reflection of the low-grade ore being used.[83] Powell's proposal fitted neatly with the apparent needs of the Onega works; and the College decided that he should be sent north to try out his new method. A three-month period was allowed for trials, during which Powell was to cast cannon from ore of his own preparing. If he substantiated his claims, the College promised to take him back into service with a new contract, and he was to have full salary and free accommodation during the trials.[84]

The tale of Powell's time at Petrozavodsk was first published in 1949 by O. I. Vasil'evskaya, in an article entitled 'Angliiskii prokhodimets Poul' i russkie pushechnye mastera na Aleksandrovskom zavode', and is summarized by Ya. Balagurov in his history of the Olonets complex.[85] The new Aleksandrovsk foundry, built between 1772 and 1774 under the direction of Soimonov and the distinguished engineer A. S. Yartsov, was a modern enterprise, of a quality different from the relics of Peter the Great's time with which the government had been trying to work in the area hitherto. But Yartsov, although a skilled metallurgist, had no experience in cannon-founding; and a major difficulty at the outset

---

[80] Ibid., *listy* 822–3.

[81] Ibid., *listy* 828–30ᵛ, College of Mines to Powell, 25 Apr. 1778.

[82] Ibid., *listy* 823, 827, Powell to College of Mines, Mar. 1778; O. I. Vasil'evskaya, 'Angliiskii prokhodimets Poul' i russkie pushechnye mastera na Aleksandrovskom zavode', *Na rubezhe* (Petrozavodsk), 1949, no. 4, p. 95.

[83] TsGADA, *fond* 271, *kn.* 2065, *list* 824, 21 Mar. 1778; Vasil'evskaya, loc. cit. (n. 82).

[84] TsGADA, *fond* 271, *kn.* 2065, *listy* 828–30ᵛ.

[85] Vasil'evskaya, see reference n. 82; Balagurov, *Olonetskie gornye zavody* (n. 6), 46–7. Balagurov quotes another article by Vasil'evskaya: 'Iz istorii pervykh let Aleksandrovskogo (nyne Onezhskogo) zavoda', *Izvestiya Karel'skogo filiala Akademii nauk SSSR*, 1949 no. 3.

was the continuing lack of a skilled work-force in the region. Yartsov succeeded in retrieving from the Urals some former Olonets workers who had been drafted there, including the veteran founder Fedor Shamarin, who arrived in 1773 before the commissioning of the new plant and became the instructor not only of the other workers but of Yartsov himself.[86] A British specialist, Bowie, sent to Yartsov by the College of Mines in October 1774, admitted that he had no skill in preparing the metal for casting, and Yartsov scornfully rejected him as a novice whose high salary would be better paid to 'the poor Russians'.[87] Much of the trained labour for the new foundry came at this stage in fact from Lipetsk. The first group, headed by 'the skilled journeyman [*khoroshii podmaster'e*] Yakov Seleznev', reached Petrozavodsk in January 1774, shortly before the works began operation; two more groups followed later in 1774. None the less, the Aleksandrovsk works' early cannon were very imperfect: of 606 guns cast in the years 1775–7 only 193 passed inspection and proof; and the death of Fedor Shamarin in 1776 was a serious loss.[88]

In the spring of the same year, 1776, there arrived another group of Lipetsk workers, headed by Petr Chekmenev. Chekmenev had worked for many years at Lipetsk, and already in the 1760s was considered a skilled cannon-founder. Cannon cast by him in 1773 'in the English manner', but without assistance, had also been attested as 'clean and without cracks, and withstood the official proof':[89] Powell's pupil, it would seem, had fully justified his teacher. With Chekmenev's arrival, both the Lipetsk founders for whose training Powell had received official credit were working at Petrozavodsk.

However, with the arrival of the new group under Chekmenev, according to documents quoted by Vasil'evskaya, the efficiency of the work-force was seen to decline. 'In the work of the Lipetsk craftsmen there began to be noticed . . . hour by hour . . . the greatest laziness and lack of zeal for their duties, and the cannon began to come out with more cracks than before his arrival.'[90] Chekmenev was also soon asserting that the local ore was unsuited to the making of cannon; and, again according to Vasil'evskaya, in his attempts to disrupt cannon production he had the support of the artillery inspector at the works, Skryabin. Skryabin rejected any gun with the slightest defect, and used particularly severe proving methods.[91]

Chekmenev's own attempts at casting gave poor results, despite exhortation and then fines imposed by the administration. Finally, in March 1778, he disappeared from Petrozavodsk. He had gone to St.

[86] Balagurov, *Olonetskie gornye zavody* (n. 6), 44.
[87] Ibid.   [88] Ibid. 45, 105–6.   [89] Ibid. 45–6.
[90] Vasil'evskaya, 'Angliiskii prokhodimets Poul'' (n. 82), 94.
[91] Balagurov, *Olonetskie gornye zavody* (n. 6), 46, quoting Vasil'evskaya, 'Iz istorii . . .' (n. 85).

Petersburg, where he laid with the College of Mines the complaint already mentioned. In the College's file on Powell, the latter's March petition immediately precedes an extract from Chekmenev's report.[92]

After delay caused by difficulties in finding an interpreter, Powell set out in June 1778 for Lake Onega. Yartsov meanwhile was instructed to release Chekmenev's family, who had been detained at Petrozavodsk, and send them on to St. Petersburg.[93] At the Aleksandrovsk works, Powell received every assistance, as ordered by the College of Mines, except in one point: instead of the former Lipetsk foundry-workers, whom he had asked for by name, he was given Olonets-trained assistants. These could find nothing new in the methods used by Powell; and the results of the trials were unfavourable to him. The iron prepared under his direction turned out worse, it was reported, than that usually obtained from the Olonets ore; and of the eight cannon which he cast, the works office declared four unfit for proof and the other four 'doubtful'—the actual proof was to take place in St. Petersburg.[94]

To check on Powell's proceedings, Yartsov ordered a second trial, smelting and casting from the same ore, to be carried out separately by Olonets- and Lipetsk-trained workmen, but without Powell's participation. The results of the Olonets-trained Ustinov, who had never cast cannon before, easily surpassed those of the Lipetsk worker Milovanov; in fact the poor quality of Milovanov's guns caused astonishment, since he was experienced and had previously cast good cannon. Under close cross-questioning Milovanov admitted that at Powell's suggestion he had added lead to the molten iron while it was cooling, which had the effect of producing roughness and cracks in the finished guns. During the investigation carried out by the works administration, evidence came out which suggested that Chekmenev had followed a similar practice.[95]

Yartsov sent samples of Powell's iron to St. Petersburg, with a scathing report. Perhaps, he said, Powell 'wished with someone else's connivance to bring this works and all previous procedures here into disrepute. Afterwards, and asking large sums ostensibly for putting things right, he would take over the casting of ordnance, by some clever means, using simpletons, on exactly the same basis as existed here previously.' At all events, Yartsov refused to have anything more to do with Powell.[96]

It is difficult to reach a balanced assessment of this episode on the limited evidence available. Powell was evidently quite unsuccessful at Petrozavodsk, and equally evidently something conspiratorial was

[92] TsGADA, fond 271, kn. 2065, listy 834-6, cf. Vasil'evskaya, 'Angliiskii prokhodimets Poul'' (n. 82), 95.   [93] Ibid.

[94] Ibid.; Balagurov, Olonetskie gornye zavody (n. 6), 47.

[95] Vasil'evskaya, loc. cit. (n. 92); Balagurov, loc. cit. (n. 94).

[96] Vasil'evskaya, 'Angliiskii prokhodimets Poul'' (n. 82), 98.

involved. But it is hard to see what Powell could hope to gain by deliberately producing bad results; and if he thought he had some special method, it would be natural enough in the context of the time for him to try to keep it from the Olonets personnel. Furthermore, he had no means of familiarizing himself directly with all the qualities of the Olonets ore (the geology of the region is very different from that around Lipetsk); and the use of additives in metal preparation is not in itself unusual. One may therefore perhaps think as much in terms of miscalculation as of villainy. And Vasil'evskaya and Balagurov in any case approach the question of foreign technicians in a somewhat xenophobic spirit: their foreigners tend to appear as swindler, ignoramus, spy, or wrecker. The point of the incident, for Vasil'evskaya, lay not only in the fact that the Russian government undervalued the skills of its native workmen—which was often true; with further investigation, she thought, 'it will probably also be proved that the causes of a series of difficulties and deficiencies in the operation of the Aleksandrovsk works . . . as of many other Russian works at that time, sometimes had roots which went beyond the boundaries of our country'.[97]

Powell's work at Lipetsk seems to have been adequate; and he had evidently won the loyalty of the men with whom he worked there, or at least some authority over them. It may be, too, that the Lipetsk men were influenced by the harsh conditions they found at the new Olonets plant: initially some even had to sell clothing to feed themselves, and apparently in an attempt to have themselves removed from the plant, claimed that they did not know the work required.[98] Nor did Powell's failure at the Aleksandrovsk works damage him in the eyes of the College of Mines—a fact from which Vasil'evskaya draws further ammunition, with objections of patronage and protection.[99] Powell returned to St. Petersburg in August 1778, ahead of Yartsov's report, and was at once reappointed on a two-year contract to Lipetsk, on rather better terms than before—in particular he was to have sole charge over the workers under him. The College made the appointment because Lipetsk had an urgent order for cannon for the Dnieper flotilla, to be completed in May or June 1779, and 'it is very necessary to have there a sufficiently knowledgeable master-founder'.[100]

Powell stayed at Lipetsk for three years, not two, and evidently succeeded in retaining the confidence of the College of Mines. In 1781 his future again came up for discussion. In February 1782 the College finally decided that, since both Lipetsk and the Aleksandrovsk foundry had passed under the control of their local *kazennye palaty* and cannon-

[97] Vasil'evskaya, 'Angliiskii prokhodimets Poul'' (n. 82), 98. Cf. Balagurov, *Olonetskie gornye zavody* (n. 6), 92 and note.   [98] Balagurov, *Olonetskie gornye zavody* (n. 6), 105–6.
[99] Vasil'evskaya, 'Angliiskii prokhodimets Poul'' (n. 82), 98.
[100] TsGADA, *fond* 271, *kn.* 2065, *listy* 838, 840–2, Minutes of College Board meeting, 23 Aug. 1778.

founding at Lipetsk for the Admiralty had stopped for the time being, the Admiralty might itself find employment for Powell, as a man 'sufficiently proven in his art and having shown no little usefulness in the introduction into Russia of a new and completely unknown method for the founding of cannon'.[101] This description seems rather extraordinary after the Olonets affair, and it is not clear what might have justified it in Powell's work at Lipetsk, unless the 'English manner' of casting demonstrated by Chekmenev in 1773 was something new. None the less, the Admiralty College took Powell on, and appointed him to the Izhora iron-works near St. Petersburg.[102] He is mentioned in the official histories of the plant, working in 1785 as head of the *liteinyi tsekh*;[103] and presumably he continued working there until his death four years later. He died on 13 April 1789, aged about 54, and was buried in St. Petersburg two days later.[104]

Powell's career is in general not untypical for foreign workers in eighteenth-century Russia, and illustrates some of the problems attaching to Russia's economic development at the time. There seems to be no trace of him in the available records of Carron Company, so that one cannot assess his standing or training in Scotland; and the sometimes contradictory evidence on his work in Russia precludes great accuracy there either. He seems to have been competent in at least the standard skills of his trade; he would also appear to have been a somewhat difficult person to deal with, and he had an eye to the main chance. Russian officials frequently made the point that the best foreign workmen either asked too much or were too well placed at home to wish to move[105]—which perhaps does not say much for Powell. But the migration of quite good workers was not at all uncommon in contemporary Europe. And the difficulty of attracting the best certainly did not deter the Russian authorities, who persisted in this practice well beyond the eighteenth century. In fact, in this respect Russia was very much in line with other industrial nations of the time. While Chernyshev, Musin-Pushkin, and other diplomats hunted cannon-founders in Britain, Sweden, and Saxony, the Swedes themselves were engaging British metal-workers, and British employers were seeking different skills which were well developed in other countries, for instance silversmiths and goldsmiths from France.[106] In 1769 the Royal Foundry at Woolwich was placed under the direction of Dutch founders; and despite the

---

[101] Ibid., *list* 902[r-v], Minutes of meeting, 18 Feb. 1782.

[102] Ibid., *list* 912, Admiralty College to College of Mines, 30 Jan. 1784.

[103] G. Gorodkov, *Admiral'teiskie Izhorskie zavody. Kratkii istoricheskii ocherk* (Spb., 1903), 31; S. Zav'yalov, *Istoriya Izhorskogo zavoda*, i (M., 1934), 28.

[104] Guildhall Library, London, Guildhall MS. 11192B, Register of the British Church in St. Petersburg, f. 111. I am indebted to Dr. A. G. Cross for this reference.

[105] Cf. the case of Watt, above, p. 62, and I. Chernyshev's remarks, *MIRF* xi, 524–5, CM 16 Dec. 1769; also Gol'denberg, *Soimonov* (n. 24), 32 (Soimonov's own comments).

[106] Robinson, 'International Exchange' (n. 65), *passim*.

success of British iron-masters in developing metal-boring techniques, it was apparently the work of the Verbruggens at Woolwich which led in 1775 to the official ruling that only cannon bored from solid castings would be accepted in future by the British Board of Ordnance.[107]

Carron's problems with cannon production in the early 1770s put the Russian difficulties of 1769–71 likewise in proper perspective. The chemistry of ferrous metallurgy at this stage was still developing. And apart from the inadequacy of contemporary understanding of the actual chemical processes involved, technical application of available knowledge was not always systematic. Carron Company, for example, built an assay furnace only in 1774, when their difficulties at Woolwich and Cronstadt had forced it upon them.[108]

More complex and difficult was the question of native skilled labour and Russian government attitudes towards it. While evidently well-informed on technical developments in other countries, and anxious to make use of them, the Russian authorities were at this time unable to develop sufficient reservoirs of reliable or skilled labour, or an administrative system for industry sufficiently flexible or responsive to function smoothly. The peasants frequently enrolled at state works were an inefficient labour force; and they were often inefficiently used—at the Kamenskii foundry in 1767, for example, cannon-casting came to a halt when the works administration insisted on the work-force carrying out its obligation to cut hay.[109] And conditions of life were such as to cause much unrest and consequent loss of production. Besides the Kizhi rising of 1769–71, which stopped all work at the Olonets complex, and similar smaller-scale disorders at Lipetsk at about the same time,[110] unrest was endemic in the Urals throughout the 1760s and 1770s. Such unrest involved both the unskilled labour force and the skilled workmen on the shop floor. At the same time, the training systems introduced under Peter I and extended during the eighteenth century were insufficient at this stage to maintain skills in depth.

The necessity of using foreign specialists compounded these difficulties. From Peter's time such people were expected both to make their own contribution and to train apprentices who would form a nucleus of skilled native Russian cadres. But some foreigners (as already indicated) did not match Russian expectations, either being insufficiently skilled themselves, or even deliberately withholding their skills from Russian apprentices on patriotic grounds, such as those cited above from the Boulton papers. Powell, who fulfilled his contract to train apprentices, shows up well on this score. But in other cases government

[107] Ffoulkes, *Gun-founders* (n. 46), 65–7.   [108] Campbell, *Carron Company* (n. 46), 87.
[109] *MIRF* xi, 311, CM 2 Oct. 1767.
[110] Cf. Semevsky, op. cit. (n. 22), i, 487–96; Martynov, Zhdanov, loc. cit. (n. 6), quoting V. A. Garanichev, 'Volneniya rabotnykh lyudei na Lipskikh zavodakh kn. Repnina v 60-kh gg. XVIII v.', *Uchenye zapiski Smolenskogo pedagogicheskogo instituta*, ii (1953).

concern with and reliance on foreign expertise could produce a vicious circle, the replacement of foreigners with more foreigners, or the neglect of native potential where it did exist. In this respect Vasil'evskaya's praise for the unsung Russian workmen at Petrozavodsk is not without justification.[111] On the other hand, specialists from abroad who were both competent and conscientious could be frustrated by the conditions under which they had to work.

Failures of organization and management in this particular area form part of the wider problems of Russian administration generally. In the case of Ramage and Powell, communication and co-ordination within the government seem to have broken down completely. Engaged on the highest authority, as a matter of urgency, after several years of unsuccessful search in different countries, and having emigrated illegally, they were reduced to appealing to their own country's ambassador, after fruitless applications to the College responsible for hiring them and which, at least initially, was paying to keep them idle in St. Petersburg.

Deficiencies or malice on the part of foreign specialists played, in fact, only a relatively minor part in the difficulties of technological advance in Russia in this period—although individual foreigners who held high positions in government service could sometimes influence affairs decisively, both for good and ill. In the field of naval artillery with which we are concerned, it was one such foreigner who was to make perhaps the most notable single contribution in this period. The progress achieved by the Russian foundries in the 1770s did not entirely resolve the problems laid bare in the 1760s; and even twenty-five years later, in the aftermath of the second Turkish war, members of the government could still be found expressing sentiments similar to those of Catherine during the first. Platon Zubov wrote to Admiral N. Mordvinov in 1795 concerning the lack of cannon for southern defence requirements:

If we specify that all the galley fleet's artillery shall be of brass, a fearful sum of money will be necessary, and we shall not fulfil the requirement in many years. . . . If of iron, then the Siberian [sc. Urals] and Batashev foundries will cast cannon more dangerous to our own forces than to the enemy.

The Olonets complex had by this time been radically reorganized. But it was too far away, and the solution (Zubov said) lay in a completely new foundry, to be set up on the southern river Lugan'.[112] The architect of this project was also the director of the Olonets development, Charles Gascoigne, Powell's former employer at Carron who had presided over

---

[111] Vasil'evskaya, 'Angliiskii prokhodimets Poul'' (n. 82), 98–9.
[112] *Arkhiv grafov Mordvinovykh*, i (Spb., 1901), 609, no. 473, 24 Apr. 1795. How far Zubov's opinion was authoritative is another matter.

the Company's Russian fiasco of 1772–3 and the subsequent establishment of its position in the later 1770s, and who was very much an 'originator or entrepreneur' of the kind sought by I. Chernyshev in 1769.[113] At about the time when Powell was ending his Russian service, in 1786, Gascoigne emigrated to Russia himself, bringing with him men, machinery, and know-how. With these he made a brilliant career, remaining in Russia until his death in 1806. A proper account and assessment of his work there remains to be written.

[113] Cf. p. 56 above. On Gascoigne, see among numerous references *Russkii biograficheskii slovar'*, vol. Gaag–Gerbel' (M., 1914), 258–9; A. G. Cross, 'The British in Catherine's Russia: a Preliminary Survey', *The Eighteenth Century in Russia*, ed. J. Garrard (Oxford, 1973), 260–1; Robinson, 'The Transference of British Technology' (n. 62), especially pp. 8–10, 14–15; Balagurov, *Olonetskie gornye zavody* (n. 6), *passim*.

Adam Czartoryski: an Advocate of Slavonic Solidarity at the Congress of Vienna

By W. H. ZAWADZKI

1

IT is generally accepted by modern historians that, although his capacity was only semi-official, Prince Adam Jerzy Czartoryski was Emperor Alexander I's chief adviser on the Polish issue at the Congress of Vienna, and played a central role in the establishment of the so-called 'Congress' Kingdom of Poland. What is less widely appreciated is that, in addition to his concern for Poland at the Congress, Czartoryski also appealed to Alexander to encourage greater cultural and political solidarity among the Slavs under Russian leadership.[1] Documentary evidence of this less known, yet important, aspect of Czartoryski's political activities in 1814–15 exists among his papers in the Public Archive in the Czartoryski Library in Cracow in the form of a hitherto unpublished memorandum in French entitled 'Remarques justificatives d'un Projet qui garantit la Nationalité aux Provinces Polonaises de différentes Dominations'. The document has been preserved in a volume of manuscripts relating to diplomatic activities at the Congress of Vienna (Czart. MS. 5238, pp. 153–64) and is reproduced in its entirety below.[2]

The document is not in Czartoryski's hand, nor is it signed; it is a neatly written copy probably made by a secretary.[3] It is undated, but

[1] This aspect of Czartoryski's activities at the Congress is not mentioned at all in such important and relevant works whose authors have used the Czartoryski archive as M. Handelsman, *Adam Czartoryski* (Warsaw, 1949); M. Kukiel, *Czartoryski and European Unity, 1770–1861* (Princeton, 1955); L. Dębicki, *Puławy (1762–1830). Monografia z życia towarzyskiego, politycznego i literackiego na podstawie archiwum ks. Czartoryskich w Krakowie* (Lwów, 1887–8); K. Bartoszewicz, *Utworzenie Królestwa Kongresowego* (Cracow, 1916); nor more recently P. K. Grimsted, *The Foreign Ministers of Alexander I: Political Attitudes and the Conduct of Russian Diplomacy, 1801–1825* (Berkeley—Los Angeles, 1969). There is some material about Czartoryski's hostility towards Prussia and Austria in 1814 in E. Wawrzkowicz, *Anglia a sprawa polska, 1813–1815* (Cracow—Warsaw, 1919), 117–18, 453.

[2] In all quotations from the Czartoryski MSS. the spelling of the original is retained. For further information about the value of the Czartoryski Archive for this period see W. H. Zawadzki, 'The Czartoryski Archive: an Important Source for the History of Russia and Poland in the Reign of Alexander I', *Canadian-American Slavic Studies*, ix (1975), 472–80.

[3] The same unidentified person made a copy of Freiherr Heinrich vom und zum Stein's memorandum on Poland to Alexander I of 12 Oct. 1814, which is kept in the same volume of documents: Czart. MS. 5238, pp. 10–13. Stein argued against a Polish kingdom under Alexander I.

its contents, as will be shown, unmistakably connect it with Czartoryski and the Congress of Vienna. The opinions expressed in it fit in well with Czartoryski's political ideas at that time: the document is extremely enthusiastic about Alexander I's involvement in the Polish Question and about the Russo-Polish *rapprochement* of 1814–15 (pp. 153–5 and *passim*); it has a high moral tone and advocates the need for great powers, and for Russia in particular, to base their policies on criteria of morality, truth, and eternal justice (pp. 156–8); it attaches great importance to enlightened social, intellectual, and political progress (pp. 154–6, 163–4); it expresses a deep distrust of and hostility towards German influence in Poland and among the Slavs in general (pp. 159–61); it appeals for greater unity among the Slavs, indicates an important role for the Poles in this context, and favours overall Russian leadership of the Slavs (pp. 158–60, 163–4); and it also expresses deep regret at the continued partition of Poland and speaks of eventual full Polish reunification under Russian auspices (pp. 155, 161–3).

Czartoryski's authorship is also indicated by the specific recommendations made in the document, which clearly reveal an intimate acquaintance with the formulation of Russian policy on the Polish issue at the Congress: it appeals for the establishment of similar constitutional principles in all parts of divided Poland, for unhampered commercial and personal movement across the borders, for the preservation of the Polish language and institutions, especially to check the danger of Germanization (pp. 155–6); and it specifically calls for guarantees of Polish nationality to be included in the final treaty (p. 163).

As will be seen, all these elements were an integral part of Czartoryski's political outlook and activity not only in this period but also, in many instances, in the early years of Alexander's reign, when Czartoryski was his foreign minister.

The document indicates that Czartoryski was to regard the Polish settlement of 1815 as a regrettable and temporary compromise, and that his ultimate objective was the reunification of pre-partition Poland. Czartoryski proposed arrangements for Prussian and Austrian Poland that would preserve 'l'unité idéale' of the Polish nation, despite the continued political division of the country, as a prelude to the full integration of these provinces with Alexander I's Polish kingdom. Castlereagh's and Metternich's misgivings, therefore, about possible Russian intervention in Austrian and Prussian Poland were not without justification.

The document also illustrates the bizarre mixture of arguments, some morally self-righteous and others flattering to Alexander, which Czartoryski skilfully used to encourage the Emperor to persevere with his 'idée favorite'—his professed desire to restore the Polish state, in union with Russia.[4] It also shows that Czartoryski still believed that Alexander could be brought to act as a champion of Polish unity, and of reform and progress in his own Russian and Polish domains.

The specific interest of the document is that it throws additional light on Czartoryski's ideas on Slavonic solidarity, and on his hostile attitude towards the two major Germanic powers of east-central Europe. The document is not only an example of the growing interest of educated Slavs in the Slavonic-speaking populations within the borders of Prussia, Austria, and Saxony; it is also one of the earliest serious appeals in the nineteenth century by a leading Slavonic statesman for Russian-sponsored resistance to the eastward spread of German political and linguistic influence at the expense of the western Slavs. The document explicitly alludes to future radical changes in the composition of the Habsburg Empire and the Hohenzollern monarchy (p. 163).

The document does not define the details of a future political association of the Slavonic peoples—what Czartoryski vaguely termed 'le système constitutif des Peuples Slaves' (p. 163). In another context he referred to a Polish–Russian union as a prelude to a federal reorganization of the Russian Empire,[5] and suggested to Alexander I that a Russo-Polish link favourable to the Poles would serve as a model of what the southern Slavs could expect from Russia.[6] What he probably had in mind was a Russian-led federal association of Slav nations, mutually respecting each other's individual characteristics, in which the reunited Poles would play an important political and cultural role.

2

The document dates from the first months of 1815 when the special commission on Polish affairs, created on 9 January of that year, was deciding the details of the Polish settlement. The rough line of the new western frontier of Alexander's Polish domains—to which the document refers (pp. 153–5)—was reluctantly accepted in January 1815 by Austria and Britain, Prussia already having done so in November 1814. The western part of the Napoleonic Duchy of Warsaw was to pass to Prussia; Austria was to recover the right bank of the Vistula opposite Cracow, including the lucrative Wieliczka salt-mines; Cracow and Toruń (Thorn) were to become neutral and free cities; and the rest of the Duchy of Warsaw was to pass to Russia.

The commission drafted the Russo-Austrian and the Russo-Prussian

[4] *Mémoires du prince Adam Czartoryski et correspondance avec l'empereur Alexandre Ier*, ii (Paris, 1887), 250–2: Alexander I to Czartoryski, 25 Dec. 1810/6 Jan. 1811. Cf. ibid. ii, 255–78.

[5] Czart. MS. 5239, p. 87: A. Czartoryski, 'Malheurs de la Pologne depuis près de deux siècles' [1813]; ibid. p. 215: 'Note du Prince Adam Czartoryski présentée à l'Empereur Alexandre Ier à Chaumont en 1814', 7/19 Mar. 1814.

[6] Ibid. p. 216.

treaties concerning Poland, signed finally on 3 May 1815,[7] which formed the basis of the Polish settlement and which were incorporated into the Final Treaty of Vienna of 9 June 1815.[8] Although Jean Protadius Anstedt was the official Russian representative on the commission, Alexander I asked Czartoryski to direct Anstedt in his work.[9] Czartoryski tried hard to include in the final treaties guarantees for national institutions in each of the separate parts of Poland, as well as for easier trading links between all parts of historic Poland.[10] The document explicitly refers to these problems and therefore probably originates from this stage in the proceedings of the Congress. It seems to have been attached to an unidentified draft of a treaty which Czartoryski submitted to Alexander.

On the basis of the Vienna treaties a small Polish kingdom under Alexander I was created, and somewhat vague discretionary provisions were made for national Polish institutions in the remaining parts of pre-partition Poland. The treaties did not go as far as Czartoryski's ambitious proposals in the document for establishing similar constitutional arrangements in all parts of Poland, and his early disappointment was understandable.[11] However, important personal and economic advantages were secured for the landowners in all parts of pre-partition Poland, whose economic unity was nominally recognized.[12] And so, while regretting the deficiencies of the settlement, Czartoryski could console himself with the thought that it was the most realistic at the time—as he wrote to his father on 9 May 1815: 'Le mal et le bien sont toujours mêlés; en général nous serons beaucoup mieux que nous n'avons été; il faut s'ettonner du bien qui s'est fait; le mal seul était vraisemblable et facile.'[13]

Czartoryski's achievement in Vienna was limited; in addition to the actual treaty terms, developments after 1815 did not augur well either for the concept of 'l'unité idéale' of the Polish nation as outlined by

[7] Comte d'Angeberg, *Recueil des traités, conventions et actes diplomatiques concernant la Pologne* (Paris, 1862), 651–61: Russo-Austrian treaty, 3 May 1815; ibid. 662–75: Russo-Prussian treaty, 3 May 1815. Also in F. Martens, *Recueil des traités et conventions conclus par la Russie avec les puissances étrangères publié d'ordre du Ministère des Affaires Étrangères*, iii (Spb., 1876), 317–33 and 333–53 respectively.

[8] See clauses I–XIV in Martens, *Recueil* (n. 7), iii. 237–43.

[9] *Vneshnyaya politika Rossii v XIX i nachale XX veka. Dokumenty Rossiiskogo Ministerstva inostrannykh del*, Series I, viii (M., 1972), 157–62: Czartoryski's note, before 30 Dec. 1814/ 11 Jan. 1815.

[10] Cf. E. Wawrzkowicz, *Anglia* (n. 1), 459: Czartoryski to J. Bentham, 8 Feb. 1815. T. Schiemann, *Geschichte Russlands unter Kaiser Nikolaus I.* (Berlin, 1904), i, 532: Czartoryski to N. N. Novosil'tsev, 5 Mar. 1815.

[11] Cf. M. H. Weil, *Les Dessous du Congrès de Vienne d'après les documents originaux des archives du Ministère Impérial et Royal de l'Intérieur à Vienne*, ii (Paris, 1917), 518: Czartoryski to J. P. Anstedt, 29 Apr. 1815.

[12] D'Angeberg, *Recueil* (n. 7), 657–9, 668–70; Martens, *Recueil* (n. 7), iii. 320–9, 337–47.

[13] Czart. MS. Ewidencja 819, p. 112: Czartoryski to A. K. Czartoryski, 9 May 1815.

Czartoryski in the document. Despite substantial political and linguistic concessions to the Poles, fundamental differences were to remain between Alexander I's constitutional Kingdom of Poland, Prussia's Grand Duchy of Posen, Austrian Galicia, the semi-independent Republic of Cracow, and the former Lithuanian and eastern provinces of pre-partition Poland now incorporated with Russia. Social and economic differences between these areas were also to increase with time, and hopes of free trade were short-lived.

3

The idea of Slavonic solidarity is very prominent in the document. The identification of the cause of Polish reunification with the general cultural, social, and political advancement of the Slav peoples under Russian auspices appears at first glance as a ruse to lure Alexander I into defending Polish interests, and such an *arrière-pensée* was certainly present in Czartoryski's ambitious plan in 1813–15 to reunite Poland with Russian support. There were also economic considerations in his views on Slavonic solidarity: for example, his long-standing concern that Poland's landowners should have an easy access to the Baltic ports contributed to his hostility towards Prussia;[14] and one of his earlier arguments for Russian involvement in the Balkans had been the need to safeguard Russia's growing Black Sea trade.[15] Nevertheless, the sincere belief that the historic interests of Poland and Russia could be harmonized and the two nations reconciled had been a central feature of Czartoryski's political credo since the accession of Alexander I.[16] The Emperor's willingness to discuss political and even social reform, and to recognize the legitimacy of Polish aspirations for national self-government justified, in Czartoryski's eyes, such an optimistic attitude.

Another important factor which influenced Czartoryski's political views on the Slavs was the growing preoccupation of scholars and men of letters in central and eastern Europe with the distant past of the Slavs and the development of the various Slavonic languages. Influenced by the ideas of Herder, Schlözer, and others, Czech, Polish, and Russian scholars became interested in the Slavs, and by the early nineteenth century close links had developed between some of the

[14] e.g. Czart. MS. 5226, pp. 78–9, 83(a): A. Czartoryski, 'Ecrit redigé en 1803 sur le Système politique que devroit suivre la Russie'. The entire text of this document (ibid., pp. 13–138) has been published in 'Czartoryski's System for Russian Foreign Policy, 1803: a Memorandum', ed. P. K. Grimsted, *California Slavic Studies*, v (1970), 19–91. This document will henceforth be referred to as 'Système'. See also Czartoryski, *Mémoires* (n. 4), ii, 261: Czartoryski to Alexander I, 18/30 Jan. 1811; and Czart. MS. 5239, p. 212: 'Note du Prince Adam Czartoryski' (n. 5).

[15] e.g. *VPR* (n. 9), i, 620, 623: Czartoryski to Alexander I, 17/29 Feb. 1804.

[16] The earliest recorded expression of this sentiment that I have found is in Czartoryski's 'Système' (n. 14), pp. 77–9.

leading academic and literary circles in Bohemia, Poland, Lithuania, and Russia. This interest was predominantly cultural, but it was not devoid of a certain political flavour, as can be seen for example already in Herder's prognosis of future Slav glory[17] or in Josef Dobrovský's warm, though not unqualified, sympathy for Russia.[18]

No detailed assessment of this Slavonic intellectual movement is possible here, but a brief account of the cultural and political interest in the Slavs among Poles and Russians in the period before 1815, and of Czartoryski's connections with Slavonic scholarship, will contribute to a better appreciation of his political ideas on the Slavs. The 'discovery' of ancient Slavonic unity by ethnographers, historians, and philologists, and the corollary that this former unity could and should be somehow restored strongly influenced Czartoryski's theoretical political concepts. Furthermore, the consciousness of a common Slavonic origin could be used to promote an understanding between the educated classes of Russia and Poland.

Interest in Slavdom was never very widespread among the educated class in Poland, but it did exist and in some respects Polish Slavonic scholarship exerted considerable influence in Bohemia and Russia.[19] Poland's links with other Slavonic peoples were emphasized in the late eighteenth century by the historian and poet Adam Naruszewicz and the court poet Stanisław Trembecki,[20] while the study of early Polish and Slav history was promoted in Leipzig by Prince Józef Aleksander Jabłonowski.[21] The versatile scholar Jan Potocki searched for Slavonic antiquities in Mecklenburg and West Pomerania in the 1790s, and continued his work on early Slavonic history in Russia, where he entered government service and where he was well known to Czartoryski.[22] Czartoryski also knew Stanisław Siestrzeńcewicz-Bohusz, the Roman Catholic Archbishop of Mogilev in Belorussia, who published works in Russia on Slavonic history,[23] and whom he encouraged to study the origins of Lithuania, a subject in which Czartoryski himself was deeply interested.[24]

[17] J. G. Herder, *Ideen zur Philosophie der Geschichte der Menschheit*, 3 ed., ii (Leipzig, 1828), 287–90. The first edition appeared in 1784–91. Cf. F. M. Barnard, *Herder's Social and Political Thought: from Enlightenment to Nationalism* (Oxford, 1965), 55–62, 171–4.

[18] F. Fadner, *Seventy Years of Pan-Slavism in Russia: Karazin to Danilevsky, 1800–1870* (Washington, 1962), 12–14.

[19] This influence is emphasized for instance by V. A. Frantsev, *Polskoe slavyanovedenie kontsa XVIII i pervoi chetverti XIX st.* (Prague, 1906), and by G. Luciani, *Panslavisme et solidarité slave au XIXᵉ siècle. La Société des Slaves unis, 1823–1825* (Bordeaux, 1963), especially 77–154.

[20] M. Handelsman, 'La politique slave de la Pologne au xviiiᵉ et xixᵉ siècles', *Le Monde slave*, xii (1936), 433–5.   [21] Frantsev, op. cit. (n. 19), 44.

[22] Ibid. 47–62; and see in particular R. W. Wołoszyński, *Polsko-rosyjskie związki w naukach społecznych, 1801–1830* (Warsaw, 1974), 264–7, 283–9. Jan Potocki's brother, Seweryn Potocki, was appointed in 1803 the first curator of the new university in Khar'kov.

[23] Frantsev, op. cit. (n. 19), 62–73; Wołoszyński, op. cit. (n. 22), 291–300.

[24] Frantsev, op. cit. (n. 19), 70: S. Siestrzeńcewicz-Bohusz to Czartoryski, 27 Apr./9 May 1814. Czart. MS. Ewidencja 707–8: A. Czartoryski, 'Wstęp do historii litewskiej'. Ibid. Ewidencja 709–10: 'Historia litewska'.

Another Pole, Prince Aleksander Sapieha, visited Istria, Dalmatia, and Bosnia in 1802–3, where he studied the simple virtues of the southern Slavs, and in 1811 called on the Poles to interest themselves in their fellow-Slavs.[25] Czartoryski knew Sapieha well,[26] and in 1817 married his only daughter.

Slavonic studies were encouraged by the Society of Friends of Learning (Towarzystwo Przyjaciół Nauk) established in 1800 in Warsaw, then under Prussian occupation. The Society gathered together many of Poland's most eminent scholars, promoted the study of the arts and sciences in the Polish language, and aimed at making Polish a leading language of scholarship. A great achievement of Polish Slavonic scholarship was the publication, between 1807 and 1814, of the first modern dictionary of the Polish language, compiled by Samuel Bogumił Linde, a leading member of the Society. While working on his dictionary in Vienna in 1794–1803, Linde acquainted himself with the cultural life of other Slav peoples and in 1801 met Dobrovský, with whom he corresponded. Linde spoke of Polish becoming the language of scholarship of the Slavs,[27] and in his dictionary he emphasized the links between Polish and other Slavonic languages, expressing the hope that his work would contribute to the creation of a common Slavonic grammar and literary language.[28] He referred to Polish as one of the best dialects of a basically unitary Slavonic language spoken from the Elbe to Kamchatka and from the Baltic to the Adriatic.[29]

Linde was assisted in his work by many wealthy Poles, in particular by the great bibliophile and literary scholar Józef Maksymilian Ossoliński, Linde's original patron in Vienna, and by Czartoryski and his father Prince Adam Kazimierz Czartoryski, who was himself an erudite linguist. The two Czartoryskis covered nearly half of the dictionary's publication costs.[30] In 1813–14 Linde sought advice from Dobrovský and from the elder Czartoryski about his project of a uniform alphabet for all Slavonic languages;[31] he also planned a comparative Slavonic dictionary, as well as a learned Polish–Slavonic society. This society was not only to help the Slavs learn more about each other's languages, but also to promote the creation of a single

[25] Z. Klarnerówna, Słowianofilstwo w literaturze polskiej lat 1800 do 1848 (Warsaw, 1926), 54–6. For a recent wider treatment of Polish-South Slav relations see L. Durković-Jakšić, Jugoslovensko-polska saradnja, 1772–1840 (Novi Sad, 1971).

[26] Frantsev suggested (op. cit. (n. 19), 99–100) that Sapieha may even have been encouraged by Czartoryski to visit the South Slavs in 1802–3.

[27] A. Kraushar, Towarzystwo Warszawskie Przyjaciół Nauk, 1800–1832, i (Cracow–Warsaw, 1900), 80–2. Czart. MS. 590, p. 384: S. B. Linde to A. K. Czartoryski, 22 Dec. 1802.

[28] S. B. Linde, Słownik języka polskiego, i (Warsaw, 1807), pp. xii–xvi. Linde's dictionary was advertised in Russia by Czartoryski's secretary V. G. Anastasevich and was well received there.

[29] Ibid. i, p. i.

[30] See the dedications and acknowledgements in vols. i, iv, and vi of Linde's dictionary.

[31] Frantsev, op. cit. (n. 19), 128–30.

Slavonic language based on Polish.[32] Czartoryski was not unsympathetic to this grandiose plan for Polish cultural pre-eminence among the Slavs and supported Linde's ideas.[33]

The Warsaw Society of the Friends of Learning also showed an interest in Czech scholarship and in November 1802, on Linde's recommendation, elected Dobrovský as an honorary member. The first member of the Society to visit Prague, in 1802, was Jan Nepomucen Kossakowski, the Roman Catholic Bishop of Vilna, who also visited Silesia and Moravia. In December 1803 Kossakowski addressed the Society on the Czech cultural revival, emphasized the need for Polish–Czech solidarity, and praised Alexander I's support for university education in the Russian Empire. In the spirit of Linde's own work, Kossakowski called on Slavonic scholars to unite the Slavonic languages under the auspices of the Russian Emperor.[34]

In November 1802 Czartoryski was elected a member of the Society; and his appointment in February 1803 as curator of Vilna University, whose Polish character was confirmed, and of the Vilna educational district won for Alexander I the gratitude of many educated Poles.[35] Co-operation between the Warsaw Society, Vilna University, and other centres of learning in Russia was encouraged,[36] and in 1804 Alexander I himself contributed 500 ducats towards the cost of publishing Linde's dictionary.[37]

In Russia at this time the political and intellectual élite was not yet deeply conscious of the wider Slavonic world. There was, however, in the period when Czartoryski held high office in Russia, a small number of influential Russians greatly interested in the Slavs. Count Nikolay Petrovich Rumyantsev, Chancellor of the Empire 1809–14, did much to promote the study of Slavonic philology and history and gave due consideration to non-Russian Slavonic languages. After 1815 he was to maintain a lively contact with Polish Slavonic scholars in Vilna, Warsaw, and Cracow, and was to contribute substantially to Russo-Polish academic co-operation. Much information about Czech, Polish, and Serb cultural life was disseminated in Russia by Mikhail Trofimovich

[32] Frantsev, op. cit. (n. 19), 131–7. Cf. Luciani, op. cit. (n. 19), 113–18.

[33] S. Askenazy, 'Polska a Europa 1813–1815 podług dziennika Adama ks. Czartoryskiego', Biblioteka Warszawska, pt. ii (1909), 19, 224. Cf. Wołoszyński, op. cit. (n. 22), 72; and Frantsev, op. cit. (n. 19), Appendix, p. cxiv: Czartoryski to S. Malewski, Rector of Vilna University, 4/16 Mar. 1819.

[34] Kraushar, Towarzystwo (n. 27), i, 250–1; Z. Klarnerówna, op. cit. (n. 25), 27.

[35] Even the pro-Napoleonic Hugo Kołłątaj spoke warmly of Alexander I on this subject in 1808. [H. Kołłątaj], Uwagi nad teraźnieyszem położeniem tey części ziemi polskiey, którą od pokoju tylżyckiego zaczęto zwać Xięstwem Warszawskim. Nil desperandum! (Leipzig, 1808), 137, 207–8.

[36] Attention should be drawn to the constructive participation of Czartoryski and other Poles in educational reform in the Russian Empire in this period; cf. S. Truchim, Współpraca polsko-rosyjska nad organizacją szkolnictwa rosyjskiego w początkach XIX wieku (Łódź, 1960); Wołoszyński, op. cit. (n. 22), 401–13. Cf. N. Hans, History of Russian Educational Policy (1701–1917) (1931), 35–41.

[37] Kraushar, Towarzystwo (n. 27), i, 266.

Kachenovsky, Rumyantsev's librarian and secretary, who was editor of *Vestnik Evropy* from 1805 to 1830. Another member of the Rumyantsev circle was Aleksandr Ivanovich Turgenev, who collected Slavonic philological material in the Austrian Empire; in 1808 Czartoryski's then close friend Nikolay Nikolaevich Novosil'tsev also travelled through Austria's Slavonic lands and, while in Vienna in 1811–12, befriended the Slovene scholar Jernej Kopitar.

A central figure in promoting Russo-Polish literary and scholarly relations until the late 1820s was Vasily Grigor'evich Anastasevich, in 1803–10 secretary to Czartoryski when he was curator of the Vilna educational district. Russian interest in other Slavs had been sufficiently awakened in this period for a chair of Slavonic studies to be created in the University of Moscow in 1811 by the Minister of Education Aleksey Kirillovich Razumovsky.

A more narrow Russian-orientated cultural interest in Slavdom was promoted by Admiral Aleksandr Semenovich Shishkov, who became President of the Russian Academy in 1813. In contrast to the Rumyantsev circle, Shishkov insisted that only the Russian language had evolved directly from the primitive Slavonic, all other Slavonic languages being merely derivative dialects. This attitude did not, however, prevent him from establishing relations with the western Slavs. In 1813 Shishkov met Dobrovský in Prague, and in the 1820s he was to extend his patronage to Linde. In 1826–7, as Minister of Education, Shishkov was even to try (unsuccessfully) to secure the appointment of V. Hanka, F. L. Čelakovský, and P. J. Šafařík as professors of Slavonic studies at Russian universities.[38]

Czartoryski's knowledge of the work and ideas of scholars in Russia, Poland, Bohemia, and elsewhere in the fields of Slavonic history, ethnography, and philology was intimate, and he personally knew most of the individuals concerned. It is worthy of note also that in 1786, as a sixteen-year-old boy, Czartoryski had met Herder in Germany,[39] and that Herder corresponded with Czartoryski's father. In 1802 Prince Adam Kazimierz had even suggested to his son that Herder should be invited to Russia to assist with educational reform.[40] It would not be surprising therefore if the enthusiasm shown by Slavonic scholars and men of letters for closer cultural relations and even for linguistic unity among the Slavs affected Czartoryski's political thinking. For political as well as academic reasons Czartoryski remained deeply interested in Slavonic scholarship and continued to encourage it in Poland and Lithuania for many years after 1815.[41]

[38] For Russian cultural interest in the Slavs, see Fadner, op. cit. (n. 18), 36–60.
[39] Czartoryski, *Mémoires* (n. 4), i, 31.
[40] Czart. MS. Ewidencja 1046: A. K. Czartoryski to Czartoryski, 2 Oct. 1802.
[41] Handelsman, *Adam Czartoryski* (n. 1), i, 113–29; Frantsev, op. cit. (n. 19), 249–59 and Appendix, lv–lvi; Wołoszyński, op. cit. (n. 22), 77.

4

It did not take long for this growing cultural interest to reflect itself in political ideas, both in Russia and Poland—especially when political circumstances and strategic considerations were favourable. Czartoryski was by no means alone in this respect. In May 1804 Vasily Fedorovich Malinovsky, a former diplomat, and the first director of the *Lycée* in Tsarskoe Selo, recommended to Czartoryski the destruction of the Ottoman and Habsburg Empires, and the formation of a South Slav federation including Bulgaria, Serbia, Croatia, Bosnia, and Dalmatia. This federation was to be part of a wider Slavo-Russian state including Poland and Bohemia.[42] In December 1804 Vasily Nazarovich Karazin, Czartoryski's assistant in educational matters, suggested the establishment of a 'royaume des Slaves' that would occupy the territory of modern Yugoslavia.[43] Appeals for the creation of Slavonic states in the Balkans also reached Alexander I through Czartoryski in 1804 and 1806 from such south Slav leaders as Stefan Stratimirović, the Serb metropolitan of Karlovac (Karlstadt) in Croatia,[44] and Petar Petrović Njegoš, the Prince-Bishop of Montenegro.[45]

Slav-orientated political projects continued to appear in Russia even after Czartoryski left the foreign ministry in June 1806. In 1807 Vladimir Bogdanovich Bronevsky, a naval officer serving with Admiral Senyavin's fleet in the Adriatic, appealed for the liberation of the Ottoman and Austrian Slavs and the creation of a Slavonic confederation under Russian auspices.[46] Official Russian policy reflecting such attitudes was in fact formulated on the eve of Napoleon's invasion of Russia; all the southern Slavs of what today is Yugoslavia were to be used to create a grand diversion against Austria, and were even to be promised a 'Slavonic kingdom'.[47] The Russo-Turkish peace of May 1812 and the French invasion of Russia frustrated this and other ambitious Slavonic schemes which Rumyantsev, the Chancellor, had

---

[42] Arkhiv Vneshnei politiki Rossii, Moscow, Chancellerie du Ministre 1804, vol. 7869, ff. 1–32: V. F. Malinovsky's memorandum. I am deeply indebted to Dr. Jerzy Skowronek of Warsaw University for kindly allowing me to make use of his copy of this document. See also V. F. Malinovsky, *Izbrannye obshchestvenno-politicheskie sochineniya*, ed. E. A. Arab-Ogly (M., 1958).

[43] *Russkaya starina*, iii (1871), 715–17: V. N. Karazin to Czartoryski, 21 Nov./3 Dec. and 27 Nov./9 Dec. 1804.

[44] *Russkii arkhiv*, vi (1868), 111–20: Stratimirović's memorandum, June 1804. Both S. B. Linde and J. M. Ossoliński knew Stratimirović and had discussed with him in Vienna a project for a Serb dictionary; see Frantsev, op. cit. (n. 19), 107.

[45] V. G. Sirotkin, 'Franko-russkaya diplomaticheskaya bor'ba na Balkanakh i plany sozdaniya slavyano-serbskogo gosudarstva v 1806–1807 gg.', *Uchenye zapiski Instituta slavyanovedeniya*, xxv (1962), 181–2.

[46] A. N. Pypin, *Panslavizm v proshlom i nastoyashchem (1878)* (Spb., 1913), 77–8.

[47] S. Goryainov, *1812: Dokumenty Gosudarstvennogo i S. Petersburgskogo glavnogo arkhivov. Izdanie Ministerstva inostrannykh del*, pt. ii (Spb., 1912), 31–2.

strongly supported.[48] Nevertheless, Alexander I ordered the Slavs and the Wallachians to be assured confidentially that Russian forces would return to the Balkans after Napoleon's defeat 'pour créer un empire Slave'.[49]

In Poland ideas of Slavonic solidarity and unity were also exploited for political purposes. In the first five years of Alexander I's reign Polish political thinking on the Slavs had a distinctly pro-Russian slant, expressed in particular by Czartoryski. However, the Napoleonic presence in Poland in 1807–13 revived hopes of independence and inspired pro-Napoleonic Slavonic combinations. Stanisław Staszic, a leading intellectual and political writer of the period, suggested in 1807 that Poland should become a bridge between western civilization, as represented by France, and the Slav peoples,[50] and Prince Aleksander Sapieha, who directed Napoleon's intelligence network in the western provinces of the Russian Empire, praised the French Emperor as the protector of the Slavs.[51]

With Napoleon's defeat sentiments of Slavonic solidarity with a definite pro-Russian flavour, influenced by political opportunism and by the establishment of a seemingly permanent and not disadvantageous political link with Russia in 1815, reappeared with great force in Poland. In 1815 the poet and Bishop of Cracow Jan Paweł Woronicz, who had earlier spoken of Poland leading the Slavs at Napoleon's side,[52] now hailed the golden age in which Slavonic Russia would defend Polish lands.[53] In a speech on 20 June 1815 Tomasz Wawrzecki, one of the leaders of the Polish uprising of 1794 and now a member of the provisional government in Warsaw, justified the new Russo-Polish union, referring to the Russians' and Poles' ethnic and linguistic affinity, geographical proximity and common possession of all the virtues attributed to the Slavs by Herder.[54] Staszic also swayed with the prevailing political wind and to what he now believed to be the irresistible march of historical progress.[55] In August 1815, some six months after Czartoryski composed the document, Staszic publicly praised the union with Russia and appealed to the Russians to complete the union

[48] VPR (n. 9), vi, 487: N. P. Rumyantsev to Alexander I, 5/17 July 1812.

[49] Ibid. vi, 90: Alexander I to P. V. Chichagov, 18/30 July 1812.

[50] S. Staszic, 'O statystyce Polski krótki rzut wiadomości w roku 1807', in: S. Staszic, Pisma filozoficzne i społeczne, ed. B. Suchodolski, ii (Cracow, 1954), 285–300.

[51] Klarnerówna, op. cit. (n. 25), 13–14.

[52] Wołoszyński, op. cit. (n. 22), 55; Luciani, Panslavisme (n. 19), 100.

[53] Klarnerówna, op. cit. (n. 25), 17. Woronicz was closely associated with the Czartoryski family from 1794 and spent much time in Puławy, the Czartoryski family residence. See Luciani, Panslavisme (n. 19), 97–8.

[54] Frantsev, op. cit. (n. 19), 25.

[55] See the revealing alterations Staszic made, probably in 1814, to his originally pro-Napoleonic and anti-Russian draft of Ród ludzki, cf. Ród ludzki, ed. Z. Daszkowski, iii (Cracow, 1959), 313–22. The third version of this work, which was eventually published in 1819–20, was markedly pro-Russian; see Staszic, Pisma (n. 50), ii, 223–4.

of all the Slavs for which nature had already laid the foundations.[56] In a theoretical classification, similar to that already made by Czartoryski in 1803[57] and repeated in this document, Staszic underlined the existence of three main ethnic groups of peoples ('rody') in Europe: the 'Gaulo-latyni', the Teutons, and the Slavs. He argued fancifully that these groups, and not states, represented the most permanent factors of political stability in Europe.

The apparent Russo-Polish reconciliation under Emperor Alexander's auspices following the Vienna settlement of 1815 was also reflected in the activity of Russo-Polish masonic lodges in Poland and the western provinces of Russia, which adopted emblems and mottos of Slavonic unity.[58] In 1823 the brothers Petr and Andrey Ivanovich Borisov, inspired by the young Pole Julian Lubliński, established the Society of the United Slavs for the liberation of western and southern Slavs from the German and Turkish yokes and for promoting a federation of Slavonic republics.[59]

5

A specific feature of the document is the concern expressed by Czartoryski at the Germanization of the lands of the western Slavs. His hostility towards what he termed 'Germanisme' was not surprising in the Polish context if one bears in mind the Prusso-Polish rivalry over the Vistula trade route and Danzig (Gdańsk) in the second half of the eighteenth century; Czartoryski attached great importance to the problems of Poland's Baltic trade. There was also the bitterness left by Prussia's betrayal of Poland in 1792 and the resentment felt by many educated Poles towards the bureaucratic, judicial, and educational systems introduced by Prussia and Austria in their areas of partitioned Poland.[60]

Furthermore, a number of learned Poles were already showing an interest in the ethnic composition of the mixed German- and Slavonic-speaking regions of east-central Europe. One of these was Staszic, who was born in Piła (Schneidemühl), which Prussia had annexed in 1772. Travelling to Italy in 1790, he commented on the inferior status of Czech and Moravian speech in Bohemia and Moravia,[61] and on his return journey in July 1791 lamented that many young Galician Poles

---

[56] S. Staszic, 'Myśli o równowadze politycznej w Europie czytane w Wydziale Literatury Towarzystwa Przyjaciół Nauk w roku 1815 w miesiącu sierpniu', *Pisma* (n. 50), ii, 301–21.

[57] See below, p. 87.

[58] Pypin, *Panslavizm* (n. 46), 80–3; Fadner, op. cit. (n. 18), 105–10; S. Askenazy, *Łukasiński, i* (Warsaw, 1908), 112–14, 220–7.

[59] Luciani, *Panslavisme* (n. 19), 33–73. M. V. Nechkina, *Obshchestvo soedinennykh slavyan* (M., 1927).

[60] e.g. Kraushar, *Towarzystwo* (n. 27), ii, 71–4: J. Albertrandi's speech to Frederick Augustus of Saxony and Grand Duke of Warsaw, 12 Dec. 1807; H. Kołłątaj, *Uwagi* (n. 35), 207–8.

[61] *Dziennik podróży Stanisława Staszica, 1789–1805*, ed. C. Leśniewski (Cracow, 1931), 14, 20.

were being Germanized in Viennese schools.[62] In October 1804, on his way to Paris, Staszic wrote extensively in his diary on the rapid disappearance of Polish speech in Lower Silesia and of Lusatian speech in Saxony, and lamented that Breslau had become a German city: 'Wraclaw [sic], the capital of Polish princes, has today no sign of Poles except its name. All [inhabitants] are Germans. Only the remains of Polish settlement still survive in some villages.'[63] He attributed Germanization to the dominant role of the Germans in the professions, trade, industry, and all forms of handicrafts. Slavonic speech, he observed, was to be found only among the peasants. And, while travelling to Hungary in August 1805, Staszic noted down the areas of old German settlement in northern Slovakia.[64]

Much information about the linguistic situation in Silesia and Lusatia reached Polish educated circles through the historian, philologist, and bibliophile Georg (Jerzy) Samuel Bandtkie, who had travelled widely in central and eastern Europe in 1794–8. In 1798 he became headmaster of a school in Breslau; he was a member of the Society of Learning of Upper Lusatia and the author of an early Polish–German dictionary. In 1801–2 Bandtkie participated in a Prussian commission which inspected the schools of Prussian Poland, and in September 1803 he advised the Prussian government against forcing the German language on Prussia's new Polish subjects, arguing that such a policy in Upper Silesia had a harmful social effect on the local Polish-speaking population.[65] In 1806 Bandtkie was elected to the Warsaw Society of the Friends of Learning and in 1811 became the librarian of Cracow University. He drew Dobrovský's attention to Polish speech in Silesia[66] and helped to spread knowledge of that region among the Poles.[67]

The growing awareness in Poland of the Slavonic populations of Prussia, Saxony, and Austria was also leading in some instances to far-reaching and extravagant political conclusions. Seven years before Czartoryski spoke of political action on behalf of these Slavs in his document, Hugo Kołłątaj, one of the authors of the Polish constitution of 1791 and Vice-Chancellor of Poland in 1791–2, had already applied the criteria of modern linguistic nationalism with deadly effect to the Hohenzollern monarchy in his treatise on the Duchy of Warsaw. He claimed that the lands to the east of the Oder—Silesia, Neumark, and Pomerania—were essentially Slavonic and Polish in speech and custom, while the East Prussians, despite the official German placenames in their land, still used either Polish or Lithuanian speech.[68]

[62] Ibid. 286. [63] Ibid. 392. [64] Ibid. 412–28.
[65] Kraushar, Towarzystwo (n. 27), i, 45–8. Cf. 'Über die polnische Sprache in Schlesien', in: G. S. Bandtkie, Historisch-critische Analecten zur Erläuterung der Geschichte des Ostens von Europa (Breslau, 1802), 270–8. [66] Frantsev, op. cit. (n. 19), 142–3.
[67] A. Brückner, Tysiąc lat kultury polskiej, 3 ed., ii (Paris, [1954]), 610.
[68] Uwagi (n. 35), 50–1, 144–6.

Kołłątaj unduly minimized the importance and size of German settlement in those areas, and stated that a restored and modernized Poland,
allied to France and acting as the eastern bulwark of the western
Napoleonic Empire, should extend from the Baltic and the Oder in the
west to the Dvina and Dniepr in the east.[69] He argued that the Oder
was the natural dividing-line between the Germanic and Slavonic
worlds, conceding that the Slavs to the west of the Oder were already
largely Germanized. Linguistically heterogeneous states were a barrier,
in Kołłątaj's opinion, to the spread of enlightenment and stability:
'The ruler and the ruled should understand one another and speak
one language. Woe to that people whose speech their ruler does not
understand!'[70]

The Russo-Polish settlement of 1815 prompted Staszic also to be
very outspoken on the subject of German–Slav relations. In his
'Thoughts on the Political Balance of Europe' he presented a very
unflattering picture of the Teutonic races as the most avaricious, cruel,
and dangerous, and drew attention to their ruthless expansion, over
many centuries, beyond the Elbe, the Oder, the Vistula, the Niemen,
and even to the Neva. The Prussians, he felt, were the greediest of the
three partitioning powers, and with the Austrians they had pursued
the most anti-national policies towards the Poles. He regretted that the
Germans still ruled over many Slavs and declared that they were the
greatest foes of Slavonic unity.[71]

6

It is against this many-faceted background of nascent cultural and
political interest in the Slavs that Czartoryski's ideas should be considered. His contribution, both as statesman and as patron of scholarship,
to the furthering of this interest in Russia and Poland was significant,
and he was early in drawing political conclusions from it. Already
in 1803, as Russia's deputy Foreign Minister, he recognized that the
new emphasis on the common origin of the Slavs could be exploited in
international politics to justify Russian involvement in Poland and the
Balkans. He recommended to Alexander I the creation of a union or
federation of Slavonic peoples based on a Russo-Polish dual monarchy,
or alternatively, on a Russia enlarged by the annexation of the whole of
Prussian and Austrian Poland.[72] He mentioned the existence of other

[69] *Uwagi* (n. 35), 133–62.
[70] Ibid. 141. It is worth noting that Kołłątaj advocated the linguistic and cultural Poloniza-
tion of the eastern provinces of the former Polish Republic, where the majority of the peasants
spoke Lithuanian, Belorussian, or Ukrainian; see H. Kołłątaj, *Stan oświecenia w Polsce w
ostatnich latach panowania Augusta III (1750–1764)*, ed. J. Hulewicz (Wrocław, 1953), 10–12.
Kołłątaj wrote this work in 1803–10.
[71] S. Staszic, *Pisma* (n. 50), ii, 305–20.   [72] 'Système' (n. 14), pp. 82–4, 128.

Slavs beyond, that is, to the west and south-west of Poland;[73] he described Prussia and Austria as 'des ennemis naturels de la Russie',[74] and as Poland's 'ennemi naturel' singled out Prussia.[75] He emphasized, re-echoing Herder, that there existed fundamental natural differences between the peoples of Slavonic and Germanic origin.

Although well aware of further subdivisions within each group, Czartoryski listed for the Emperor three leading groups of peoples ('races') on the continent of Europe: the French, the Germans, and the Slavs, each with its own very different characteristics.[76] He therefore suggested, and was to repeat in the document, that an equilibrium between these three 'races' would contribute to peace. Not surprisingly, the expulsion of the German powers from Poland was for him an essential condition of such an equilibrium.[77]

Between 1803 and 1807 Czartoryski on several occasions recommended the Russian annexation of Prussian Poland and even parts or the whole of East Prussia,[78] as well as the liberation of the Balkans from Ottoman rule and the establishment of separate Balkan states under Russian protection.[79] He emphasized Russia's religious links and linguistic and racial bonds with the Balkan Christians.[80] However, the practical need of preserving the alliance with Turkey to offset the French threat in the Mediterranean, reluctance to alarm Great Britain and Austria by overtly excessive demands in the Balkans, as well as Alexander's indecision, all hindered the implementation of Czartoryski's projects for European Turkey, just as Alexander's ambivalence and the need for Prussian and Austrian assistance against the growing power of Napoleonic France tied a Gordian knot on the Polish issue.[81]

Czartoryski also recommended on various occasions the transfer to Austria of such Slav-inhabited areas as Bosnia, parts of Serbia, and

[73] Ibid., p. 128.   [74] Ibid., p. 70.   [75] Ibid., p. 79,
[76] Ibid., p. 124. As an afterthought Czartoryski added the Italians as a fourth group.
[77] Ibid., p. 125.
[78] Ibid., pp. 83(a), 128; Czartoryski, *Mémoires* (n. 4), ii, 76–7: A. Czartoryski, 'Mémoire sur les rapports de la Russie et de la Prusse', 17/29 Jan. 1806. In the 1820s Czartoryski still regretted that Poland had not annexed East Prussia in the past; A. Czartoryski , *Essai sur la diplomatie. Manuscrit d'un Philhellène, publié par M. Toulouzan* (Marseille–Paris, 1830), 392. I am grateful to the late Professor Marian Kukiel for allowing me to use his rare copy of the 1830 edition of this book.
[79] e.g. 'Système' (n. 14), pp. 85–7, 127. *Sbornik Imperatorskogo Russkogo istoricheskogo obshchestva* (hereafter *SIRIO*), lxxxii (1892), 244–78: Czartoryski's memoranda, 11/23 Jan. 1806.
[80] 'Système' (n. 14), pp. 85–9; *VPR* (n. 9), i, 621–3: Czartoryski to Alexander I, 17/29 Feb. 1804. See also *SIRIO*, lxxxii, 244–51.
[81] Recent studies of these subjects can be found in E. Halicz, *Geneza Księstwa Warszawskiego* (Warsaw, 1962); N. E. Saul, *Russia and the Mediterranean, 1797–1807* (Chicago–London, 1970); V. G. Sirotkin, *Duel' dvukh diplomatii. Rossiya i Frantsiya v 1801–1812 gg.* (M., 1966); J. Skowronek, *Antynapoleońskie koncepcje Czartoryskiego* (Warsaw, 1969); A. M. Stanislavskaya, *Russko-angliiskie otnosheniya i problemy Sredizemnomorya 1798–1807* (M., 1962). Cf. also W. H. Zawadzki, 'Prince Adam Czartoryski and Napoleonic France, 1801–1805: a Study in Political Attitudes', *The Historical Journal*, xviii (1975), 245–77.

Montenegro in return for Vienna's consent to Russia's policies in Poland and the Balkans.[82] The need for Austrian assistance against Napoleon in 1803-5 and later, as well as Czartoryski's respect for the ruling dynasties of central Europe, inhibited him at this stage from suggesting major alterations in the status of Austria's Slavonic territories along the lines recommended by Malinovsky or Bronevsky, except of course for the surrender of ex-Polish Galicia. As the document indicates, by 1814-15 Czartoryski had adopted a more radical attitude towards the Habsburg state.

Yet, despite the internal contradictions in his policies as minister, the lack of precise information about the Slavs, and the complications created by the demands of international politics, Czartoryski envisaged in this period a considerable degree of political unity among the Slavs under Russian leadership with Poland playing second fiddle. In December 1806 he argued that by restoring Poland Russia 'commencerait ce lien heureux qui doit rattacher un jour autour d'elle toutes les branches éparses de l'antique famille des *Slaves*'.[83] In 1807, virtually single-handed, he tried to dissuade the Poles from turning to Napoleon with geo-political arguments and appealed to Slavonic solidarity: Poland should

... préférer à toute chose sa réunion à la Russie, où une même dialecte, une même origine l'attachent déjà, et sa soumission au Sceptre du Souverain, sur le quel tous les peuples Slaves, qui ont des vœux à former, ont fixé leurs yeux. Les Polonais voudraient-ils seuls se séparer de leur propre tige, et se livrer à un joug étranger?[84]

In May 1807 he explained to his mother that his project of reintegrating Poland under Alexander I was

le seul practicable au sujet de la Pologne; c'est le seul qui conserve une chance de probabilité, et qui en reunissant la nation polonaise à la cause de toutes les nations Slaves, la rendrait solidement heureuse.[85]

Several weeks later he wrote to his friend P. A. Stroganov that he regretted that the Poles had become associated with Napoleon, and wished 'que leur cause soit celle de tous les peuples Slaves, dont ils ne doivent pas se séparer'.[86] He was certain, however, that Poland's future would eventually be decided by Russia '. . . car un système

[82] 'Système' (n. 14), pp. 87-8, 127; *Mémoires* (n. 4), ii, 65-6: A. Czartoryski, 'Article pour l'arrangement des affaires de l'Europe à la suite d'une guerre heureuse' [late 1806 or early 1807]. The document is erroneously dated 1804.

[83] Ibid. ii, 151: A. Czartoryski, 'Mémoire sur la nécessité de rétablir la Pologne pour prévenir Bonaparte', 5 Dec. 1806 [O.S.?].

[84] Czart. MS. 5231, p. 131: A. Czartoryski, 'Circulaire du Prince à quelques personnes eminentes de Pologne, 1807'.

[85] Czart. MS. Ewidencja 816, p. 9: Czartoryski to I. Czartoryska, 12 May 1807.

[86] Le Grand-Duc Nicolas Mikhailovitch, *Le Comte Paul Stroganov*, ii (Paris, 1905), 256: Czartoryski to P. A. Stroganov, 23 May/4 June 1807.

fédératif des *nations* slaves est le grand & unique but auquel elle [Russia] doit nécessairement tendre'.[87]

Czartoryski did not share the enthusiasm of many Poles for Napoleon's invasion of Russia in 1812. When the tide of war turned in Alexander's favour, Czartoryski again brought into the open his concept of a Russo-Polish dual monarchy and resumed his lobbying of the Emperor. The idea of Slavonic solidarity also reappeared. In March and June 1813 Czartoryski twice met S. B. Linde and discussed projects for a Polish-centred Slavonic academy.[88] In May 1813 Czartoryski, fully aware of Metternich's hostility to his attempts to arrange a last-minute alliance between Alexander I and the Duchy of Warsaw, warned Alexander of Austria's 'politique double', and argued that Vienna's apprehensions regarding Russia were based on fears of Russian influence on Austria's Slavs.[89] At Chaumont in March 1814 Czartoryski appealed to Alexander I, as a Slavonic monarch, to free the Slavs of Turkey from foreign oppression and to lead them towards that stage of civilization and power to which they were entitled by virtue of their numbers and natural abilities. And he argued that by giving autonomous status to Poland Alexander would show the Slavs what advantages they could expect from Russia.[90]

Czartoryski's interest in Prussia's ethnic composition and the economic importance of Prussia for Poland was also evident in 1813–14. In July 1813 he commented in his private diary on the Lithuanians and Protestant Masurians of East Prussia,[91] while at Chaumont in March 1814 he recommended to Alexander I detailed arrangements for the release of Polish trade in the Baltic from the stranglehold of Prussia: free trade in Danzig, Elbing, Königsberg, and Memel; free navigation on the Vistula and the Niemen; and free commercial passage across Prussian Silesia.[92] Czartoryski's other main concern—that similar national institutions should be established in all parts of Poland if some form of partition proved unavoidable—was also well expressed before the Congress of Vienna,[93] and was articulated again in the document.

In his advice to Alexander I at the Congress Czartoryski reaffirmed the general principles of his 'système politique' of 1803, emphasizing that only the reconstruction of the continent on the basis of nationality

[87] Ibid.   [88] Askenazy, 'Polska' (n. 33), loc cit.
[89] Czart. MS. Ewidencja 1039(a), p. 323: Czartoryski to Alexander I, 24 Apr./5 May 1813.
[90] Czart. MS. 5239, pp. 215–16: 'Note' (n. 5).
[91] Askenazy, 'Polska' (n. 33), pt. ii, 235.
[92] Czart. MS. 5239, p. 212: 'Note' (n. 5). In the summer of 1814 a representative of the city of Danzig named Keidl was in London and Paris attempting to acquire international support for Danzig's political independence of Prussia. Czartoryski was in touch with him and lent him support; see Wawrzkowicz, *Anglia* (n. 1), 117–18, 383–414; Askenazy, 'Polska' (n. 33), pt. iii, 51.
[93] Wawrzkowicz, *Anglia* (n. 1), 347–53: Czartoryski's Pro-memoria for Castlereagh [June 1814].

would secure stability in Europe.[94] He admitted that his ideas on national self-government had ominous implications for the Habsburg and Hohenzollern monarchies, and suggested that Prussia should turn away from the east to involve herself in purely German affairs.[95]

7

The fear of 'Germanisme' is the most striking feature of the document. It would be a mistake to think that Czartoryski, an enlightened magnate brought up in the eighteenth century, was hostile to all things German. On the contrary, he read Goethe,[96] was on friendly terms with Stein, Stadion, and Hardenberg,[97] had advocated greater German unity (but without Prussia and Austria!) at least since 1803,[98] and in the document praised Germany's intellectual and cultural achievements (p. 164). Nevertheless, Czartoryski did react strongly against German political and economic power and linguistic influence in east-central Europe, and in the ethnically mixed German–Polish borderlands in particular. When it became clear at the Congress of Vienna that Prussia and Austria would retain parts of pre-partition Poland, he assured his father: 'But the fate of even those Poles will not be neglected, and they will be protected against Germanization'.[99] Czartoryski's associate, Andrzej Horodyski, a former Polish 'Jacobin', was also concerned lest the Poles in Prussia and Austria suffer the fate of the Slavs along the Baltic, in Pomerania, and Mecklenburg.[100]

In the spring of 1815 Czartoryski noted in his diary that '. . . the Austrians are against nationality [narodowość] to the end'; that Prussia was double-dealing; and that 'only Stein is perfect; the other Germans are insincere and in their hearts want to Germanize'.[101] Attempts to introduce greater uniformity in the Habsburg and Hohenzollern states, and to promote *Amtsdeutsch* at the expense of regional native institutions and languages, were viewed by Czartoryski as vindictive measures to 'denationalize' the Poles. Hence his concern for preserving national Polish institutions and the Polish language in what was to be Prussian and Austrian Poland after 1815.

One can detect in Czartoryski's political ideas the germs of a more aggressive attitude in German–Slav relations, based on the principles

---

[94] Wawrzkowicz, *Anglia* (n. 1), 453: Czartoryski to Alexander I, 2/14 Nov. 1814.

[95] Ibid.

[96] Cf. the reference to Goethe's *Faust* in Czartoryski's diary; see Askenazy, 'Polska' (n. 33), pt. ii, 442.

[97] Ibid., pt. ii, 230–1, 439, 442; pt. iii, 69.

[98] e.g. 'Système' (n. 14), pp. 91–3; Czart. MS. 5533, p. 52: Czartoryski to A. R. Vorontsov, [1803]; *VPR* (n. 9), ii, 151: Secret instructions for Novosil'tsev, 11/23 Sept. 1804, additional notes, article 2; *Mémoires* (n. 4), ii, 63: 'Article' (n. 82); *Essai* (n. 78), 296–302, 398–400.

[99] Czart. MS. Ewidencja 819, pp. 107–8: Czartoryski to A. K. Czartoryski, 16 Nov. 1814.

[100] Czart. MS. 3945, p. 80: A. Horodyski to Czartoryski, 29 Mar. 1815.

[101] Askenazy, 'Polska' (n. 33), pt. iii, 69.

of ethnic and linguistic nationalism.[102] Staszic and Kołłątaj provide other contemporary examples of such militancy which went beyond the desire to promote Slavonic scholarship or the cultural awakening of the Slavs. New ideas of linguistic nationality (largely Herderian in inspiration), awareness of Slavonic unity in the distant past, and forecasts of a glorious Slav future assuaged feelings of resentment and inferiority with regard to the German powers and added new and ominous elements to the otherwise purely political ambition of restoring the Polish state.[103] Czartoryski was conservative in so far as he hoped to re-create Poland within its pre-partition frontiers and with its own national, though not unreformed, institutions. Yet, he had also espoused the revolutionary idea (ultimately incompatible with Poland's pre-partition frontiers) that political frontiers should coincide with the boundaries of language and race,[104] and applied it to the western limits of Slavdom. However imprecise and confusing these ideas still were and despite existing inter-Slav rivalries, they were to find an increasing number of adherents among western Slav and Russian intellectuals and publicists as the century progressed and were to resound loudly at the Slav Congress in Prague in 1848.

APPENDIX

Remarques justificatives d'un Projet qui garantit la Nationalité aux Provinces Polonaises de différentes Dominations

Czart. MS. 5238, pp. 153–64

Toute la confiance de la Nation Polonaise répose uniquement sur la Personne de l'Empereur. Tandis que sur la grande scène de l'Europe les Polonais apprenaient avec tant d'autres Peuples à apprécier la grandeur d'Ame & la force de caractère de l'Empereur, Il voulut encore leur en fournir à eux-mêmes des preuves particulières bien plus touchantes, & parvint à remporter le triomphe le plus complet sur tous leurs sentimens. Les Polonais, de quelque Domination qu'ils soyent, n'admirent maintenant qu'Alexandre; ils n'aiment, ils ne rêvent que Lui; ils ne parlent que de Lui, & ce n'est que de Sa Main qu'ils attendent leur bonheur. Aucun des Souverains voisins ne pourra en dire autant: aucun ne pourra dire que dans leur malheur ils ayent invoqués son appui de quelque manière que ce soit.

Ce sont là des faits notoires & incontestables. Ces sentimens dérivent des motifs les plus solides; & c'est ce qui garantit leur durée.

---

[102] Characteristic was Czartoryski's praise of General Henryk Dąbrowski for being 'bon Polonais, anti-allemand'; *SIRIO*, ix (1872), 443: Czartoryski to N. N. Novosil'tsev, 8/20 May 1814.

[103] In some respects one could draw an analogy between the Polish resistance to German influence and the contemporary reaction in Germany of J. G. Fichte, E. M. Arndt, and F. L. Jahn against French political and cultural domination.

[104] e.g. 'Système' (n. 14), p. 124; *VPR* (n. 9), ii, 142: Secret instructions for Novosil'tsev, 11/23 Sept. 1804; *Essai* (n. 78), 126–33, 187–93, 205–17, 222–30.

Une confiance nationale & illimitée s'est tellement emparée de l'imagination active des Polonais, qu'ils ne conçoivent plus la possibilité d'être déchûs de ce qu'ils espèrent & de ce qu'ils désirent si ardemment.[105]

Voilà ce qui explique pourquoi, malgré les bruits les plus sinistres que les Allemands ne cèssent de répandre sur le sort futur des contrées du Duché limitrophes aux etats de l'Autriche [p. 154] & de la Prusse,[106] tout le monde y reste dans une parfaite sécurité, & personne n'ajoute foi aux nouvelles de ce genre.

D'après ces données on pourra aisément juger du degrès de douleur et du désespoir que causera dans toute la Nation la nouvelle du Partage qui va séparer de la Patrie la portion du Pays la plus populeuse, la plus riche, la plus industrieuse & la plus avancée dans la culture sociale;[107] & qui en outre fait perdre les salines, source intarissable d'un très grand revenu & d'une sorte de certitude rassurante pour le Peuple qui n'y voit qu'un article indispensablement nécéssaire pour la vie.[108] Quelle secousse funeste, portée à l'ésprit public! quel abattement dans le gros de la Nation, qui n'est pas à même de juger des motifs & des moyens du Cabinet, & qui ne se dirige que d'après l'impression de ce qui est palpable!...

La crainte d'un mal aussi immédiat, & la nécéssité d'une mesure propre à en néutraliser les effets, a d'abord motivé le Projèt dont il s'agit ici. On avait en vue la gloire de l'Empereur, on était conduit par le désir ardent de consoler & même d'augmenter encore, s'il est possible, la force de ce dévouement que Lui porte tout ce qui a un cœur Polonais.

Il faut que toute l'Europe soit forcée de convenir que, si les difficultés insurmontables n'ont pas permis à l'Empereur de parvenir au Rétablissement complet de la Pologne, Il a au moins sauvé l'individualité de la Nation; Il a perpetué la vie Nationale des Polonais; Il les a rendus tous au bonheur, les a tiré de l'humiliation, & leur a obtenu les moyens de se procurer tous [p. 155] les perfectionnemens sociaux; Il les a remis enfin sur la voye de participer aux travaux qui ont pour but d'avancer les grands intérêts de l'humanité.

Un tel bienfait ne s'efface jamais de la mémoire des hommes. Des exemples d'une conduite, pareille à celle d'Alexandre envers la Nation Polonaise, manquent encore aux plus belles époques de l'histoire, & il est vrai de dire

---

[105] High hopes of the restoration of Polish statehood were held in 1814–15 by many of Poland's leading political figures as a result of Alexander I's definite assurances on the subject. See in particular Czart. MS. Ewidencja 1140, pp. 1–7: T. Matuszewicz, 'Précis de ce qui s'est dit [sic] et traité dans le Cabinet de S.M. l'Empereur Alexandre lorsqu'il a daigné y appeler Mr. Zamoyski, Linowski et Matuszewic, le 21 Sept. 1814 à Puławy'. Also published in S. Askenazy, Szkice i portrety (Warsaw, 1937), 369–73.

[106] Despite the treaties of Breslau (Feb. 1813) and Töplitz (Sept. 1813), Prussia's and Austria's claims to large parts of the Duchy of Warsaw were not finally settled with Russia until May 1815.

[107] The western districts of the Duchy of Warsaw to be lost to Prussia, namely the departments of Poznań, Bydgoszcz, and a part of Kalisz, were economically some of the most advanced areas of the former Polish Republic. There were more towns, fewer magnate latifundia, a higher proportion of free peasants than elsewhere in Poland, and the process of replacing compulsory unpaid labour (pańszczyzna) by rents to the noble landlord was quite advanced.

[108] The royal salt-mines of Wieliczka, 15 km. south-east of Cracow, already lost by Poland to Austria in 1772. In 1809–13 the Duchy of Warsaw shared the right to exploit the mines. The Russo-Austrian treaty of 3 May 1815 was to grant full ownership of the mines to Austria.

qu'il n'y a dans la vie de l'Empereur que le Titre de *Libérateur* & de *Pacificateur de l'Europe*, qui puisse par l'immensité de ses résultats, l'emporter sur celui de *Sauveur de la Pologne*.

Mais un tel bienfait est trop grand, trop beau, pour que l'on puisse se borner à ne le faire qu'à demi: & c'est précisément cette idée qui a présidé à la rédaction du Projèt.

Si une partie considérable du Territoire de l'ancienne Pologne reste encore partagée entre les mains de deux gouvernemens Allemands, le Projèt en question rétablit au moins *l'Unité idéale* de la Nation, en la séparant d'une race étrangère par des marques distinctives & inéffaçables. Tous les Articles de ce Projèt tendent plus ou moins à consolider cette *Unité idéale*, & à faire ensorte que, malgré l'éxistence des frontières Autrichiennes & Prussiennes, il n'y ait point de séparation *réelle* entre les Enfans de la même Patrie qui sous cette forme nouvelle ne cessera jamais d'occuper l'imagination de chaque Polonais, & dont le vrai Trône sera toujours envisagé par eux comme fixé dans la capitale du Royaume.[109] L'identité des Principes constitutionnels pour chaque Partie de la Pologne; — la liberté des communications sociales & commerciales entre toutes ces [p. 156] Parties; — la conservation de la Langue & de la Nationalité, garantie par de nombreuses institutions; — enfin les dénominations proposées pour chaque Partie de ce Royaume: — tout ceci concoure à cimenter & perpétuer cette Unité de Patrie; à concentrer dans un foyer commun toutes les forces morales des Polonais, & à calmer la profonde douleur que la Nation va ressentir en apprenant que des Portions si précieuses ont été sacrifiées à la cupidité d'une race étrangère.

Mais, outre l'intérêt de la Gloire, outre l'importance qu'il y aurait à subjuguer les sentiments de tous les Polonais, n'y a-t-il pas encore des motifs d'une Utilité (: pour ainsi dire:) *plus Immédiate*, qui puisse parler en faveur du Projet?

On pourrait d'abord répondre par une observation générale dont la force & l'évidence tient à l'infaillibilité d'un ordre supérieur de choses. Si les motifs & toute la tendance du Projèt est essentiellement juste, morale & humaine, ses résultants ne pourront jamais manquer d'être éminement utiles, & d'une influence décisive en faveur de l'humanité. Laissons les Etats subalternes & faibles chercher quelquefois des moyens de salut dans les déviations du devoir moral: les maximes de la Politique des Grands Etâts ne devraient jamais être que celles de la *vérité* & de la *justice* éternelle. Pour qu'une Puissance prépondérante dévienne réellement *Tout-puissante*, elle n'a besoin d'autres armes que de celles des *maximes rigoureusement morales*.[110]

On a déjà dit plus d'une fois que si Napoléon, après avoir atteint une prépondérance décisive sur le continent, se fût constitué Défenseur sincère de

---

[109] Warsaw.

[110] Czartoryski was consistent over many decades in his Utopian view that great powers should base their foreign policies on the principles of morality and justice. Cf. 'Système' (n. 14), pp. 15–47; Czart. MS. 5239, pp. 93–110: A. Czartoryski, 'Malheurs de la Pologne depuis près de deux siècles', [1813]; Wawrzkowicz, *Anglia* (n. 1), 307–24: A. Czartoryski, 'La Politique de la Grande Bretagne, mémoire présenté au cabinet anglais en faveur de la Pologne, Puławy', 9 Sept. 1813; *Essai* (n. 78), *passim*.

tout [p. 157] ce qui est vrai, équitable & humain, la plus grande partie du monde politique auraient déjà obei aux lois d'une seule Nation.

La Russie ayant la 1/9ᵉ partie du globe terrestre pour sa bâse physique, & réunissant désormais sous son scèptre la plus grande et la meilleure partie de la Slavonie, forme un Univers à part qui *se suffit à lui-même*, dans toute la force de l'acceptation de ce terme. Elle n'a plus besoin de rien sous le rapport physique. La seule alliance permanente avec les forces irrésistibles de l'Ordre moral, pourrait La rendre en peu de tems Toute-Puissante. Elle n'a vis-à-vis d'Elle que des Etâts, corrompus en grande partie jusques dans les sources mêmes de la civilisation & luttant avec assez de peine contre les progrès continus de la *dissolution* des liens sociaux de leur ordre actuel.[111] L'élévation des sentimens de l'Empereur Aléxandre a déjà remis la Russie sur la vraie route qui convient à la Politique d'un Empire aussi solidement puissant. Les succès les plus éclatans & les plus mémorables, ont heureusement couronné ses efforts, & l'Europe Lui a déjà voué un hommage de reconnaissance & d'admiration. L'exemple d'une conduite souvairenement [*sic*] morale envers la Nation Polonaise, ne manquera pas de même de produire [*sic*] des résultâts bienfésans: mais il ne faut pas que ce bel ouvrage présente des Parties qui attristent. L'Empereur est trop au-dessus de son siècle: Il peut imprimer un caractère de grandeur à tous les Actes de Sa Politique, pour que l'on puisse y reconnaître l'aurore d'un avenir plus fortune — [p. 158] Quoique ces considérations générales suffiraient déjà seules pour appuyer le fond du Projèt, il sera pourtant utile d'indiquer encore quelques avantages de détail, qui ajouteront à la justification de la mesure proposée —

La pensée d'imprimer une espèce *d'Unité idéale, & un caractère distinctif* à toute la masse des Peuples de l'origine *Slavonne*, devrait désormais être mise à la tête des Maximes Politiques du Cabinet de l'Empereur. Elle est comme la bâse & la garantie des grandes destinées qui attendent l'Empire de la Russie.[(a)]

Le Projèt en question tend directement à réaliser en partie cette Pensée de l'Unité idéale & du caractère distinctif des [p. 159] Peuples Slaves. On y entreprend de maintenir *dans le lien de cette Unité*, des Provinces Polonaises très étendues, & qui sont de la plus grande importance sous le rapport de la civilisation ainsi que sous celui de leur position: On y tâche de conserver &

(a) L'Observation suivante ne sera pas déplacée dans cet endroit. — Puisque, considérant l'excès de l'égoisme actuel des gouvernemens, il devient impossible de consolider la paix pour bien long-tems: la sagesse commande au moins de penser à un ordre de choses qui mette fin au scandaleux fratricide des Peuples d'une même race. La Paix consolidée dans l'intérieur de chacune des Trois Races Européennes,[112] contribuerait le plus à réaliser en partie le beau rêve d'une *Paix perpétuelle*: & il paraît même que la marche de l'esprit humain a pris une tendance plus dirècte vers ce grand but, en éveillant avec plus de force les sentimens de fraternité entre les Peuples de l'Origine Allemande,[113] ainsi que dans une partie des Peuples de l'origine Slavonne.[114]

111 Czartoryski almost certainly had the Ottoman Empire in mind; since 1803 he had often spoken of its ultimate downfall. He probably also thought of the Habsburg Empire and Prussia, to which he refers by name on p. 163 of the document.

112 See above, p. 87.

113 A reference to the growing movement for greater German unity in this period.

114 A reference to the current ideas of Slavonic solidarity and the prospect of Russo-Polish reconciliation under Alexander I.

de consolider leur Nationalité qui renforcera le caractère distinctif de la Race Commune. Par ce moyen on sauve pour bien longtems cette Unité & ce caractère dans les contrées plus éloignées, telles que la Bohême, la Silésie, la Lusace, la Prusse Orientale & Occidentale, & autres, où l'action plus immédiate du *Germanisme* tend avec plus de succès à les anéantir: — On n'a qu'à observer, avec quelle souplesse & par combien d'artifices le Germanisme continue à s'introduire par des progrès imperceptibles jusqu'au cœur même de la Slavonie, & l'on sentira qu'il est urgent de lui opposer l'action d'une Politique plus combinée & plus suivie.

Par suite d'une espèce de *Suicide Politique* on a permis déjà que le Germanisme s'établisse & s'enracine bien au-délà de la Vistule.[115] Malgré tous les changemens arrivés postérieurement,[116] il ne cèsse d'y déployer une action sourde, & d'affaiblir peu à peu le caractère National: & ce n'est peut-être qu'au moyen des mesures indiquées dans le Projèt, que l'on serait à même de détourner les suites funestes d'une grande faute en Politique.

Ce serait une grande erreur de croire que les Provinces Polonaises, laissées ainsi tout-à-fait (: sans aucune stipulation:) à la mercie de la Politique vindicative des Allemands, & de leurs efforts pour nous dénationaliser, se détâcheront d'autant plus [p. 160] vîte de leurs oppresseurs, & viendront réjoindre leur Patrie Commune.[117] Une telle tentative ne pourrait avoir lieu qu'au moyen des événemens beaucoup trop favorables, sur lesquels on ne peut pas compter de sitôt. Ces Provinces se sentiraient trop faibles vis-à-vis de la masse des Peuples Allemands, toujours trop enclins à réunir leurs efforts pour nous maintenir dans les chaînes. Elles sont découragées par de terribles expériences; elles le seraient encore plus par l'aspect de ce grand Pacte Européen[118] qui paraîtra garantir la permanence de leur sort: & il est plus que probable qu'après avoir été ainsi sacrifiées à une époque décisive, il ne leur resterait plus de motifs de confiance envers la Russie. Peut-être même un sentiment de dépit leur donnerait-il des tentations à se rapprocher des Allemands. D'ailleurs la Politique de ces Voisins est devenu maintenant plus mesurée & plus sage par les leçons de l'expérience:[119] leurs moyens d'oppression ne seront plus si patens comme par le passé, & leurs mesures pour nous dénationaliser, suivront une marche mieux combinée; imperceptible, mais sûre & continuë. — Le mal pourrait donc devenir irréparable, & une grande partie de la Slavonie (: à-peu-près la Partie la plus belle:) courrait risque d'être germanisée sans retour. On sacrifierait gratuitement & sans aucun motif fondé, le bonheur de ces Provinces; & un tel acte ne répondrait nullement au grand caractère qui doit signaler la Politique de l'Empereur.

On serait encore dans une grande erreur, si l'on croyait que les Provinces détâchées par le Partage & conservées dans [p. 161] leur nationalité, pourraient opérer une espèce d'attraction dangereuse pour la Pologne Russe, &

---

[115] Reference to East Prussia and probably the Baltic provinces of the Russian Empire.
[116] Reference to Prussian and Austrian losses of territory in Poland in 1807 and 1809 respectively. [117] i.e. the Polish kingdom united to Russia.
[118] The forthcoming final treaty concluding the work of the Congress of Vienna.
[119] Reference to greater Austrian and Prussian moderation towards the Poles resulting from the re-opening of the Polish Question in 1806–15 and Alexander I's insistence at the Congress of Vienna on creating a Polish state.

qui tendrait à détâcher celle-ci du corps de l'Empire. C'est une supposition qui est contraire à l'Ordre naturel de choses. Les Allemands, quelque chose qu'ils fassent pour plaire aux Polonais, ne pourront jamais parvenir à se les attacher: ils ne sauront jamais faire en sorte, que les Polonais puissent sous leur direction s'envisager comme ayant une *Patrie*. La volonté même des Allemands ne sera jamais sincère à cet égard: leurs prévenences [*sic*] envers nous seront toujours faites de mauvaise grace, & les motifs en seront ordinairement entâchés par quelque arrière-pensée. La nature a tracé ici une ligne de séparation, impossible à effacer: les obstacles resteront invincibles. — D'ailleurs, le moyen de concevoir qu'une seule *Partie* exerce une attraction éfficace envers la *masse totale*, au lieu d'en subir elle-même la loi! — Cette appréhension n'a donc pas le moindre fondement, & d'autres motifs très forts concourent précisément à nous démontrer le contraire. — D'abord, peut-il y avoir lieu à quelque crainte raisonnable lorsqu'on tourne ses regards sur la solidité de l'Empire de Toutes les Russies que l'Empereur vient d'entourer récemment de toutes la prépondérance de l'opinion morale des *Peuples*? Peut-on concevoir des craintes lorsqu'on considère ce degré de dévouement, de reconnaissance & d'amour que les Polonais rendus au bonheur d'avoir une Patrie, un nom & une existence politique, vont ajouter à cette Puissance déjà prépondérante? Croit-on sérieusement que les Polonais des Provinces séparées par le partage, conservant religieusement tous les traits de leur nationalité (: comme le plus grand bienfait reçu [p. 162] par l'intercession de l'Empereur:) pourront jamais songer à remuer la masse de prèsque toute la Pologne, & s'exposer par là aux hazards les plus terribles, tandis qu'à la première circonstance favorable ils n'auraient qu'un pas à faire pour être réunis sans aucune secousse au corps de leur vraie Patrie?

Si le Projèt en question tend réellement à assurer à l'Empereur la reconnaissance, l'amour & le dévouement des Polonais qui habitent les Provinces cedées, il Lui assure par là des avantages incalculables qui ne peuvent être contre-balancés par aucune considération de quelque importance qu'elle puisse être. Si le Projèt viendra à être réalisé par le consentement des Puissances rassemblées en Congrès, les Polonais séparés du Duché recevront alors le plus grand bienfait, & ils ne méconnaîtront point la Main Protectrice à laquelle ils le doivent. — Or il est généralem[en]t connu, combien on gagne sous tous les rapports, si sur une grande partie des frontières l'on est entouré des contrées où les habitants vous sont devoués par sentiment & par conviction: l'experience pendant les guèrres françaises a donné à cette vérité la plus grande évidence.[120] Ces sentimens de dévouëment, qui dans leur source n'ont été consacrés qu'à la Personne de l'Empereur, resteront à jamais à la Russie vû que les Polonais des dites Provinces seront essentiellement intéressés à l'envisager comme garante de leur droits constitutionnels & même (: s'il est permis d'employer cette expression:) comme héritière éventuelle de chaque Province Polonaise qui par l'effet de quelque événement, viendrait à se détacher du système allemande.

---

[120] Reference probably to the difficulties created for the Russian authorities by the considerable pro-Napoleonic sentiments of the Poles in the Duchy of Warsaw and in the western provinces of the Russian Empire in 1806–13.

[p. 163] Par un hazard très heureux pour la Russie les deux Etâts qui l'avoisinent, c'est-à-dire l'Autriche & la Prusse, inséparablem[en]t associés à toutes les métamorphoses éventuelles de l'Empire germanique & de l'Italie, n'ont pas encore terminé le développement de leurs déstinées politiques, & se trouvent encore bien loin de les avoir fixées. Ils sont pour ainsi dire, au plus fort de leur travail pour arriver à un systême definitif: & voilà ce qui présente à la Russie la perspective de beaucoup de chances favorables, qui La mettront peu à peu à même d'étendre & de consolider le systême constitutif des Peuples Slaves dont la suprématie Lui appartient par le cours naturel de choses. Peut-être arrivera-t-il encore bien de conjonctions où, sans effusion de sang & simplement au moyen des coopérations amicales, ou des secours accordés à propos, ou bien au moyen des acquisitions procurées aux voisins &c., l'on pourra faire des progrès vers le grand but. — Cette considération suffirait seule pour convaincre le Cabinet de Pétersbourg, qu'il est du plus intérêt pour la Russie, d'adopter une conduite analogue à l'ésprit qui règne dans le Projèt en question. Il est même de nécéssité absolue, que l'Empereur en procurant aux Polonais la garantie de leur nationalité, fasse paraître & ressortir autant qu'il est possible Son influence à cet égard, & que cette influence soit même constatée dans l'Acte à jamais mémorable de la Pacification Européenne.

Au reste, on pourrait encore ajouter à l'appui du Projèt une remarque, dont l'objet intéresse essentiellement l'Humanité. Il s'agit ici d'activer les progrès de la culture sociale & intellectuelle [p. 164] des Peuples Slaves. Le systême qui par effet d'une désastreuse nécéssité, partagerait la Nation Polonaise en quatre ou cinq Individualités séparées, pourra contribuer beaucoup à accélérer & perfectionner sous tous les rapports cette culture, *pourvû qu'elle soit empêchée de dévier jamais de la Nationalité* qui est propre aux Polonais. Nous en avons un exemple très frappant dans les progrès étonnans des lumières dans l'Empire germanique divisé en tant de différens Etâts. — Une raison de plus pour favoriser le Projèt, & pour arranger les choses de manière à ce que — *du malheur même il résulte un grand bien* pour la Nation Polonaise dont chaque progrès tourne aussi, par un résultât tout naturel, au profit des autres Peuples de la même origine.

R. W. Blackmore (1791–1882), an English Chaplain in Cronstadt

By MARK EVERITT

THE family of Blackmore is an ancient one in Dorset. It shares its name with the vale which borders on the neighbouring county of Wiltshire, and it was in Shaftesbury, the chief town of the area, where his father was vicar of St. James's church, that Richard White Blackmore was born in 1791. In his native countryside in and around Shaftesbury he was to spend most of his long life, except for his undergraduate years at Oxford and the one long interlude with which this essay is chiefly concerned.

Blackmore went up to Merton College in 1809 at the age of 18. He took his B.A. in 1813, and his M.A. four years later. He took Holy Orders, and went first to be curate to his father in Shaftesbury. He was apparently in no hurry to proceed to priest's orders, and was only ordained priest two years later, when he moved to a curacy at East Knoyle, some seven miles away. Here he spent three years, at the end of which he would normally have been looking for a living. Instead, for what reasons we do not know, he applied to the Russia Company for the post of Chaplain to the Company in Cronstadt, then vacant. Letters of recommendation from his rector and other clergymen, and a testimonial from the principal inhabitants of East Knoyle proving satisfactory, he was appointed in September 1819, set off soon after, and arrived in Cronstadt before the end of the year. He was to remain there for nearly thirty years, and while there to do pioneer work in interesting English churchmen in the affairs of the Russian Orthodox Church.

The Cronstadt chaplaincy was one of four maintained by the Russia Company[1] at this time. That in St. Petersburg was naturally reckoned the senior post, so that when any of the more desirable chaplaincies fell vacant there was some vying for promotion. The chaplain in Archangel had wished to be transferred to Cronstadt in 1819.

Blackmore arrived in Cronstadt to find much activity in progress. His predecessor, Marshall, had suffered ill health, and had, it seems, been a difficult man to deal with. But this was not too important, since the affairs of the chapel, as of all the Company's chapels in Russia, were in the exclusive management of a superintendant, Charles Moberly,

---

[1] See A. G. Cross, 'Chaplains to the British Factory in St. Petersburg, 1723–1818', *European Studies Review*, ii (1972), 125–42.

who was at that time organizing the building of a new church and parsonage. The old church and parsonage buildings, bought in 1806, were in a bad state, and the tenure of the land was uncertain. A new site had already been acquired, and the year after Blackmore's arrival the new parsonage was completed. The church was begun two years later, and opened for divine worship on 20 July 1824. Not long after, the new tsar Nicholas I presented it with a cross for the roof, to the scandal of Protestant-minded visitors. Unfortunately, the church was a mile from the commercial port, and so the 2,000 or so sailors who were generally in Cronstadt had every excuse for not making their way there very often.

The Company paid the chaplain's salary (which was increased from time to time) and furnished his parsonage (at an initial cost of £150), 'including mattresses, beds, and pillows, but exclusive of linen, plate, and crockery'.[2] He was provided with wax and tallow candles, firewood, and a servant, and there was a small library attached to the parsonage. The Company also paid bonuses to its chaplains from time to time, but with other grants (such as the payment of removal expenses) it was not always generous.

Things took a long time. The post between Russia and England was expensive and slow. In 1827 the masters of vessels trading to Cronstadt petitioned to be allowed to subscribe for an organ in the chapel, but it was not until 1832 that the Company finally acquired 'a good hand organ' (whatever this might be: an organ without pedals, perhaps), which was sent out from England, together with prayer and psalm books.

The duties of the chaplain were various. Besides providing the regular services for the resident English community, Blackmore had to minister to a large occasional population of visiting seamen. In 1839, when the Company increased his salary, they noted: 'Mr. Blackmore has established a school in Cronstadt, and having a numerous congregation of British and American Seamen has given Evening Lectures every Sunday during the winter, which have been well attended and met general approbation.'[3] Weddings and christenings were rare, but burials, particularly of seamen, were quite frequent. When the cholera first appeared in Cronstadt in 1831, the Russian authorities had a number of British seamen removed to the hospital, where they died and were buried. The first the chaplain knew of it was when he received an official list of their names.

Another duty of the Company's chaplains was to entertain and show around English visitors of various kinds. One such visitor, who was to have a considerable influence on Blackmore, was William Palmer of

---

[2] Guildhall Library, London, Russia Company MS. 11, 741/9, Court Minute Books of the Russia Company, 13 Feb. 1835.

[3] Guildhall Library, London, Russia Company MS. 11, 749.

Magdalen College, Oxford, who travelled to Russia in 1840–1 with the intention of opening discussions with Russian churchmen, and hoping to be accepted by them as a communicant by right in a sister Church, since, in his view, the Russian and English Churches had never formally condemned one another or broken off relations. The story of Palmer's abortive mission can be read elsewhere.[4] But it is clear that Blackmore was able to give him considerable help with his project, and in return was much influenced by Palmer, who seems to have told him about the Oxford Movement, then still at its height, and gained his adherence to its principles in some degree. The English colony in Russia was very isolated, and books were hard to come by, so that, although Blackmore had been a contemporary of Keble at Oxford and remembered his name, until Palmer enlightened him he knew nothing of the *Christian Year*. Blackmore had made friends with various Russian churchmen, and had a sympathetic knowledge of the Russian Church, unlike the chaplain in St. Petersburg, Law, who took a much more critical and 'Protestant' view. He told Palmer that he had been admitted within the sanctuary at the consecration of a new Russian church, 'a kind of recognition of my orders'. He thought that the Eastern Church was right on the vexed question of the *Filioque*, and (on another notorious theological issue) from living much with Russians he had come to think that the invocation of saints, as practised by the Russians 'does not interfere with the one mediation of Christ, nor is their veneration of icons really idolatry, though there may be superstition mixed with it'.[5] With some of the local Russian clergy he was on quite close terms. We hear of his lending a local priest one of the classical works of Anglican theology,[6] and he took the *protopop* of the main church home with him when he found him early one morning out in the rain and the worse for drink.

Yet, for all his sympathy with the Russian Orthodox Church, Blackmore was no uncritical admirer of it. Thus, in his translation of an article 'On the Orthodoxy of the Russian Church', he notes against a rather bombastic sentence ('Thus then in Russia alone has the beautiful idea of the sage and pious Emperor Justinian been realised and fully justified.') his own ironic comment, 'I am not as other men are!' (See Appendix, No. 4). And later in his translation of the same article he takes occasion to relate the following incident:

A recognised sign of Saintship is the incorruption of the body—they apply the words of the Psalmist Thou wilt not suffer thy holy one to see corruption not only to Christ but also to his Saints—

---

[4] See W. Palmer, *Notes of a Visit to the Russian Church*, ed. J. H. Newman (1882).
[5] Ibid. 75–6.
[6] A book 'in defence of the Apostolic Canons' by Bishop Beveridge: probably *Codex canonum ecclesiae primitivae vindicatus ac illustratus* (1678).

This I need not say is a very doubtful test. I saw the body of the Prince de Croix, killed in a battle with Peter the Great, near Revel, 1725, quite as perfect as that of any recognised Saint in the Cathedrals of Novgorod and Moscow. The Prince was a very profligate person and deeply in debt: his creditors prevented his burial, and laid him in his full dress, in one of the Catacombs till his debts were paid. I saw him in 1829.

Blackmore had translated other works of Russian theology into English. Palmer mentions

(i) Some sermons by Michael, late Metropolitan of Moscow [actually of St. Petersburg and Novgorod], and by Philaret. (One of Metropolitan Michael's sermons was subsequently published, in a volume entitled *Lives of Eminent Russian Prelates*, of which more below.)

(ii) The History of the Russian Church by A. N. Mouravieff. (Written in 1838; this was subsequently printed.)

(iii) The Full Catechism of the Orthodox Church. (Also printed later.)

(iv) The official account of the return in 1839 of a million and a half of Lithuanian Uniats. (This translation does not survive.)

And he relates, 'Mr. Blackmore and I read and translated together at Cronstadt the *Orthodox Confession* of Peter Mogila, the XVIII Articles of the Synod of Bethlehem of 1672, and the *Imperial and Patriarchal Letters* which were the occasion of that Russian version.'[7]

On his return to England, Palmer acted as intermediary in getting two of Blackmore's translations published. First to appear was the translation of Mouravieff's *History*, which Blackmore dedicated to the Governor and Court of Assistants of the Russia Company. It was published in 1842, and for it he wrote an Introduction which shows very clearly the influence of his conversations with Palmer.

Although there is a great similarity between [the Eastern Church] and the Communion of Rome in the splendour and pomp of their external rites and ceremonies, and in many of those customs which they have in common derived from the earlier age of our religion, and which we in our zeal for getting rid of corruptions have—perhaps hastily and inconsiderately— dropped, yet in essentials, both of Faith and Discipline, and in its spirit, as well as in its differences from the modern Roman theology, it has very many points which bear a striking resemblance to our own. Derived from the same high source, the Greek patriarchs and the British Churches have indeed for centuries ceased to hold intercourse with each other, but yet our Christian intercommunion has never been formally broken off by any open act of either party. It is only by long custom and mutual prejudice that it is assumed to have become impossible, neither party sufficiently considering that all the Churches of the world were not necessarily implicated in the temporary quarrels and reconciliations of the archbishops of Rome and Constantinople.

7 Palmer, op. cit. (n. 4), 63, 72.

This is exactly Palmer's argument to the authorities of the Russian Church. Later in his Introduction Blackmore goes on to consider the position of the English clergy, in comparison with the Russian, in language which vividly recalls the *Tracts for the Times*.

... we have been too often looked upon merely as the teachers of an Act of Parliament Religion, or as ministers of the most wealthy and influential of those sects or persuasions, with which our country abounds. Our ministry has been therefore esteemed and respected for our learning, eloquence or piety, or been despised for our want of them, and we have been either preferred or postponed to the sectarian preacher who has intruded into our charge, from our superiority or inferiority to him in these qualifications; whilst our Apostolical descent, the true point of difference between us, and to which he does not even make any pretensions, has been ridiculed by our enemies and too often but coldly and doubtfully defended by our friends.

'Our Apostolical descent': the phrase is Newman's in Tract I. Did Palmer bring some of the *Tracts for the Times* with him for Blackmore— and others—to read?

Three years later, in 1845, was published the Full Catechism referred to by Palmer, under the title *The Doctrine of the Russian Church, being the Primer or Spelling Book, the Shorter and Longer Catechisms, and a Treatise on the Duty of Parish Priests*. This volume, too, shows the influence of Palmer in the dedication 'To the Most Reverend, the Primus and the other Bishops of the Apostolic Church in Scotland . . . as to the other remaining successors and representatives of those British bishops, who in the reign of Peter the First held a correspondence with the Russian Synod; a correspondence, which was dropped on the death of Peter with an assurance from the Imperial Government that it should be renewed at some future and more convenient opportunity.' This dedication is verbally very similar to that of Palmer's compilation, entitled *A Harmony of Anglican Doctrine with that of the Eastern Catholic Church*, a catena of extracts from Anglican writers and official documents written as an Appendix to Blackmore's volume, and often bound with it.

By this time Blackmore's stay in Russia was drawing to its close. In 1847 his father died at the age of 89, and he notified the Company that he must return home. He had been in Cronstadt for twenty-eight years, during which time he had returned home only three times. The first time, in 1824–5, was for his honeymoon: in April 1824 he had married a widow named Harriet Hembry, the daughter of Admiral Elliott. The second time was in 1835–6, because his aged father had expressed an anxious wish to see him once more; and the last was from September 1844 to June 1845, when his replacement was the Revd. George Williams, who was later to become a prime mover in founding the Eastern Churches Association and continuing the work of acquainting

English churchmen with the Eastern Church. On leaving Cronstadt, Blackmore was presented with an address from the British Factory, expressing the Company's regret at his leaving 'a post he had filled for upwards of twenty-seven years with the most steady and persevering attention to his several duties, by which he had obtained the good opinion of his parishioners, the respect of all the authorities of Cronstadt &c.'[8] All the same, he had some difficulty in getting the Company to pay the expenses of his removal to England.

He came back to his home country of west Wiltshire, and succeeded his father in the parish of Donhead St. Mary. (His father had bought the advowson of this parish from Lord Arundell in 1810, presented himself to the living in 1816, and afterwards sold it to New College, Oxford, which still retains it.) It was only seven miles from his birthplace; a large, scattered, rural community, with two churches and a good stipend of £1,200.

He brought back with him to England his unpublished translations from Russian and some at least of his Russian books, and for a while he carried on his literary work.

His name is first among the acknowledgements in the Preface to the massive General Introduction to J. M. Neale's *History of the Holy Eastern Church* (1850). (This, though Part I of the unfinished work, was in fact the second part to be written.) We do not know how Neale and Blackmore became acquainted, though it was very probably through the intermediary of George Williams. We learn from the Preface that Blackmore lent Neale 'the entire store of his MS. translations from the Russ and Slavonic', and that he read the whole work in proof and made many valuable suggestions. It is clear that Blackmore also lent him some of his Russian printed books. And there is among the Neale papers in Lambeth Palace Library a manuscript translation by Blackmore, 'The Answer of the Orthodox Eastern Church to a circular letter lately sent by Pope Pius IX to the Orthodox in the East'.[9] As the Russian translation from which Blackmore worked was published in Moscow in 1849, this is the only translation which Blackmore certainly made after his return to England.

A few years later, in 1854, a volume appeared, entitled *Lives of Eminent Russian Prelates*. The editor was the Reverend R. Thornton, then a fellow of St. John's College, Oxford. But, as he explains, 'The Lives of St. Demetrius and Michael in this volume are simply translations from the Russian, for which the Editor is indebted to the Rev. R. W. Blackmore . . .', and his own part was simply to compile the life of Nikon from English materials and to write the Introduction. Even in the Introduction he is in fact much indebted to Blackmore, who had

[8] Guildhall Library, London, Russia Company MS. 11, 749.
[9] Lambeth Palace Library, Lambeth MS. 2678, 154–95.

evidently allowed him the use of his manuscript material. He gives extensive quotations from the Letters of Orders of a Deacon and a Priest, as specimens of ecclesiastical documents and of the teaching of the Russian Church. These excerpts, and the explanatory footnotes that go with them, are the work of Blackmore, though not acknowledged as such (see Appendix). The authorship of the original of the two latter Lives is not disclosed, and I have not been able to trace the original in any English library. But the same is true of the Russian originals of all Blackmore's translations. It seems that, having made the translations, he did not bother to bring the originals home with him.

With the publication of the *Lives of Russian Prelates*, Blackmore's literary activity came to an end. He had his manuscripts bound into a quarto volume in 1857, and they were forgotten. Nor did he care to keep in touch with any of his friends and acquaintances in the Russian Church. In the Church of England, interest in the Eastern Orthodox Churches was growing, but it was Neale and others who were now to carry on the work of informing English churchmen about the Church in Russia. Blackmore took no part in it. The Eastern Churches Association was founded in 1865, but he did not even become a member. It was as though the Russian interlude in his life had never been.

Blackmore had returned to his native country, and to his hereditary occupation as a country parson. In Donhead he led the life of a conscientious Victorian country priest, and tried, though not very hard, to put into practice some of the principles of the Oxford Movement which he had learned through William Palmer. (The evidence is to be found in his answers to the Bishop of Salisbury's questions in successive Visitation Articles.) Two of the main aims of the Oxford Movement were to revive the daily service in churches, and to establish a celebration of Holy Communion, at least every Sunday. On each of these points, Blackmore met with very limited success in his remote rural congregation, though he was able to establish Communion monthly and on festivals. He had marked in his manuscript translations the sections about daily services in the Russian Church. And his answers to the Bishop's question about daily service in successive Visitations seem to show an uneasy conscience. 'No, I have tried it and found the attendance so very small that I did not continue' (1870). 'No I do not neither does my curate. We think it would in part prevent our performing other duties and we should get scarcely anyone to attend' (1873). Later (1879) he had tried at any rate services on Saints' days, but no-one came. Still, during his long incumbency the attendance at Sunday services in both his churches increased steadily, in spite of a declining population. He kept a curate; sometimes two. He founded a charity to supply coal for the poor, a church trust, and a Sunday School.

And he was not allowed quite to forget about his years in Russia.

Two years before Blackmore's arrival in Donhead St. Mary a new rector had been instituted to the parish of Broadwindsor, over the border in Dorset. His name was Solomon Caesar Malan, and even among the learned country clergy of the nineteenth century he stands out as a prodigiously learned man. Oriental languages and theology, on both of which he wrote prolifically, were only two among his many interests.[10] He and Blackmore were neighbours for thirty-five years, and they became friends. We do not know at what stage Malan added Russian to the number of languages of which he had a practical knowledge, but clearly Blackmore was a help to him in his Russian studies. By 1870, he was himself publishing translations from Russian, and it was to him that Blackmore finally bequeathed all his Russian books and translations. The Russian printed books formed part of the large gift with which Malan helped to establish the library of the Indian Institute in Oxford, whence they passed into the Bodleian Library.

One more reminder of his days in Russia was to come to Blackmore shortly before his death. In December 1881 he unexpectedly received a letter from no less a person than Cardinal Newman. Newman wrote to inform him of his intention to publish a volume of notes from the journals of Palmer's visit to St. Petersburg in 1841. He asked whether Count Pratosoff (sic) and M. Mouravich (sic) were alive or dead, and expressed a wish 'to record the friendly intercourse which existed between Mr. Palmer and Mr. Blackmore to whom the former owed so much in the way of information and advice'. The letter led to a brief correspondence between the two men. Blackmore answered Newman's questions, and added: 'As to myself I feel that I may give Carte Blanche to you to transcribe and print any thing my dear friend W. Palmer may have recorded of my intercourse with him.' In acknowledging this letter, Newman took the opportunity to put to Blackmore one or two more questions of detail (to which Blackmore replied), and asked him to accept the volume when it was published.[11] But before the book appeared, Blackmore was dead. He died on 28 June 1882, and was buried in the churchyard of his own parish church. His death was duly noted in the columns of the *Guardian* and the *Church Times*, but he was not thought worth an obituary notice. In his will, among other bequests, he left his Russian books and papers, as we have seen, to Malan. There were also a Turkish sabre and a Circassian pistol which went to the Trustees of the Salisbury and South Wilts Museum, and a diamond ring which he had received from Nicholas I, the Emperor of Russia, and which went to his niece, one of his few surviving relatives. And lastly, he left £200 for painted glass to be placed in the East Window of

[10] For biographical details of S. C. Malan, see A. N. Malan, *Solomon Caesar Malan* (1897).
[11] See *The Letters and Diaries of John Henry Newman*, xxx (Oxford, 1976), 32, 56. Blackmore's two letters to Newman are held in the library of The Oratory, Birmingham.

Donhead Church. This window (of good Victorian glass) survives, and is his visible memorial.

APPENDIX

A List of the Contents of Lambeth MS. 1550

This quarto volume (ii+326 ff.) contains translations of documents about the Russian Orthodox Church, bound up and signed 'R. W. Blackmore; Donhead St. Mary 1857'. There are many notes and comments by Blackmore on the verso pages, which are left blank in all the translations except the last. This list of contents is Blackmore's own.

1. The Oustaff or Code of Laws of the Russian Spiritual Consistories together with other documents relating to the Church in Russia. Printed by order of the Most Holy Governing Synod (St. Petersburg 27 March 1841). 119 pages.
2. Table of Contents of the Oustaff. 12 pages.
3. The Oath to be taken by a Priest at his Ordination. 4 pages.
4. A Translation of An Extract from the 'Christian Reading', a periodical published at the Spiritual Academy of St. Petersburg—July 1843—and approved of by the Spiritual Censors. Article II—Page 47: 'On the Orthodoxy of the Russian Church'. 74 pages.

   [At this point is bound in a copy of a letter (? to W. Palmer), dated 'Cronstadt 19/31 August 1843', asking for comments, apparently on the preceding translation.]

5. A Translation of the Short Russian Catechism published in 1843 (by the Synodal Press and approved for use in schools). 18 pages.
6. An Appendix to the above containing instructions for those engaged in Military Service (St. Petersburg 1843). 6 pages.
7. The same, for Military Schools. 6 pages.

   [At this point is interleaved a copy of a letter to W. Palmer, dated 'Cronstadt 1843']

8. Deacon's and Priest's Letters of Orders. 12 pages.
9. General Instructions from a Bishop to a Priest at his Ordination for his private perusal (St. Petersburg November 1815). 38 pages.
10. An Analysis of Baron Rosencampf's History of the Russian Church. 60 pages.

Some Unpublished Poems of Nicholas Bachtin

By R. F. CHRISTIAN

THE poems published for the first time below have been deciphered from draft versions scribbled in pen and pencil in a number of old exercise books bequeathed to me some years ago, and represent only a very small selection from a very short period in the life of a brilliant and colourful, but little-known Russian *émigré*, Nicholas Bachtin. Bachtin was born in 1896 in Orel, where his father was a civil servant and a member of the hereditary gentry, and died in Birmingham in 1950. Nicholas Bachtin never enjoyed the scholarly reputation of his elder brother, Mikhail Mikhailovich Bakhtin, well-known in academic circles in Russia and abroad for his seminal book on Dostoevsky, *Problemy tvorchestva Dostoevskogo* (first published in 1929, and recently translated into English), and for his important studies on Rabelais. By contrast, the younger Bachtin published very little in his lifetime, but left behind a great many manuscript articles, texts of lectures, unfinished books, notebooks, and diaries, and several exercise books containing many hundreds of poems in various stages of completion. Much of this material is now in the Birmingham University archives; some of it—in particular the notebooks and poems—has come into my possession through a mutual friend and colleague. As a result of the enthusiastic collaboration of Professor A. E. Duncan-Jones at Birmingham University, Professor George Thomson, Emeritus Professor of Greek at the same University, and Miss Francesca Wilson, the author and relief worker who gave Bachtin his first home in England, a selection of Bachtin's unpublished writings was issued privately in 1963 in a limited edition of 100 copies, containing essays of an autobiographical nature, lectures on aspects of Greek, Russian, and English literature, and a short biographical introduction. The main stages of Bachtin's career—pieced together from information in this introduction, his own notebooks, and the reminiscences of his close friends—are as follows. After an unusually precocious childhood in Orel and Vilna, and a short period of study in Odessa, he matriculated in 1913 at the University of St. Petersburg, where his philological and philosophical studies, and the inspiration of the outstanding Greek scholar, Professor Zelinsky, aroused in him a passionate love for the language, literature, and civilization of ancient Greece. An irrepressible spirit of adventure led him to enlist as a hussar in 1916, although as a student he could have claimed exemption from military service. From then until 1923 he fought in the First World War, sided with the White Army after the Revolution (a matter of profound regret in later life), and eventually joined the Foreign Legion, in which he served for several years in North Africa and was decorated for gallantry. Severely wounded in 1923, he spent eight months in hospital in Algiers before obtaining his discharge from the Legion and moving to Paris early in 1924. The poems printed below were nearly all written during this period, when he held a variety of casual and menial jobs and was often on the verge of starvation. Before long, however, his remarkable erudition and great talent as a public speaker were rewarded by his appointment to the editorial board of the Russian *émigré* journal *Zveno* (*The Link*), and by requests to lecture on classical Greece to the Russian community in Paris. *Zveno*, whose title alluded to its purpose of serving as a link between the past and future of Russian culture as a branch of a common European spiritual tradition, was edited successively by M. M. Vinaver and M. L. Kantor, and attracted contributions from most of the Russian writers in Paris in the 1920s—Bunin, Merezhkovsky, Gippius, Remizov, Berdyaev, Mochul'sky, Khodasevich, and many others. Bachtin was responsible for editing the philosophical section of the journal and for helping to shape its policy. He himself published over fifty articles and book reviews in *Zveno*, which give a good indication of his range of interests and the quality of his mind. Many of his contributions understandably had to do with contemporary French literature and ideas—Paul Valéry, Jacques Maritain, André Maurois, Anatole France, Jean Cocteau, the impact made by Freud and by neo-Thomism in France. Further afield there were articles on Nietzsche and Dostoevsky, Nietzsche and music, and Spengler and France. His book reviews embraced Tomashevsky's and Zhirmunsky's important Formalist writings on Russian prosody and rhyme, Berdyaev's *The New Middle Ages* and Zelinsky's *Ancient Greek Religion* in French translation. From time to time he also wrote philosophical dialogues or so-called 'conversations' on a number of abstract themes such as 'contemplation', 'optimism', 'reason', 'in praise of death', and—on a more concrete level—the problems involved in translating from one language and culture into another. His public lectures, on the other hand, were mainly devoted to the subject in which as a classical scholar he felt most at home—ancient Greece and Greek religion.

The last issue of *Zveno* appeared in June 1928, and in the same year Bachtin was invited by Francesca Wilson, on the initiative of Professor S. Konovalov, to come to England for a period of study and to enjoy the hospitality of her Birmingham home. Konovalov was at the time Professor of Russian at Birmingham University and had described Bachtin as one of the most brilliant men of the Russian *émigration*. His

five-month visit was to shape the course of his later life, for after returning to Paris to study at the Sorbonne and the École des Langues orien-
tales, he came back to England in 1932 and obtained his Ph.D. degree
from Cambridge University for a thesis on Thessaly in the thirteenth
century B.C. and the origins of the Centaur-Lapithai myth. In 1935 he
was appointed assistant lecturer in classics at University College,
Southampton (now Southampton University), and in 1938 he became
a lecturer in classics at Birmingham University, where his friend George
Thomson had recently been appointed to the chair of Greek. After the
Second World War, Bachtin transferred his formal allegiance from
classics to the science of language, and from 1945 until his death in
1950 he constituted in effect a one-man Department of Linguistics at
Birmingham. Towards the end of his life, his deep loyalty to Russia re-
asserted itself, although he never returned to his native country and
never joined any political party.

These bare biographical facts give no indication of the extremely
fertile influence Bachtin exercised on his literary and academic colleagues, or of the outstanding contribution he made as a teacher of
language and literature. His friends at Cambridge and Birmingham,
including Professors Cornford, Dodds, Duncan-Jones, Konovalov,
Pascal, Thomson, and many others, have borne ample testimony to that
side of his activity. His literary output, however, remained regrettably
small. His only published book was his *Introduction to the Study of Modern
Greek* (1935), which grew out of his belief that the historical development of Greek shows a unity unparalleled in any other Indo-European
language; that 'there is no modern Greek language, there is only the
present state of Greek'; and that the spoken Greek language of today—
the only *living* survival of the classical past—is the only real key to the
study of ancient Greek. As a result of his views, and with the active
support of Professor Thomson, spoken Greek became an integral part
of the syllabus of the Department of Greek at Birmingham 'as the last
link', to quote Duncan-Jones, 'in a chain which led back, without a
break, to the earliest known form of the language'. In 1938 Bachtin
edited the first issue of the short-lived periodical *The Link*, a review of
medieval and modern Greek which took its name from *Zveno* and was
produced with the collaboration of a group of scholars of international
distinction. His article in the first issue on 'English Poetry in Greek'
stemmed from his interest in problems of poetic translation, and was
designed to show, on the basis of Seferis's translation of Eliot's *The
Waste Land*, some of the fundamental divergences and 'significant in-
commensurabilities', as he called them, between modern Greek and
English poetic idioms, and the significance of the 'interference' of two
linguistic systems which can be observed in a verse translation. The
Birmingham University archives include *inter alia* a course of ten

lectures on general linguistics, essays on Greek history and on Homer and the Greek spirit, general talks on 'Linguistics and classical studies' and on 'The place of poetry in capitalist society', and a number of more specialized lectures on various Russian authors, delivered at Birmingham and Oxford. Two of these lectures—one on Mayakovsky and one on Pushkin—were published posthumously in volumes ii and xi of *Oxford Slavonic Papers*, in 1951 and 1964 respectively. There are also notes for a book on Plato's *Cratylus*, as well as numerous fragments of a literary and linguistic nature.

The purpose of this introduction, however, is not so much to indicate the range of Bachtin's intellectual interests as to introduce the reader to his considerable talent as a poet. Professor Thomson, in the Introduction to his book *The Greek Language* (1960), which is dedicated to Bachtin's memory, says that his friend was 'by nature a poet, but, compelled by circumstances to forgo the writing of poetry, he devoted himself to the science of language, to which he brought . . . a poet's passion'. Georgy Adamovich recalls in a long obituary notice in *Novoe russkoe slovo* that it was as a poet that he was particularly remembered by his contemporaries at St. Petersburg University, but adds—mistakenly—that he apparently gave up writing poetry in his mature years, despite continuing to be passionately, and indeed 'almost convulsively' interested in it. Adamovich was not, of course, aware of the many hundreds of poems which Bachtin wrote in his twenties and thirties and which, to the best of my knowledge, have never yet been published. Technically and academically speaking, his qualifications as a poet were impeccable—a scholar's mastery of prosody, a remarkable facility at handling metre and rhyme, a passionate interest in words and images, and a profound knowledge of the poetry of Greece and Rome, England, France, Germany, and Russia. He was gifted by nature with a photographic memory, and was at one time able to recite entire poems by heart after one reading or hearing. These attributes made him an admirable versifier, but they could not by themselves make him a great poet. Nevertheless, a careful reading of several hundred of his poems—unrevised and not intended for publication—has confirmed my belief that some of them at least deserve to be rescued from oblivion, and that they will illuminate yet another facet of an unusually gifted and many-sided writer, teacher, and scholar.

For the purposes of this article, I have chosen 24 poems out of 118 written between 30 November 1923 and 31 March 1924—many of them short autobiographical lyrics which were his favourite means of expression. This four-month period was interrupted by a move from hospital in Algiers to a new existence in Paris, and the poems have been selected in part to illustrate Bachtin's changing approach to life at a critical time in his career, immediately after leaving the Foreign Legion. The first eight poems were written in Algiers, some in hospital, and the rest were written in Paris where he arrived in February 1924. The early ones reveal his preoccupation with childhood and youth, and particularly with memories of the year 1918 when he found himself in Alushta, in the Crimea—memories of the spring, of the Black Sea coast and mountains, of the grape harvest, and of himself and his friends reciting Homer while Soviet troops were retreating before the German advance and Bachtin was selling tickets in a people's cinema. There is an interval of two months between No. 8, inspired by a line of Heraclitus and announcing Bachtin's stoical determination to cling to life, and No. 9, written in Paris when he was no doubt already living, as he later put it, 'on old tea-leaves and a few cigarettes', but feeling once again the joy of reawakened creativity. No. 11 is presumably addressed to his brother, who stayed behind in Russia. No. 12 expresses the nostalgia Bachtin was to experience from time to time for the life of a soldier (the first line is a reference to the wounds in his chest and arm sustained while leading an attack for which he was later awarded the Croix de Guerre avec Palmes). Echoes of the Russian Civil War and of the legionary's life in Africa are heard again in Nos. 16 and 20 respectively, while the other poems of the same period mostly reflect the ups and downs of his days in Paris, the moments of passion, despair, and hope, culminating at least temporarily in the calm acceptance of his lot in the final poem of the group (No. 24).

Bachtin often spoke of the qualities he particularly admired in Pushkin's poetry—restraint, definition, a sense of measure, clarity, and a high level of craftsmanship—and within his own limits he aspired towards them, while following with keen interest, but without the desire to emulate them, the poetic experiments of the 1920s in Soviet Russia and abroad. He saw poetry as a highly conventional, perceptibly ordered, and distinctively patterned form of utterance depending on a constantly changing balance between repetition and variety, which gives rise to a subtle interplay of recognition and suspense, surprise and anticipation. He saw the poet's task as being to recall the minds of his readers and listeners—and the *oral* side of poetry came to assume greater and greater importance for him in his later years—to the simple and essential; 'to integrate into our living experience', as he put it, 'the few things which really matter and which we know so well that we are no longer aware of their existence'.

Bachtin's own poetry did not measure up to his high ideals, and perhaps for that reason he preferred to keep it to himself, while treasuring to the end of his life the cheap exercise books containing it. In preparing this small selection for publication, I have been guided by the wish to present a fairly typical cross-section of the poems written in the winter of 1923–4, and have therefore not limited myself to choosing only the best. I have taken liberties with the punctuation, which in places is obscure, and have corrected some careless spelling mistakes. I have also transposed the poems into the new orthography.

1

В моей печали вновь раскрылось мне
Бесценное и мудрое наследство.
Все, что мечталось смутно, в полусне,
В садах медлительного детства,
Все, что ковалось в боли и в борьбе
И крещено огнем в моих глубинах
Приемлю, верный цельному себе.
И признаю себя в своих личинах
Жить. Властно налагать свою печать
На дни, на дни. И вожделеть. И снова
Грядущее мятежно зачинать
Всей мощью плодотворного былого!

30.11.1923

2

У вод речных, вблизи могил, себе
Я ископал, среди камней, могилу —
Мой тесный дом — чтоб медленно застыло
Все, что кипело в буйстве и борьбе;
Чтоб чуждые часы, года, века,
Спокойно проходили предо мною,
Как долу тихая течет река
Среди песков — покорная — к покою.

2.12.1923

3

Дай мне забыть все буйное, дневное,
В твоей тиши,
Дай мне испить от светлого покоя
Твоей души.

Я всю тоску, что в смуте жизни крепла,
Тебе принес.
Коснись с улыбкой золота и пепла
Моих волос,

И на меня свой взгляд из тихой дали
Приподыми,
В твое бесстрастье, в свет твоей печали
Меня прими.

1.1.1924

4

Весна 1918 (Алушта)

Нет, не было блаженней и белее
Той медленной весны.
Всей нежностью, всей легкостью лелея,
С прозрачной вышины
Она сошла в долины, к шумам моря,
И сладко зацвела,
Пасхальные в сияющем просторе
Будя колокола.
И розовел миндаль и неустанно
Сбегая с гор, ручьи
Несли, звеня, в мой круг благоуханный
Немолчные струи.

2.1.1924

5

А. А. Смирнову

Зарозовел и звоном полон сад.
Затихло море и цвели фиалки.
Недолог путь от нашей тихой балки
До городка. Прерывисто шуршат,

Туманно-фиолетовы и серы,
Валы, ложась у самого пути.
Там в сумерках, скандируя Гомера,
Любили мы, спокойные, брести.

Грозя бедой, кругом вставал мятеж,
Но, чуждые смятенья и тревоги,
Беседы были благостны и строги,
А чуткий вечер светел был и свеж.

2.1.1924

6

Пути клубятся золотою пылью,
Несут ослы тяжелых гроздий груз.
Не молкнет гам: осеннему обилью
С трудом и песней дружный люб союз.

Полны до края каменные чаны.
Высоко солнце. Сбор богатый снят.
Благоухая, золотой и рьяный,
Ждет легких ног и вянет виноград.

Правь с песней мерный труд: на камень серый,
Сминая гроздья теплые, пролей
Сок тусклых лоз, испивших полной мерой
Тяжелой мощи лучезарных дней.

4.1.1924

7

Хрупкие гребни ленивы,
Тусклы сырые пески побережий.
Дует на лоно залива
Ветер неслышный, широкий и свежий.
Тронуты зыбью неяркой
Серые воды и стынут устало.
Радуга тающей аркой,
Легкая, облики гор увенчала.

8.1.1924

8

Πῦρ ἀείζωον, ἁπτόμενον μέτρῳ καί
ἀποσβεννύμενον μέτρῳ (Heraclitus)

Не все ль равно — на миг или навек!
Бери глубоко, жадно все земное.
Есть просветы лазури — в смуте боя
Есть тишина и свет на ложе нег!
Испытано до дна — сквозит иным
Все буйное, чем сердце жадно дышит,
И сердце упоенное земным
Призыв родных глубин яснее слышит.
И тлеет в дрожи мук, блаженств, тревог
Живой огонь, что, неподвластный смене,
Течет как пламенный немолчный ток
Под косною раздельностью явлений.

14.1.1924

9

Всей дрожью мышц, всей мощью рук
Опять развязываю, споря,
Назревший трепет. Узел туг
И темен труд в скупом затворе.
Мой день суров. Но тверд и прав
Искус, что судьбы мне судили,
И, цепкий узел развязав,
Я дам полет крылатой силе.

13.3.1924

10

Забрызгана сияньями течет
Вечерняя река: мосты крутые
Шлют фонарей отсветы золотые
В тускнеющую гущу вешних вод,
И легкие сплетаются лучи
И в мягкий мрак вливаются, истаяв,
И властен наростающий в ночи
Гул по мостам несущихся трамваев.

14.3.1924

11

Одному из оставшихся

Делила нас тревожная вражда,
Что с каждым годом строже и упорней.
Но в глубину — как прежде, как тогда —
Уходят волю черплющие корни.

Пусть нет пути между тобой и мной,
Но два непримиримые хотенья
Питаемы единой глубиной,
Которой не коснулось разделенье.

Здесь — долу — предначертаны пути
И вольно был предызбран и измерен
Земной удел. Избравший, будь же верен,
И смей, упорней, до конца идти.

Но в высший миг прозренья и свободы
Двух разных душ коснется та же дрожь,
Мой враг и брат; — и сквозь вражду и годы
Ты мой привет услышишь и поймешь.

18.3.1924

12

Твоя печать клеймит мне грудь и руку;
И благостно отмеченный тобой,
По трубному, рокочущему звуку,
Зовущему в веселый бой —

Из тихого и ласкового дома,
Где жизнь прозрачна, как затон,
Я вновь уйду под веянье знамен
Тропой суровой и знакомой.

И сладко мне носить твою печать,
И любит сердце жадное, земное
Веселой, звонкой меной променять
На радость песни — радость боя.

19.3.1924

13

На краткий срок сошел я в эти долы,
И тесен мне твой скудный, пестрый дом.
Я взял тебя рабынею веселой,
Наложницей — покуда я в земном.

Я не хочу во времени приюта,
Упорный, гневный и чужой тебе —
Я лишь беру по праву — крепко, круто —
Твою любовь, подвластную судьбе.

О жизнь моя, случайная подруга,
Покуда горьким странствием души
Не пройдены пути земного круга —
Люби меня и, смуглая, пляши.

20.3.1924

14

Эта песнь замерла недопета,
Встали вихри, мутя и круша —
И в затонах глубокого света
Затонула безгласно душа.
И до срока молчанья вкусила,
Чтобы выйти опять к бытию,
Чтобы втайне созревшая сила
В час вечерний покорно свершила
Предреченную волю твою.

20.3.1924

15

Не нам, случайным, ведать срок и меру
Себя чрез нас познавшей полноты,
Нам только боль немолчную и веру
Он дал в залог средь смуты и тщеты.

Нас только неустанное горенье
От часа к часу жертвенно ведет.
А малый дар познанья и прозренья
Лишь он, Пославший, примет и сочтет.

21.3.1924

16

Встреча

Нет забвенья отошедшим дням.
Властны годы — буйные, крутые.
Мы служили разным знаменам
На полях потоптанных России.

Кто же нас насмешливо связал,
Свел мечтать под сень одной палатки?
Но врага в тебе я угадал:
Не укроешь вражеской повадки.

И деля с тобой вино и хлеб,
Я слежу упорно за глазами.
Ты почуял. Взор твой тускл и слеп,
Но на дне — глухое тлеет пламя.

И тревожат старые мечты,
Наростают, глухо беспокоя:
Я рубил бы вновь таких, как ты,
Как бывало — в остром взлете боя.

21.3.1924

17

Холодная и легкая рука
Замедлила на миг в моей — горячей.
Ты вся проста, печальна и легка,
Спокойная в покорном, тихом плаче.

Ты нежная, ты верная, и все же
Я не хочу тебя. Хмельной и грубый
Уйду делить мою глухую дрожь
С подругами, которые мне любы.

Ни кротости твоей я не люблю,
Ни нежности, ни пристального взгляда,
Чью тишину, прозрачная наяда,
Я пел когда-то в призрачном хмелю.

22.3.1924

18

Настороженный, чуток день,
И просты, пусты эти дали.
А сердце, с каждым днем бедней,
И примиренней и усталей.

Да и откуда почерпнуть
Бывалой дрожи — непокорной —
· Когда так тих, так светел путь,
А мир — застылый и просторный.

22.3.1924

19

В окне — облака, и тревожный и серый
Расширенный свет.
Разбита, разметана строгая мера,
Но радости нет.
И входит сырая весна дуновеньем
В затвор мой, хмельна.
И веет простором, зачатьем и тленьем
Сырая весна.

25.3.1924

20

Сухие ветры жестко дуют с юга,
Метут пески, слепят глаза верблюду,
Шуршат кружа. Прокрался зной повсюду.
И мутный очерк солнечного круга —
Сожженный, без лучей, в сожженном небе.
А ночь в огне, в сухих шуршаньях страха.
И всюду он — в плодах, в иссохшем хмеле,
В вине прокислом — горький привкус праха.

27.3.1924

21

Современный мистик

Когда в кафэ заказывал ликеры,
Стуча перстнем о мрамор, чахлый франт,
И в наглом свете плыли сутенеры
С подругами в грохочущий жаз-банд;

Когда в мельканьи света, в гулах, в звонах
Текла толпа; и щелкали шары
В дыму сигар; и у столов зеленых
Взрывались крики, метя ход игры;

— Все, все он променял на том Плотина,
На чад диалектических нирван,
На жесткий, с выпирающей пружиной,
Измазанный, просиженный диван.

Наглее сутенеров и скуднее
Бездельников, пьянеющих спеша,
— Рвалась к высотам, мутно вожделея,
И пыжилась обрюзглая душа!

28.3.1924

22

Я чью-то радость приютил
Сегодня в сердце. Залетела,
Коснулась чуткой лаской крыл
И, благодарная, запела.

Открыто сердце всей весне:
И часто, с песней, прилетали
Чужие радости ко мне
Клевать зерно моей печали.

28.3.1924

23

Все полно голосами живыми.
Всюду зовы. Но праха печать
На душе, что бессильна назвать,
В горькой немощи, светлое имя.

Смутно, ощупью ищет она
В тайниках подсознанья глухого.
— Не достигнуть глубокого дна,
Не найти благодатного слова!

Как отсветы далеких зарниц
В тесный дом мой живое стучится:
Бьются белыми крыльями птиц
В душном мраке отсветы — зарницы.

30.3.1924

24

Иду, как Он велел. И вижу только путь
Прямой и неизбежный.
Не должно, не дано — в иной предел свернуть
По прихоти мятежной.

И зовы чуждые смолкают, прозвенев,
Но я не внемлю зовам,
И твердость горькую коплю, как давний гнев,
В стремлении суровом.

31.3.1924

Theses in Slavonic Studies Approved for Higher Degrees by British Universities, 1972-1976

By J. S. G. SIMMONS

THIS list, covering theses approved for higher degrees by British universities during the quinquennium 1972–6, continues the basic 1907–66 list and the first supplement to it, which were published in *Oxford Slavonic Papers*, xiii (1967), 139–59, and n.s. vi (1973), 133–47, respectively. The numeration of the previous lists has been followed, i.e. the first thesis has been numbered 475 and the last 712, giving an apparent total of 238 theses for the period. The net figure, however, is 219, as five of the theses listed date from 1970 (Nos. 496, 514, 522, 589, and 622), thirteen from 1971 (Nos. 497–8, 513, 519, 523, 556, 623–5, 665–6, and 679–80), and one entry (No. 621) has been withdrawn. The 219 total (which includes 61 masters' degree theses and 10 Oxford B.Litt. dissertations), represents a 25 per cent advance on the comparable net figure (175) for the previous quinquennium, and is evidence that the research-explosion referred to in the introduction to our 1967–71 list rumbles on. The number of centres has also increased: the Universities of Belfast, Bradford, East Anglia, Exeter, Hull, Kent, Leicester, Newcastle, St. Andrews, Ulster, and York, and the Colleges of the University of Wales at Aberystwyth and Cardiff can now be added to the tale of those at which research degrees in Slavonic subjects have been awarded.

The distribution by subject indicates that international relations, history, economics, literature, and politics have attracted increased interest, while the number of theses in linguistic studies has declined. It has, moreover, proved necessary to add new rubrics covering art and architecture, law, and military and naval history, and to include the word 'sport' in the education heading.

The proportion of theses devoted to Russian (including Soviet) studies increased from the previous quinquennium's two-thirds to something over three-quarters of the total in the five years under review.

The colleges of the University of London together continued to produce the largest number of theses, though their proportion of the total

(67 out of 219 as against 64 out of 175) declined. The runners-up, Oxford (40), Birmingham (19), and Cambridge (16) all increased their totals by comparison with the previous five years.

In the 'date column' of the list the date is recorded in the form of the second element in the relevant academic year, e.g. 1972 for the year 1971–2, except in the case of London University, where the calendar year of acceptance is entered.

Once again the list has been compiled on the basis of information recorded in the annual volumes of the Aslib *Index to Theses*—supplemented by the unpublished materials for the most recent volume which were made available to me by the Editor of the *Index*, Mr. G. M. Paterson. Additional details were received in form of replies to a circular addressed to Slavonic Departments at British universities. My thanks are due to all those who provided me with information, and I hasten to combine with this expression of gratitude an assurance that the errors and omissions in the list are the reflection of my inadequacies rather than theirs. At the same time, I hope that they and others who may note imperfections in the list will inform me of them so that they may be corrected in the next five-year supplement which, if all goes well, should be published in 1982.

ABBREVIATIONS

B	B.Litt.	LS	London: School of Slavonic Studies
B	Birmingham	LU	London: University College
Brd	Bradford	LX	London (External)
C	Cambridge	M	Master of Arts
D	D.Phil., Ph.D.	M	Manchester
D	Durham	ME	M.Educ.
E	Edinburgh	ML	M.Litt.
EA	East Anglia	MP	M.Phil.
Es	Essex	MS	M.Soc.Sc. (**B**); M.Sc. (Econ.) (**LE**)
Ex	Exeter		
G	Glasgow	N	Nottingham
H	Hull	Ne	Newcastle
K	Keele	O	Oxford
Kt	Kent	Q	Queen's, Belfast
La	Lancaster	StA	St. Andrews
LB	London: Birkbeck College	Sx	Sussex
LCC	London: Chelsea College	U	Ulster
LE	London: School of Economics	WA	Wales: Aberystwyth
Le	Leeds	WB	Wales: Bangor
LEd	London: Institute of Education	WC	Wales: Cardiff
Leic	Leicester	WS	Wales: Swansea
Li	Liverpool	Y	York
LK	London: King's College		
LQ	London: Queen Mary College		

LIST OF THESES

I. ART, ARCHITECTURE

475. Bowlt (J. E.), The 'Blue Rose' Movement and Russian **StA** D 1972
Symbolist painting.

476. Crossley (B. P.), The architecture of Kasimir the Great: **C** D 1975
a study in the architecture of Lesser Poland, 1320–70.

II. DIPLOMATIC HISTORY, FOREIGN POLICY, INTERNATIONAL RELATIONS

A. *Czechoslovakia*

477. Easby (M.), The Brezhnev doctrine and the Czechoslovak **M** M 1972
crisis of 1968.

478. Mannion (M.), British policy towards Czechoslovakia, **Ne** ML 1972
1936–9.

479. Vyšný (M. P.), A study of Czechoslovak–Russian relations, **M** D 1972
1900–14.

480. Kett (D. F. B.), British attitudes to the Czechoslovak state, **WA** MS 1973
1914–26.

B. *Poland*

481. Żur (S.), British policy and the Polish western frontier, **LQ** D 1974
1941–5.

482. Raffel (K.), The German march into Prague and the ori- **O** B 1975
gins of the British guarantee to Poland of March 1939.

483. Żurowski (M. A.), British policy towards the Polish– **LE** D 1975
Soviet border dispute (1939–45).

484. Coutouvidis (J.), The formation of the Polish government- **K** D 1976
in-exile and its relations with Great Britain, 1939–1941.

485. Fedorowicz (J. K.), Anglo–Polish relations in the first **C** D 1976
half of the seventeenth century: a study in commercial
diplomacy.

C. *Rumania*

486. Braun (A.), Romanian foreign policy under Nicolae **LE** D 1976
Ceauşescu, 1965–72: the political and military limits of
autonomy.

487. Lungu (D.), The problem of Soviet–Romanian relations in **LQ** D 1976
Romanian foreign policy under Nicolae Titulescu.

D. *Russia to 1917*

488. Scott (G. A. K.), The formation of the Turkestan frontier **O** D 1972
between Russia and China in the eighteenth century.

489. Sweet (D. W.), British foreign policy, 1907–9: the elabora- **C** D 1972
tion of the Russian connexion.

490. CHEN (C.-Y.), The development of relations between   O   B   1973
China and Russia to the Treaty of Nerchinsk (1652–89).

491. McFIE (A. L.), The Straits Question, 1908–36.   LB   D   1973

492. SHEPARD (J. E. B.), Byzantium and Russia in the eleventh   O   D   1974
century: a study in political and ecclesiastical relationships.

493. THRASHER (P. A.), The diplomatic career of Pozzo di   LB   D   1974
Borgo . . . 1805–40.

494. ZAWADZKI (W. H.), The views of Prince Adam J.   O   D   1974
Czartoryski on reconstructing Europe, 1801–30.

495. HSU (Y-t. A.), Procedure and perception in the making of   O   B   1975
Chinese foreign policy: a study of the 1896 treaty with
Russia.

E. *R.S.F.S.R., U.S.S.R., 1917 onwards*

496. MARCHANT (J. R.), Russian involvement in Cuba, with   U   M   1970
particular reference to the crisis of September–November
1962.

497. HELLIAR-SYMONS (P. E.), Germany, the Soviet Union and   WS   M   1971
world disarmament, 1923–33.

498. MOORE (M. A.), The Cuban missile crisis: an essay in   U   M   1971
interpretation of the perception and motivation of Khrushchev and Kennedy.

499. LEE (C. D.), The interplay of political and economic   LE   MP   1972
factors in Soviet foreign economic relations (with special
reference to the period 1945–53).

500. EDWARDS (G. R.), Sir A. Chamberlain's and Sir J. Simon's   LE   D   1973
conduct of Anglo-Soviet relations: a case-study of the rela-
tionship between the House of Commons and the Foreign
Secretary.

501. LARGE (J. A.), Soviet foreign policy, 1930–3: the new   G   D   1973
alignment, with special reference to the non-aggression
pact as an instrument of Soviet diplomacy.

502. RADICE (E. A.), Negotiations for an Eastern security pact,   LE   D   1973
1933–6.

503. SELLA (A.), Surprise attack: Soviet response to German   E   D   1973
threats, December 1940–June 1941.

504. STEVENS (C. A.), Relations between the USSR and Africa   LE   D   1973
between 1953 and 1972, with special reference to Ghana,
Guinea, Kenya, Mali, Nigeria, Somalia and Tanzania.

505. BRUNT (K.), East–West relations in Europe: the state of   Sx   M   1974
Finno-Soviet relations at the beginning of the seventies.

506. CONDREN (P. L. S.), The Soviet Union and conference   G   D   1974
diplomacy: a study of Soviet attitudes and policy towards
international conferences in the period 1933–39.

507. GORODETSKY (G.), Anglo-Soviet relations, 1924–7.   O   D   1974

508. WHITE (S. L.), Anglo-Soviet relations, 1917–24: a study in   G   D   1974
the politics of diplomacy.

509. YERGIN (D. H.), The rise of the national security state: **C**   D   1974
anti-communism and the origins of the Cold War.

510. DARWISHA (K. L.), The foundations, structure and dyna-   **LE**   D   1975
mics of Soviet policy towards the Arab Radical regimes,
1955–1961.

511. BAYER (J. A.), British policy towards the Russo-Finnish   **LE**   D   1976
War, 1939–40.

512. FREEDMAN (L. D.), The definition of the Soviet threat in   **O**   D   1976
strategic arms decisions of the United States, 1961–74.

F. Yugoslavia

513. VAN CREFELD (M.), Greece and Yugoslavia in Hitler's   **LE**   D   1971
strategy, 1940–1.

III. ECONOMICS

A. General and comparative

514. NUTI (D. M.), Problems of investment planning in socialist   **C**   D   1970
economies.

515. HANSFORD (N.), The CMEA as a vehicle for economic and   **Sx**   M   1976
political integration in Eastern Europe.

B. Hungary

516. HARE (P. C.), Hungarian planning models based on input–   **O**   D   1974
output.

C. Poland

517. GALLAGHER (C. C.), Factory organization in Poland.   **B**   D   1972

518. CHAWLUK (A. L.), Social forces and economic reform: the   **LE**   D   1975
case of Poland, 1956–73.

D. Rumania

519. SPIGLER (I.), The economic reform in Rumania.   **O**   B   1971

E. Russia to 1917

520. DAS GUPTA (K. K.), N. Chernyshevsky's economic views   **K**   D   1972
with particular reference to the agrarian situation in mid-
nineteenth-century Russia.

521. MUNTING (R. D.), Improvements in the peasant farm   **B**   D   1975
economy in early twentieth-century Russia: Tula
guberniya.

F. R.S.F.S.R., U.S.S.R., 1917 onwards

522. MILL (M. R.), Standardization of policy and practice in   **B**   D   1970
the Soviet machine-tool industry.

523. HANSON (P.), The Soviet consumer sector.   **B**   D   1971

524. ELLMAN (M. J.), The optimally functioning Socialist   **C**   D   1972
economy: a study in Soviet mathematical economics.

525. McCauley (G. M. A.), Khrushchev and Soviet agri- LS D 1973
culture, 1963–4: some economic and political aspects.

526. Harry (V. P.), The history of agricultural advice in B MS 1974
Russia and the role of the Soviet agricultural advisory
service during the period 1917–27.

527. Jefferies (I.), The Stalinist economic system as a model LE D 1974
for underdeveloped countries: the development of Soviet
thought since 1953.

528. Andrle (V.), Managerial power in the Soviet Union: the B D 1975
social position of industrial enterprise directors, 1963–72.

529. Harrison (R. M.), Theories of peasant economy: critique O D 1975
of the works of the 'organization-production' school of
agricultural economy, with particular reference to A. V.
Chayanov.

530. Vyas (A.), The behaviour of real wages in the Soviet B D 1975
economy, 1929–37.

531. Cooper (J. M.), The development of the Soviet machine- B D 1976
tool industry, 1917–41.

532. Davis (K. C.), Soviet-Japanese trade and economic rela- B D 1976
tions, 1956–73: a study in Soviet commercial policy.

533. Lewis (R. A.), Industrial research and development in the B D 1976
USSR, 1924–35.

G. *Yugoslavia*

534. Benson (L.), Class, party, and the market in Yugoslavia, Kt D 1974
1945–68.

535. Mancevski (P.), Yugoslavia's entry into the international Brd MS 1974
division of labour.

536. Waller (J. C.), The Yugoslav banking system. Brd MS 1974

537. Havranek (V.), Some aspects of Yugoslav investment LS MP 1975
policy, 1952–62.

IV. EDUCATION, SPORT

538. Dobbie (A. O.), The *Panorthosia* of Comenius. G ML 1972

539. Faloon (B. S.), The work of the *zemstvo* in public educa- B M 1972
tion, 1864–1890.

540. Badrock (J. E.), Fifty years of physical culture and sport M ME 1974
in the Soviet Union, 1917–1967.

541. Andel (J. J.), The role of the Czech labour movement in M ME 1975
the development of adult education.

542. Howard (J. B.), Changing opinions in the Soviet Union LEd D 1975
about American educational thinkers, 1920–1970.

543. O'Dell (F. A.), Soviet child socialisation: children's B D 1975
literature: a case study.

544. Riordan (J. W.), Sport in Soviet society: development and B D 1975
problems.

545. Higgins (J. M. D.), The Soviet teaching profession, with **B**   MS   1976
particular reference to the secondary school teachers
during the 1950s and 1960s.

546. Vlasceanu (L.), Decision and innovation in the Romanian **LEd**   D   1976
educational system: a theoretical exploration of teachers'
orientation.

V. GEOGRAPHY

547. Hadzalić (H.), Population redistribution: Bosnia-Herce-   **E**   MS   1972
govina, 1948–61.

548. Mazowiecki (M.), The political geography of the Poland/   **LB**   MP   1972
USSR boundary of 1945.

549. Shaw (D. J. B.), Settlement, urbanism, and economic   **LU**   D   1973
change in a frontier context: the Voronezh Province of
Russia, 1615–1800.

VI. HISTORY, HISTORIOGRAPHY

A. *Czechoslovakia*

550. Pravda (A.), The Czech reform movement (January to   **O**   D   1973
21 August 1968), with special reference to the role of the
workers.

551. Riff (M. A.), The assimilation of the Jews of Bohemia and   **LS**   D   1974
the rise of political anti-semitism, 1848–1918.

552. Appleby (B.), The relations between the Slovaks and the   **G**   ML   1976
central government of the First Czechoslovak Republic,
1918–64.

B. *Hungary*

553. Barcsay (T. J.), The Károlyi Revolution in Hungary,   **O**   D   1972
1918–19.

554. Lomax (W. A.), The politics of revolution: opposition and   **Sx**   D   1975
revolution in the Hungarian Uprising of 1956.

C. *Poland*

555. Łukowski (G. T.), The *szlachta* and the Confederacy of   **C**   D   1976
Radom, 1764–1767/8: a study of the Polish nobility.

D. *Russia, U.S.S.R.*

556. Dimond (J. M.), The peasantry in the Russian revolution   **LE**   MP   1971
of 1905–6, with special reference to the All-Russian Peasant
Union

557. Barber (J. D.), The Bolshevization of Soviet historio-   **C**   D   1972
graphy, 1928–32.

558. Bartlett (R. P.), Foreign settlement in Russia, 1762–   **O**   D   1972
1804: aspects of government policy and its implementa-
tion.

559. McKEAN (R. B.), Russia on the eve of the Great War: EA D 1972
revolution or evolution.

560. WHITE (J. D.), M. N. Pokrovsky and the origins of Soviet G D 1972
historiography.

561. PEARSON (R.), The Russian moderate parties in the Fourth D D 1973
State Duma, 1912–February 1917.

562. TURNER (C.), The Russian village under war communism LS M 1973
with special reference to social differentiation.

563. BIDELEUX (R. J.), Social and economic conditions and Sx M 1975
trends in rural Russia in the last decades of serfdom.

564. CHRISTIAN (D. G.), Reform of the Russian Senate, 1801–3. O D 1975

565. JONES (R.), The role of the factory committees in 1917. Sx M 1975

566. GILL (G. J.), The role of the peasants in revolution in LE D 1976
European Russia between March and November 1917.

E. *Yugoslavia*

567. OKEY (R. F. C.), Cultural and political problems of the O D 1972
Austro-Hungarian administration of Bosnia-Herzegovina.

568. SHEPHERD (D.), The royal dictatorship in Yugoslavia, D ML 1976
1929–1934, as seen from British sources.

VII. LANGUAGE

A. *Belorussian*

569. TAMUSHANSKI (R. J.), The German loan-words in Middle LS D 1974
Byelorussian.

B. *Rumanian*

570. HURREN (H. A.), A linguistic description of Istro- O D 1972
Rumanian.

C. *Russian*

571. COMRIE (B. S.), Aspects of sentence complementation in C D 1972
Russian.

572. GUILD (D. G.), The development of the aorist and im- E D 1972
perfect in some Slavic and Baltic languages.

573. SUSSEX (R. D.), Aspects of the syntax of Russian adjectives. LS D 1972

574. BALDWIN (J. R.), A formal analysis of the intonation of LU D 1973
modern colloquial Russian.

575. GRAYSON (P. J.), A comparison of Vladimir Nabokov's O D 1973
Russian and English prose: an investigation of those works
of which versions exist in both languages.

576. HADEN (R. G.), A comparison of the use of prepositions M M 1973
and oblique cases in Old Russian and Old Polish.

577. KILBY (D. A.), Deep and superficial cases in Russian. E D 1973

578. CLARKE (J. E. M.), Karamzin's linguistic ideas, with par-   O   B   1974
    ticular reference to his conceptions of the Russian literary
    language.

579. GREEN (B. D.), The criteria for case choice for direct   B   M   1974
    objects of negated transitive verbs in Russian.

580. KERAWALLA (G. J.), A comparative study of factors in-   LX   D   1975
    fluencing the language policies in India and the USSR.

581. SOWERBY (J. G.), The pronunciation of groups of three or   LS   D   1975
    more consonants in modern Moscow Russian.

582. PHILLIPS (K.), The influence of German romanticism on   K   D   1976
    Russian linguistic philosophy, with particular reference to
    the period 1844–91.

D. *Serbocroat*

583. YARWOOD (D.), The vocabulary of knowledge and under-   E   D   1973
    standing in Serbocroat and English.

584. HERRITY (P.), The literary language of Emanuil Janković.   LS   D   1974

VIII. LAW

585. GROVE (E.), Soviet commercial contract in the light of   LK   MP   1973
    economic reform.

586. OLAJUMOKE (W. O.), Legal aspects of the forms of inter-   E   D   1974
    national cooperation between the Soviet Union and
    African states.

587. PALAT (M. K.), Labour legislation and reform in Russia,   O   D   1974
    1905–14.

588. ŠEBEK (V.), The attitudes of the East European states to the   LE   D   1975
    law of the adjacent marine and submarine areas.

IX. LITERATURE
A. *Czech*

589. DOMIN (J. P. C.), Czech social poetry of the late nineteenth   G   ML   1970
    and early twentieth centuries.

590. DOWDING (L. M.), The treatment of contemporary society   O   B   1972
    and the individual in the Czech novel from 1948 to 1968.

591. HORSFALL (S.), Some critical attitudes to the plays of   Le   MP   1973
    Karel Čapek in Czechoslovakia, 1920–63.

B. *Russian*
i. *Literature to 1700*

592. KITCH (F. C. M.), An analysis of *pletenije sloves* in Russian   LS   D   1975
    with special reference to Epifanij Premudrij.

ii. *Literature, 1701–1800*

593. BUDGEN (D. E.), The works of F. A. Emin (1735–70): literary and intellectual transition in eighteenth-century Russia. — O D 1976

iii. *Literature, 1801–1917*

594. GRAHAM (S.), The lyric poetry of A. K. Tolstoy. — E ML 1971

595. BEAUMONT (B. J.), Flaubert and Turgenev: an examination of the parallels in their intellectual and literary development. — Leic D 1972

596. COLLINS (P.), Turgenev and his French associates. — O B 1972

597. GARLIŃSKI (J. E. J.), Chekhov in France, 1893–1939. — LS MP 1972

598. KATZ (M. R.), The literary ballad in early nineteenth-century Russian literature. — O D 1972

599. LEATHERBARROW (W. J.), The force of circumstances: a study of the hero and his environment in the works of N. S. Leskov. — Ex M 1972

600. LITTLE (T. E.), P. A. Vyazemsky as a critic of Russian literature. — LS D 1972

601. WADDINGTON (P. H.), Courtavenel: the history of an artist's nest and its role in the life of Turgenev. — Q D 1972

602. WILKS (R.), K. N. Batyushkov (1787–1855): a critical and biographical study. — LS D 1972

603. COOPER (B. F.), The history and development of the ode in Russia. — C D 1973

604. DEWEY (J. C.), Dostoevsky and Hesse. — N MP 1973

605. TULLOCH (J. C.), Anton Chekhov: a case study in sociology of literature. — Sx D 1973

606. CARTER (R. A.), The works of Aleksei Remizov (1896–1912). — B M 1974

607. GŁOWACKI-PRUS (X.), The literary significance of S. T. Aksakov's memoirs. — LX MP 1974

608. HACKEL (S.), Aleksander Blok and *The Twelve*: a study in iconography. — Sx D 1974

609. HASLETT (D. M.), The influence of populist ideas on the literary works of V. G. Korolenko. — C D 1974

610. BRADBURY (D. L.), Formal structural analysis of Dostoevsky's *Besy*. — E ML 1975

611. CROOKENDEN (J.), The symbolic system of Bely's *St. Petersburg*. — Sx M 1975

612. ELLIOT (E. M.), The early prose work of Fedor Sologub. — O D 1975

613. GILL (L. F.), Chekhov's concept of dramatic time. — LS MP 1975

614. MANGO (A.), Derzhavin and the poetry of enlightened absolutism in the reigns of Catherine II and Paul. — LX MP 1975

615. RATHBONE (C.), Problems of pattern in Lermontov's verse and prose. — O D 1975

616. TUDGE (O. E.), V. M. Garshin (1855–88) and his works in   **O**   **B**   1975
Russian and Soviet literary criticism.

617. KAY (S. E.), Saltykov's theory and practice of writing: an   **LS**   **D**   1976
analysis of the work of M. Ye. Saltykov-Shchedrin, 1868–84.

618. KNIGHT (S. C.), The function of quotation in Dostoevsky.   **Es**   D   1976

619. MARTIN (D. W.), Stylistic devices and narrative technique   **O**   B   1976
in Chekhov's short stories, 1888–1903.

620. MUCKLE (J. Y.), The Protestant spirit in the works of   **Le**   D   1976
Nikolay Leskov.

621. *Withdrawn*

iv. *Literature, 1917 onwards*

622. PAVLOV (A.), The work of Yuriy Kazakov.   **U**   MP   1970

623. HAIGHT (A. C.), Anna Akhmatova: life and work.   **LS**   D   1971

624. MARCH (M.), Esenin: a historical and sociological analysis.   **K**   M   1971

625. RECK (V. T.), Boris Pil'nyak: the literary scandals of 1926   **LS**   D   1971
and 1929.

626. TAIT (A. L.), The literary works of A. V. Lunacharsky   **C**   D   1972
(1875–1933).

627. TALBOTT (N. S.), Mayakovsky Agonistes: the myth of self   **O**   B   1972
in the poetry of Vladimir Mayakovsky

628. TULLOCH (A. R.), A study of the principal themes in the   **Q**   M   1972
works of Boris Pil'nyak.

629. WILSON (D. N.), A study of the works of Mikhail Prishvin   **O**   B   1972
in the period 1906–28.

630. BAINES (J. C. A.), The poetry of Mandel'shtam.   **O**   D   1973

631. BIRCH (C. J.), Fusions: an analysis of theme and technique   **U**   M   1973
in Olesha's *Zavist'*.

632. READER (M.), The works of Vsevolod Ivanov, 1917–32.   **M**   M   1973

633. BAUER (F. C.), V. F. Panova: a study of conflicting ethics   **Li**   M   1974
in post-war Soviet society.

634. COOKE (R. F.), Khlebnikov's revolutionary *poemy*: a study   **Sx**   M   1974
in imagery.

635. LAFFERTY (V.), A. S. Serafimovich: a study of his works   **LS**   D   1974
with a biographical introduction.

636. LE FLEMING (S.), Aspects of the fantastic grotesque in the   **D**   M   1974
works of V. Mayakovsky, M. Bulgakov, and E. Schwartz.

637. LILLY (M. A.), Vladimir Nabokov: a study of selected   **WA**   M   1974
texts, largely exegetical.

638. MURRAY (J.), The Union of Soviet Writers: its organization   **B**   D   1974
and leading personnel, 1954–1967.

639. PATRON (J. F. M.), Valentin Katayev: a biographical and   **O**   D   1974
critical study.

640. WORRALL (J. N.), The major productions of V. E. Meyer-   **H**   M   1974
hold, 1921 to 1924.

641. MILNE (L. M.), The emergence of M. A. Bulgakov as a dramatist. — C D 1975

642. MUNNS (P.), Epic qualities in A. Platonov. — Sx M 1975

643. NICHOLSON (M. A.), Aleksandr Solzhenitsyn and the Russian literary tradition. — O D 1975

644. RULLKÖTTER (B.), The depiction of the hero in Soviet Russian scientific fantasy: aspects of alienation in a peripheral genre. — G ML 1975

645. SHUKMAN (A. M.), Structural literary criticism in the Soviet Union, 1962–1970, with special reference to the work of Yu. M. Lotman. — O D 1975

646. DOYLE (P.), Mikhail Bulgakov. — M D 1976

647. KNIGHT (C.), Communication in the works of V. V. Khlebnikov. — Sx MP 1976

648. KEMP-WELCH (A.), The origins and formative years of the Writers' Union of the USSR, 1932–6. — LE D 1976

649. PENNY (S.), The short prose works of K. Paustovsky. — Sx M 1976

C. Yugoslav

650. GRAHOR (O.), France in the work and ideas of A. G. Matoš. — LS MP 1972

651. JURIČIĆ (Z. B.), Russian repertory in the Croatian national theatre, 1874–1914. — N D 1972

652. ČURČIĆ (N.), The ethical elements in the works of Dositej Obradović. — LS D 1974

653. WALKER (M. H.), Russian repertory in the Serbian National Theatre, Belgrade, 1870–1929. — N D 1974

654. McGREGOR (G.), Aspects of the development of Miroslav Krleža as a novelist. — N MP 1975

655. REID (G. W.), Reflections of rural/urban migration in contemporary Macedonian poetry. — Brd M 1976

X. MILITARY AND NAVAL HISTORY

656. ALDRIDGE (D. D.), Sir John Norris and the British naval expeditions in the Baltic Sea, 1715–27. — LE D 1972

657. MAWDSLEY (E.), The Baltic fleet in the Russian revolution, 1917–21. — LS D 1972

658. SWEETMAN (J.), The effect of the Crimean War upon the administration of the British army, 1852–6. — LK D 1972

659. MILLER (M. L.), Bulgaria in the Second World War. — O B 1973

660. TOWLE (P. A.), The influence of the Russo-Japanese War on British military and naval thought, 1904–14. — LK D 1973

661. BEAUMONT (J. E.), Great Britain and the Soviet Union: the supply of munitions, 1941–5. — LK D 1975

662. MALET (M. I. G.), Nestor Makhno in the Russian Civil War, 1917–1921. — LE D 1975

663. Siegelbaum (L. H.), The War Industries Committees and O   D   1975
the politics of industrial mobilization in Russia, 1915–17.

664. Screen (J. E. O.), The entry of Finnish officers into LE   D   1976
Russian military service, 1809–1917.

XI. MUSIC

665. Cook (A. T.), An analysis of Béla Bartók's six string WC   M   1971
quartets, with special reference to sources of influence
and the harmonic background.

666. O'Riordan (C. L.), Aspects of the interrelationship be- C   D   1971
tween Russian folk and composed music.

667. Blackwood (B. W.), The music of the Ballets Russes, C   D   1972
1909–19

668. Wightman (A. R.), The music of Karol Szymanowski.   Y   D   1973

669. Goodall (C. J.), Percussive effects in the music of Bartók. WB   D   1974

670. Wilson (A. G.), Form and harmony in the orchestral works C   D   1976
and string quartets of Bartók.

XII. POLITICS, SOCIOLOGY, THE REVOLUTIONARY MOVEMENT

A. Czechoslovakia

671. Sutton (P. R.), Relations between Czechoslovak trade M   M   1972
unions and the Czechoslovak Communist Party, 1945–69.

672. Porket (J. L.), Authority in communist Czechoslovakia LE   D   1973
prior to 1968.

673. Rybář (J.), The influence of Soviet ideology on the La   ML   1973
Czechoslovak intelligentsia, 1918–39.

674. Hards (P. W. G.), The concept of revolution in Czech C   D   1975
writing, 1918–1938.

B. Hungary

675. Zsuppan (F. T.), Electoral reform in Hungary, 1916–19. LX   D   1972

C. Poland

676. Sakwa (G.), The role of parliament in a Communist LX   D   1974
political system: the Polish Sejm, 1952–1972.

677. Lewis (P. G.), The politics of the Polish peasantry: the B   D   1975
socialisation of political party organisations in the Polish
countryside, 1956–70.

678. Berka (M.), Political development in Poland, 1968–70.   Sx   M   1976

D. *Russia, R.S.F.S.R., U.S.S.R.*

i. *To 1917*

679. HANEY (J. V.), Maxim the Greek and the intellectual O D 1971
movement of Muscovy.

680. KELLY (A. M.), Attitudes to the individual in Russian O D 1971
thought and literature, with special reference to the *Vekhi*
controversy.

681. CHAPMAN (M. C.), Ivan V. Kireevsky (1806–56): life and Li D 1972
thought.

682. JONES (M. I.), A critical assessment of the non-fictional Le MP 1972
work of Konstantin N. Leont'ev.

683. MATHURA (E.), The social thought of N. K. Mikhailovsky. K M 1972

684. PERRIE (M. P.), The social composition and structure of B M 1972
the Socialist-Revolutionary Party, and its activity among
the Russian peasantry, 1901–7.

685. DOWLER (E. W.), The native soil (*pochvennichestvo*) move- LE D 1973
ment in Russian social and political thought, 1850–70.

686. SAPIETS (M.), The Russian intelligentsia, the old believers, Sx M 1973
and the sectarians, 1870–1918.

687. OFFORD (D. C.), Revolutionary populist groups in Russia LB D 1974
in the 1880s.

688. DENNY (S. L.), Sofia L'vovna Perovskaya, 1853–1881. Sx M 1975

689. MALCOLM (N. R.), Ideology and intrigue in Russian O D 1975
journalism under Nicholas I: *Moskovskii telegraf* and *Sever-*
naya pchela.

690. O'FLAHERTY (D. M.), Tsarism and the politics of publicity, O D 1975
1865–1881.

691. ACTON (E. D. J. L.-D.), Alexander Herzen and the role of C D 1976
the intellectual revolutionary, 1847–1863.

692. JACKSON (J.), Russian marxism and populism. Sx M 1976

693. OWEN (R. C.), The revolutionary career of M. A. Natan- LE D 1976
son, 1868–1906.

694. VALI (A.), Some dilemmas of Russian populism. K M 1976

ii. *1917 onwards*

695. GISSIS (H.), Outline of the formation of the Soviet govern- B MS 1972
mental structure.

696. ALI (J. D.), The development, structure, and functions of Le MP 1973
the Russian Communist Party's central apparatus, 1917 to
May 1924.

697. SPIER (H.), Felix Dzerzhinsky, founder of the Soviet secret M D 1973
police: a biography.

698. KNAPHEIS (B.), The social and political thought of Leon O D 1974
Trotsky.

699. COLLINS (D. N.), The origins, structure and role of the   **Le**   D   1975
Russian Red Guard.

700. POTTS (D. R.), Lenin's debt to the *narodovol'tsy*.   **Li**   M   1975

701. HOGG (H. N.), The plausible illusion: an interpretation of   **Li**   M   1976
ideology in the first quarter century of Soviet Russia.

E. *Yugoslavia*

702. ROSENBLUM (K. R.), The communal system in Yugoslavia;   **LE**   D   1974
participation, coordination, and development: the ex-
perience of Mostar Commune, 1965–9.

703. TERRY (G. M.), The origins and development of the Mace-   **N**   MP   1974
donian revolutionary movement, with particular reference
to the Tayna Makedonsko-Odrinska Revolutsionerna Or-
ganizatsiya from its conception in 1893 to the Ilinden
uprising of 1903.

XIII. PSYCHOLOGY

704. SIMSOVA (S.), An evaluation of Nicholas Rubakin's concept   **LU**   MP   1976
of bibliopsychology in the light of current psychological
research.

XIV. RELIGIOUS HISTORY, THEOLOGY

705. HAROŃSKI (B.), Reform in the Polish Church in the thir-   **O**   D   1973
teenth century.

706. CREWS (C. D.), The theology of John Hus, with special   **M**   D   1975
reference to his concepts of salvation.

707. READ (C. J.), Religion and revolution in the thought of the   **LE**   D   1975
Russian intelligentsia from 1900 to 1912: the *Vekhi* debate
and its intellectual background.

708. GEEKIE (T. H. M.), The Church and politics in Russia,   **EA**   D   1976
1905–1917: a study of the political behaviour of the Rus-
sian Orthodox clergy in the reign of Nicholas II.

709. LANE (C. O.), The impact of communist ideology and the   **LE**   D   1976
Soviet order on Christian religion in the contemporary
USSR (1959–74).

710. WILLIAMS (R. D.), The theology of Vladimir Nikolaevich   **O**   D   1976
Lossky: an exposition and critique.

XV. SCIENCE, TECHNOLOGY

711. LAMPERT (N.), The technical intelligentsia in the USSR,   **B**   D   1976
1928–35.

712. SMITH (J. R.), Persistence and periodicity: a study of Men-   **LCC**   D   1976
deleev's contribution to the foundations of chemistry.

INDEX